# RE-CONSTRUCTING THE BOOK

*For*
*John Barnard*

The editors would like to thank the School of English, University of Leeds, for assistance in publication; Rachel Becker and Sarah Cowan, students in the Department of Typography and Graphic Communication, The University of Reading, for the jacket cover design; and Pat FitzGerald for her skill in producing the camera-ready copy.

# Re-constructing the Book

## Literary texts in transmission

*Edited by*

MAUREEN BELL
SHIRLEY CHEW
SIMON ELIOT
LYNETTE HUNTER
JAMES L.W. WEST III

# Ashgate

Aldershot • Burlington USA • Singapore • Sydney

Published by
Ashgate Publishing Limited
Gower House
Croft Road
Aldershot
Hampshire GU11 3HR
England

Ashgate Publishing Company
131 Main Street
Burlington, VT 05401-5600 USA

Ashgate website: http://www.ashgate.com

**British Library Cataloguing in Publication Data**
Re-constructing the book : literary texts in transmission
    1. Criticism 2. Booksellers and bookselling - History
    I. Bell, Maureen, 1953-
    801.9'5

**Library of Congress Control Number:** 2001088193

ISBN 0 7546 0360 1

Printed and bound in Great Britain by MPG Books Ltd, Bodmin, Cornwall

# Contents

# List of Illustrations

(between pages 41 and 42)

# Notes on Contributors

**Maureen Bell** was Leverhulme Fellow at the Institute of Bibliography, University of Leeds (1990–92) where she worked on the quantification of English printing 1475–1700 and, with John Barnard, published *The Early Seventeenth-Century York Book Trade* and *John Foster's Inventory of 1616* (1994). She has published widely on women in the seventeenth-century book trade and is contributor and Assistant Editor to volume 5 of the Cambridge *History of the Book in Britain* (ed. J. Barnard and D.F. McKenzie). Currently Senior Lecturer in the Department of English at the University of Birmingham, she is working on *A Chronology and Calendar of Documents Relating to the London Book Trade 1641–1700*, to be published by Oxford University Press.

**Martin Butler** is Professor of English Renaissance Drama at the University of Leeds. He is currently completing an edition of *Cymbeline* for the New Cambridge Shakespeare, and is a General Editor of the Cambridge edition of the *Works of Ben Jonson* (forthcoming in 2005).

**Shirley Chew** is Professor of Commonwealth and Postcolonial Literatures at the University of Leeds. Her publications include the co-edited *Translating Life: Studies in Transpositional Aesthetics* (1999). A work in progress is the *Blackwell History of Postcolonial Literature*.

**Martin Dodsworth** is Professor of English at Royal Holloway, University of London, and one of the editors of the Oxford edition of Burton's *Anatomy of Melancholy*. He is the author of *Hamlet Closely Observed* (1985) and editor of *The Survival of Poetry* (1970), *English Economis'd* (1989) and *The Penguin History of Literature* vol. 7: *The Twentieth Century* (1994). He has a long-standing commitment to the English Association.

**Simon Eliot** is Professor of Publishing and Printing History at the University of Reading and is Director of its Centre for Writing, Publishing and Printing History. He is also Associate Director of the Research Centre in the History of the Book based at London University. He is the author of many articles, and his publications include *Some Patterns and Trends in British Publishing 1800–1919* (1994). He is co-editor (with David McKitterick) of the volume covering 1830–1914 in the Cambridge *History of the Book in Britain*. He edits the journal *Publishing History* and is General Editor of the monograph series *History of the Book – On Demand Series (HOBODS)*. Currently he is President of the Society for the History of Authorship, Reading and Publishing (SHARP).

**Inga-Stina Ewbank**, Emeritus Professor of English Literature, University of Leeds, has written extensively on Shakespeare and early modern drama and on Scandinavian drama and has translated plays by Ibsen and Strindberg. Via translation she has returned to the Brontës, on whom she published her first book, *Their Proper Sphere* (1966).

**David Fairer** is Professor of Eighteenth-Century English Literature at the University of Leeds. He is the author of *Pope's Imagination* (1984), *The Poetry of Alexander Pope* (1989), and editor of *Pope: New Contexts* (1990), *The Correspondence of Thomas Warton* (1995), and a facsimile edition of Thomas Warton's *History of English Poetry* (1998). With Christine Gerrard he has edited *Eighteenth-Century Poetry: An Annotated Anthology* (1999).

**C.Y. Ferdinand**, Fellow Librarian of Magdalen College, Oxford, has written on the eighteenth-century provincial book trade and the history of libraries. She met John Barnard when she first came to England to study at the Institute of Bibliography and Textual Criticism at the University of Leeds.

**Paul Hammond** is Professor of Seventeenth-Century English Literature at the University of Leeds. His books include *Love between Men in English Literature* (1996) and *Dryden and the Traces of Classical Rome* (1999). He is joint General Editor with John Barnard of the Longman Annotated English Poets Series, for which he has also edited the poems of Dryden in four volumes (1995–2000).

**Lynette Hunter** is Professor of the History of Rhetoric at the University of Leeds, and has worked for many years with John Barnard at the Institute for Bibliography and Textual Studies. She has written widely on the impact of printing, publishing and computing, on oral and written rhetoric in the western world, and has particular interest in the book history of household management and conduct. She is currently co-editing *Romeo and Juliet* for the Arden Third Edition.

**Hermione Lee** is the Goldsmiths' Professor of English Literature at Oxford and Fellow of New College, Oxford. She has previously taught at the College of William and Mary, the University of Liverpool and (from 1977 to 1998) the University of York, where she had a personal Chair. She is well known as a reviewer and broadcaster and has done a number of editions and anthologies, including two collections of short stories by women, *The Secret Self*. She is the author of critical books on Elizabeth Bowen, Willa Cather, Virginia Woolf, and Philip Roth, and of a biography of Virginia Woolf (1996). She is currently working on Edith Wharton.

**Roger Lonsdale**, until his recent retirement, was a Fellow of Balliol College (1960–2000), and Professor of English Literature, University of Oxford (1992–2000). His publications include *The Poems of Gray, Collins and Goldsmith* (1969), *The New Oxford Book of Eighteenth-Century Verse* (1984) and *Eighteenth-Century Women Poets: An Oxford Anthology* (1989).

**Peter D. McDonald** is a lecturer in English Literature at the University of Oxford and a Fellow of St Hugh's College. He has published articles on Anglo-American modernism, British literary culture in the 1890s, the history of the book, and South African literature. His first book-length study, *British Literary Culture and Publishing Practice* (Cambridge), appeared in 1997. He is currently working on a study of censorship in South Africa and the international reception of South African writing during the Apartheid era.

**D.F. McKenzie** The late D.F. McKenzie was Professor of Bibliography and Textual Criticism at the University of Oxford and Fellow of Pembroke College. His publications include *Stationers' Company Apprentices, 1605–1800* (3 vols, Oxford, 1961–78); *The Cambridge University Press, 1696–1712* (2 vols, Cambridge, 1966); and *Bibliography and the Sociology of Texts* (1986). He enthusiastically supported the idea of this collection, but his intended contribution to this volume was prevented by his untimely death in 1999 and we are very grateful to his wife, Christine Ferdinand, for her permission to include an edited extract from his unpublished work.

**David Richards** is Senior Lecturer at the School of English, University of Leeds, and his interests are in post-colonial literatures, anthropology and fine art. His publications include *Masks of Difference: Cultural Representations in Literature, Anthropology and Art* (1994), and he is currently working on two books on archaeology and post-colonial and modernist writing and on ethnographic representations of Morocco.

**Christopher Ricks** is Warren Professor of the Humanities and Co-director of the Editorial Institute at Boston University. He recently edited *The Oxford Book of English Verse*. He is a member of the Association of Literary Scholars and Critics.

**Alistair Stead** is Senior Fellow in English at the University of Leeds. He is co-editor of *James Joyce and Modern Literature* (1982), *Forked Tongues? Comparing Twentieth-Century British and American Literature* (1994), and *Translating Life: Studies in Transpositional Aesthetics* (1999). He co-edits the *James Joyce Broadsheet* and has published essays on Henry Green and Janette Turner Hospital.

**James L.W. West III** is Edwin Earle Sparks Professor of English at Pennsylvania State University. He is one of the textual editors of the Pennsylvania Dreiser edition and is General Editor of the Cambridge edition of the *Works of F. Scott Fitzgerald*. His most recent book is *William Styron, A Life* (1998).

Chapter One

# Introduction: The Material Text

Maureen Bell

Students of English literature today face a demanding programme of study in a discipline which, over the past few decades, has developed dynamically (and often painfully) even as teachers and institutions of education have grappled with social and economic changes and financial constraints. In the late twentieth century 'literature' has enlarged its scope, absorbing into its syllabuses the non-canonical as well as the canonical, popular as well as 'high' literature, female as well as male writers, black as well as white authors and readers, and the variety of Englishes written and spoken in the post-colonial world. One legacy of the critical theory wars of the 1980s is that an understanding of the theory and history of literary criticism is now routinely and rigorously required of students. And in the final decades of the twentieth century, driven in Britain at least in part by the application of Marxist theory to the study of literary texts, came the development of a cultural materialist analysis in alliance with bibliography and with approaches from other disciplines – notably the French *annales* school of history – to produce the new and interdisciplinary field signalled variously by the terms 'sociology of the text', *histoire du livre* and, more broadly, 'book history' and 'print culture'.

Thus within the space of an academic working lifetime the old clear and central focus on *literary criticism*, with bibliography and textual criticism firmly positioned as ancillary skills in the service of aesthetic and moral judgement, has shifted; as has the relationship between those three aspects of the discipline. This book is intended as both argument for and demonstration of the potential of this realignment of literary criticism, textual criticism and the history of the book. Literary critics, textual editors and bibliographers, and historians of publishing have hitherto tended to publish their research as if in separate fields of enquiry. Our purpose here is to bring together in one volume contributions from some of the leading scholars in each of these fields in order to offer a dialogue which exemplifies, explores and encourages the practice of literary criticism rooted in the context of the transmission of texts. Arranged chronologically, so as to allow the use of individual sections relevant to period literature courses, this book offers students and teachers a set of essays designed both to reflect these approaches and to signal their potential for fruitful integration. Some of the essays therefore answer the demand, 'Show me what literary critics (or textual editors; or book historians) do and how they do it', and stand as examples of the different concerns, methodologies and rhetorical strategies employed by these branches of literary study. Others draw attention to the potential of these approaches in combination and demonstrate the extent to which literary critics are incorporating the 'history of the book' approach in their interpretative strategies. All are concerned not simply with literary texts *per se*, but with the way in which the *transmission* of those texts is itself a process productive of meaning.

And literary criticism is, above all, about *meaning*. At every level of the text (word, phrase, image, style, form, genre) the critic has always been concerned with interpreting the meaning of what has been written, but our perspective on what constitutes meaning has changed radically. Whereas at the beginning of the twentieth century the text itself was heralded, notably by I.A. Richards, as the sole focus of critical attention, critics at the century's end have found that looking only, as it were, 'inside' the text is wholly insufficient to an understanding of both the *what* and the *how* of meaning. Indeed, the problems inherent in that innocent word 'text' are now familiar to every student of literature. The task of establishing the required 'authoritative' text has traditionally been the province of the textual editor and the bibliographer, whose skills were thereby rendered secondary (from the point of view of the literary critic) or fundamental (from the point of view of the bibliographer). Literary history has traditionally been the assistant of both literary and textual criticism, but the combined effect of modern critical approaches – notably new historicism, feminism, cultural materialism and the sociology of texts – is a more complex historicism which, at its best, raises new and fascinating issues. The kinds of questions about textual meaning with which literary critics have hitherto been concerned – *What and how does it mean now?* and *What and how did it mean at the time it was written?* – may now be extended to *What and how did it mean at any given point between then and now?*

A common feature of both the new theoretical approaches in literary criticism and of the 'new bibliography' characterized as the sociology of the text is their stress on contingency. In literary criticism, the assumption of the existence of universal aesthetic values transcending time and place has been radically and repeatedly questioned – not least by Marxists, historicists, feminists and theorists of reader-response and reception. At the same time, and partly in response to the same pressures, in bibliography the old chimerical search for the 'ideal' text – a reconstructed text which, though it never existed materially, would represent most closely what (in the opinion of editor or bibliographer) the *author intended* – has been replaced by a critical awareness of the book as an inherently unstable form. Different printed (as well as manuscript) embodiments of the text deserve attention, therefore, not only in relation to each other but also in their individual and particular relation to their circumstances of production, distribution and consumption. The long-held expectation of the discovery or re-creation of an *originary* text, 'superior' to all others, has been replaced by a (more democratic?) respect for each manuscript or printed witness in its own right. In the case of Shakespeare, for example, the 'bad' quartos are being reinspected, reassessed and revalued in terms of printing history and performance practice.

Central to all of this is a developing and vital concern with the book as a *material* object. Transformations of meaning are effected by the very matter from which the book is constituted; differences in paper, format, typefaces, page layout, illustrations and bindings can make the same text *mean* differently. And the technology of print, far from *fixing* texts, has in practice proved as fluid a technology as scribal production. D.F. McKenzie, advocating the 'sociology of the text', argues that it is in its very *instability* as a physical form that the book offers evidence for the history of the book as 'a study of changing *conditions* of meaning and hence of reading' (1992, 297). Moreover, the details of those physical forms must be set in the wider context of the systems and agents of textual transmission:

> the physical signs in a book ... make sense only in terms of our assumptions about the historical conditions and processes by which they were made. Meanings are not therefore inherent but are constructed by successive interpretative acts, both by those who write, design, and print books, and by those who buy and read them. (McKenzie 1992, 297)

This wider context of historical conditions and processes is most familiarly represented to students by Robert Darnton's diagrammatic model of a 'communications circuit'.[1] Darnton's model elucidates not only the economic and material agents and processes of book production and distribution but also the wider political, legal, social and cultural circumstances within which the material text is produced and produces its meaning. The history of the book thus directs critical attention not to the study of an 'ideal' text but rather to a specific material text which can be studied not only diachronically – in its relation to other embodiments of the same text – but also synchronically, in relation to other texts produced at the same time (by the same printers and publishers, for example, or within the printed output of a particular time or place) and in relation to the wider conditions of cultural formation.

The materiality of the text is central to any consideration of textual transmission just as the processes of transmission are central to Darnton's formulation of the history of the book. The materials which embody the text are made and supplied by several different specialists (in the hand-press period, for example, these included manufacturers and suppliers of paper and inks, typefounders and binders) and the text may pass through many hands on its way from author to printed form: those of scribe or copyist, amanuensis, secretary, typist, editor, translator, compositor, printer, proofreader and publisher. The work of all these agents alters the text (directly or indirectly, intentionally or not) and – by the addition or deletion of material, by errors and accidents in copying or typesetting, by supplying new contexts (prefaces, dedications, postscripts, indexes) or by repackaging the text among other texts (in compilations and anthologies) – substantially conditions what and how the text *means*. The texts we now study as 'literature' have of course always been a very small proportion of the total output of the printing press, and investigation of the details of printing house practices and of the businesses of specific individuals in the book trades has already proved a valuable corrective to theories built solely on physical evidence internal to the book.[2] Happily, students of literature in English have ready access to directories and biographical dictionaries of book trade personnel and the record of their output as represented by short-title catalogues such as *ESTC* and *NSTC*. But much remains to be done both in terms of mapping the trade in general and in relation to the economic and business practices of specific periods and individuals.[3]

The material processes of production are not, however, the end of the story in terms of the text's transformation. Darnton's 'communications circuit' ends with the reader; and readers, in McKenzie's phrase, construct meanings.[4] This argues for an investigation of the processes and institutions which mediate their reading of the text. In material terms this includes not only the agents and processes of distribution (booksellers, hawkers, pedlars, religious and political networks, commercial and institutional libraries, book auctions, informal lending) and questions of people's access to books (literacy, prices and geographical location) but also the very practices of reading. How, where and in what circumstances does the reader read? Is the book bought, borrowed, freely distributed or stolen? Is it read alone or communally, in secret or within a particular social or institutional setting? Annotations in surviving books and in the catalogues of private libraries yield answers to these questions for some readers, and can be supplemented by evidence from diaries and letters in which readers describe or discuss their reading. But for other kinds of reader, particularly provincial readers of lower social status, the evidence is often fragmentary and is not easily recoverable.[5] And since, as Darnton indicates, authors too are readers, the investigation of the reading practices of authors themselves is a pertinent issue.

The third element of the Darnton model crucial to the elucidation of textual meaning is that of the wider social, political, legal and economic spheres which impinge on the production, distribution and reading of the text. Social, religious and legal institutions – as various as the monarch's exertion of prerogative rights, parliamentary statute, the actions of clergy as licensers, trade regulations and trade practices enforced by bodies such as the Stationers' Company or trade unions – provide the complex conditions within which printing operates. This wider social and cultural formation may directly circumscribe the text's production by, for example, imposing constraints upon what can be legally published. An obvious case is the imposition of censorship regulations which operate directly and formally on authors, publishers and readers alike or, more subtly, might produce a climate of caution and self-censorship. Similarly, economic circumstances both national and local have both direct and indirect effects on printing, affecting the supply and costs of labour and materials, and influencing the size and relative wealth of the potential market for books.

The research implied by the history of the book may seem daunting or even, as McGann indicates, impossible: 'the entire socio-history of [a] work – from its originary moments of production through all its subsequent reproductive adventures – is postulated as the ultimate goal of critical self-consciousness' (McGann 1988). Indeed, the very range of questions to be asked, lines of enquiry to pursue, skills to acquire and knowledge assumed has led some teachers to argue that it is inappropriate to expect undergraduates to engage with it at all.[6] Not surprisingly, therefore, many of the courses in North America and in Britain which announce themselves as 'history of the book' courses are aimed at graduate students;[7] but there is growing evidence and experience that the 'history of the book' approach is one which undergraduate students of literature find exciting and one which they benefit from exploring. Our reaction is, therefore, not a counsel of despair but an excitement about the richness of the field. The history of the book opens up new areas of enquiry with abundant potential for informing the practice of literary studies and for enthusing students about the nature of literary study. Our suggestion is not prescriptive – that any one individual (teacher, student, researcher) should (or could) master all these skills – but, conversely, that every teacher, student and researcher can engage with some aspect of the materiality of the text and its transmission, and in so doing will enrich and enliven their engagement with literary texts. As a developing interdisciplinary field,[8] the history of the book has much to offer literary studies, not least in raising new and pertinent questions, placing the literary text in the wider context of printed books, and in helping to interpret the individual text. This collection of essays is intended to exemplify current practice, to encourage discussion, and to stimulate teaching and research by demonstrating that, in the twenty-first century, a study of the 'literariness' of texts cannot be adequately compassed without attention to the material forms and processes through which those texts have been and are still being transmitted. That 'transmission' is in itself a potentially fruitful focus for literary critics is amply signalled in many of the essays collected here.

Finally, a word about this book's origin. Few scholars are equipped to make a substantial and lasting contribution to all three of the branches of literary study addressed here and the retirement of John Barnard, Professor of English Literature at the University of Leeds, spurred this effort to celebrate his rare achievement. Well known for his editions of *John Keats: The Complete Poems* (1973) and *John Keats: Selected Poems* (1988), he has also edited Congreve's *The Way of the World* (1972) and Etherege's *The Man of Mode* (1979). Appointed General Editor of Longman Annotated Poets in 1975, as successor to F.W. Bateson, he has supported and influenced editions of the poems of Arnold, Tennyson, Shelley, Blake, Browning, Dryden and Milton. Further volumes of Shelley, Dryden, Browning, Marvell and Herbert are currently in active preparation. His literary criticism includes books on Pope (*Pope: The Critical Heritage*, 1973) and Keats (*John Keats*, 1987) as well as many papers on these and other poets and on Restoration drama.

That John would become a leading figure in the future of book history is aptly signalled by the title of his first article, published in 1963: 'Dryden, Tonson, and Subscriptions for the 1697 *Virgil*' (*Papers of the Bibliographical Society of America*, 67). Happily, that initial desire to elucidate the circumstances of Tonson's publication of Dryden's *Virgil* has remained and his most recent publications include two papers which return to this theme: one on Tonson's investment (*PBSA* 92, 1998) and another on the patrons of the *Virgil*, published in *John Dryden: Tercentenary Essays* (ed. Paul Hammond and David Hopkins, 2000). His growing commitment to the history of the book during the intervening years is evident from both his teaching and his research interests. Closely involved since 1982 in the work of the Institute of Bibliography and Textual Criticism at Leeds, first as Acting Director and, since 1996, as Director, he was responsible for the MA in Bibliography, Publishing and Textual Studies and forged working links for his students with *ESTC* and other projects. In 1988, as General Editor with the late D.F. McKenzie of volume 4 (1557–1695) of *History of the Book in Britain* (Cambridge University Press), he began the research project which has absorbed much of his research time in the last decade and which has placed him at the forefront of the history of the book as it has developed in Britain. The project, supported by the Leverhulme Trust, has already led to much published work, including his investigations of the stock of the Stationers' Company (in *Publishing History*, 36, 1994, and *The Library*, 21, 1999) and *The Early Seventeenth-Century York Book Trade and John Foster's Inventory of 1616* (1994, with Maureen Bell). In 1998 he was elected Vice-President of the Bibliographical Society.

A highly respected scholar, an advocate of his subject and of his profession at every level from departmental to national, and an immensely generous and humane teacher and colleague, John Barnard and his career supply the occasion and the unifying principle of this book. We intend it to be a *useful* book for teachers and students by showing what it is to study literature in exactly the way that John has taught his colleagues and students: by good-humoured example, with spirited enthusiasm, and through energetic scholarly engagement with the many aspects of literary texts and their transmission.

## Notes

1 Darnton's model has been modified and challenged: see Adams and Barker (1993) and McDonald (1997).
2 See, for example, Hinman (1963) and McKenzie (1966); the argument is stated in McKenzie (1969).
3 The availability of short-title catalogues in easily-searchable electronic form (on CD-ROM as well as on-line) is a notable recent development. Other trade records are also becoming available electronically, such as the *British Book Trade Index* established by Peter Isaac.
4 In fact, Darnton supplies a dotted line to complete the circuit, indicating that authors are themselves readers.
5 This is particularly true for the period before 1700: for recent work on early modern readers of lower social status, see for example Colclough (2000); for provincial readers see Hunter et al. (1999) and Bell (forthcoming). The Reading Experience Database project, directed by Simon Eliot at the Open University, is collecting much valuable evidence on the material practices of reading across the centuries.
6 The SHARP Newsletter and e-mail discussion list (SHARP-L) frequently carry contributions to this debate between teachers of the history of the book, many of whom are members of the Society for the History of Authorship, Reading and Publishing.

7    British MA courses taking a 'history of the book' approach currently exist at, for example, the Universities of Birmingham, Edinburgh, Leeds, London, Reading and at the Open University; at Birmingham a History of the Book course is available to undergraduates. Several departments of Library and Information Studies and of Communications Studies have relevant courses. North America has seen a similar flourishing of graduate provision.
8    That the subject has 'come of age' is demonstrated not only by its increasing visibility in graduate and undergraduate courses, but in its increasing institutionalization. Centres for the book proliferate, national and international conferences are well established and the several national histories of the book are bringing the subject to prominence.

## Bibliography

Adams, T.R. and N. Barker (1993), 'A New Model for the History of the Book', in N. Barker (ed.), *A Potencie of life: Books in Society: The Clark Lectures 1986–1987*, London: British Library.

Bell, M. (forthcoming, 2001), 'Reading in Seventeenth-Century Derbyshire: The Wheatcrofts and their Books', in P. Isaac and B. McKay (eds), *The Moving Market*, Winchester/Delaware: St Paul's Bibliographies/Oak Knoll Press.

Colclough, S. (2000), '"A Catalogue of My Books": The Library of John Dawson (1692–1765), "Exciseman and Staymaker", c. 1739', *Publishing History* 47, 45–66.

Darnton, R. (1982), 'What is the History of Books?', *Daedalus* 3, 65–83.

Hinman, C. (1963), *The Printing and Proof-reading of the First Folio of Shakespeare*, 2 vols, Oxford: Clarendon Press.

Hunter, M. et al. (eds) (1999), *A Radical's Books: The Library Catalogue of Samuel Jeake of Rye, 1623–9*, Woodbridge: D.S. Brewer.

McDonald, P. (1997), 'Pierre Bourdieu and the History of the Book', *Library* 6th ser. 2, 105–21.

McGann, J. (1988), 'Theory of Texts', *London Review of Books*, 18 February.

McKenzie, D.F. (1966), *The Cambridge University Press, 1696–1712*, 2 vols, Cambridge: Cambridge University Press.

McKenzie, D.F. (1969), 'Printers of the Mind', *Studies in Bibliography*, 22.

McKenzie, D.F. (1992), 'History of the Book', in P. Davison (ed.), *The Book Encompassed: Studies in Twentieth-Century Bibliography*, Cambridge: Cambridge University Press, 290–301.

Chapter Two

# Why has Q4 *Romeo and Juliet* Such an Intelligent Editor?

Lynette Hunter

## Background[1]

The question sounds insulting. But as we find out increasingly more about editorial processes in the period 1600–1623, it needs to be asked. Correctors (Bland), scribes (Honigmann), theatre-related workers in printing houses (Jowett 1998), have recently been added to compositors as important agents in the textual transmission of playtexts. These additions offer complexity to the production of the printed texts that matches a similar development in studies of the collaboration among writers and theatre workers in the production of the performed texts. In the process of answering the question here, it becomes apparent that all the early quartos of *Romeo and Juliet*, Quarto One (Q1: 1597), Quarto Two (Q2: 1599), Quarto Three (Q3: 1609) and Quarto Four (Q4: 1616–26), have been intelligently edited, and S.W. Reid (1982) has suggested an intelligent hand in the production of the Folio (F: 1623) as well. This essay will focus on the editing of Q3 and Q4, but it has to be said that *Romeo and Juliet* received remarkable attention while it was being printed for successive audiences over the first twenty-five to thirty-year period of its history in print.

The edition to which most editors today turn is ostensibly Q2, but to all intents and purposes they adopt a text that is usually closer to Q4 except in a few instances where they retain Q3 changes instead. Q3 is a carefully modified version of Q2 with over 100 significant changes and a probable use of Q1. Q4 offers an even more intelligent modification and makes a further 100 changes, again using Q1. By today's standards, these texts have been edited. It is unclear why Q3 is not taken as copytext when so many editors follow its modifications, but it is possibly because it has clearly been typeset page for page from Q2 and may have led readers into thinking that it is unedited. G.H. Evans calls it a 'reprint' (Evans 206). Nor is it clear why Q4 editing is not better collated. Only Evans's Cambridge edition pays much attention to this text.[2] While most collations indicate in Q3 and Q4 substantive changes to words, they rarely indicate changes to punctuation, grammar, spelling, layout or metre, even where these substantively change the significance of the text. That they do not is attributable to coincidence of the earlier editorial choices with those of many editors since: later editors make exactly the same changes, often without consultation of either Q3 or Q4. Of course, this is standard editorial experience. At the same time, the coincidence of practice is precisely what makes Q4 and Q3 appear so intelligent when they are consulted.

The story of the relationship between Q1 and Q2 is a matter which is taken up in the introduction to the commentary on Q1 in the forthcoming Arden Three edition. It is worth remarking here, however, that not only are there instances in Q3 of an attempt to bring Q1 and Q2 together at difficult moments, but also there are over 45 changes to the 25 per cent of the text where Q1 is not present and only around 55 changes to the 75 per cent of the text where Q1 is present. Q4 follows Q3, but consistently questions its retention of Q2 text, questions its use of Q1, and questions its inattentiveness to some issues. The bibliographical and theatrical issues Q4 raises, either on its own or following Q3, are to a large extent identical with those editors raise today. This is hardly surprising on the bibliographical front since the methodology of bibliography is largely derived from analysis of the practice of earlier editors of Shakespeare. But the consistency of attention to theatrical issues that preoccupy us today is more startling.

## Quarto 3

Starting with Q2, the ostensible copytext, and Q4, there are five main areas of change to which this essay will attend. First, Q4 makes many changes to words, phrases and passages of text, and to punctuation, grammar, spelling, layout and metre, throughout the text. Second, Q4 follows Q3 in nearly all Q3's changes to Q2, with a few exceptions. Third, Q4 takes care with stage directions (SDs) and speech prefixes (SPs) in ways that at times recall Q1 and F. Fourth, Q4 makes the same choices as Q1 in many places where Q3 does not change. Fifth, Q4 introduces a number of differences to Q2 which have no correspondence with any of Q1, Q3 or F.

The extent to which Q4 uses Q3 itself raises questions. Does the editor of Q4 have no access to Q2? There are a few Q2/4 similarities not in Q3, including among others: 1.1.127 humour (2/4) honour (1/3), the reincorporation of a comma in 1.3.95 No less, (2/4) lesse (3) with a significant change in meaning and rhythm, the shift back to 3.3.152 the Prince (2/4) thy Prince (3), or to 5.3.75 Mercutio's (2/4) Mercutius (3). Yet apart from the first example, these changes do not form a strong argument that Q4 held a copy of Q2. The remarkable consistency with which it follows Q3's changes to Q2 (over 100), and the fact that in no case that I have found does it change Q2 where Q3 is not either identical with Q2 (over 50), or has not already made a slight change (13), back up the idea that Q4 is using Q3 alone, or at least as the most dependable text. For example, Q2 has 2.4.205 dog, name, where Q3 has dogsname and Q4 has Dogges name.

The most unusual aspect of Q4's use of Q3 is that it hardly ever changes the text where Q3 has already changed it, even where Q1 has a different solution. The few examples that I could find, less than 10, look far more like an imposition of spelling or layout style than considered changes: 3.1.136 be gone (2) begone (3) be gone, (4); 3.3.16 here, of (2) hereof (3) here of (4); 4.2.14 self wild harlotrie (1) selfweild harlottry (2) self willde harlotry (3) self willed harlotry (4); 4.4.15 alack the day (1) wereaday (2) weleady (3) weladay (4). Given the independent frame of mind that Q4 brings to many other changes (over 100), and given that many of the Q3 changes to Q2 (over 100) are concerned with difficulties of meaning that might tempt someone into alternative solutions anyway, the thoroughgoing resistance to changing Q3's decisions implies an editorial policy of some kind that this essay will attempt to understand.

Leaving aside this question for the moment, whether the Q4 editor could not get a copy of Q2 or decided that Q3 was more dependable, why would the Q4 editor trust Q3's changes? Possibly because theatre practitioners said so, possibly because this was the most-produced version and hence conventional wisdom, possibly because the printing house already had Q3 easily available, and possibly because the Q4 editor understood what the Q3 editor had done. They may even have been the same person. Q3 had been printed by John Windet for John Smethwicke in 1609. In 1607, having earlier that year received a number of titles transferred from Cuthbert Burby, Nicolas Ling had assigned the titles of *Hamlet, Love's Labour's Lost, The Taming of the Shrew* and *Romeo and Juliet* to Smethwicke with whom he may have worked (Arber 2:832), but *Romeo and Juliet* was not published for another two years.[3] Windet's printing house was substantial: he served as Printer to the City from 1603–10 (McKerrow 295). But the last book entry under his name in the Stationers' Register is on 14 May 1604 (McKerrow 295), and in 1611 he assigned his copyrights to William Stansby (Arber 3:465–7). Stansby had been apprenticed to Windet and bought a share in the business in 1609 (Bland). He may well have been involved in the printing of Q3. Bracken (1985) argues that many books printed at Windet's press in the first decade of the seventeenth century were in fact the work of Stansby, who was responsible for printing Q4 for Smethwicke, somewhat later. Windet appears to have employed a corrector (McKerrow 194–5), although the 1608 edition of *I Henry IV* that Windet printed for Matthew Law is apparently little changed (D. Kastan, personal communication).

The person who produced Q3 worked through the text of Q2, either from marked-up copy or possibly reading for solutions to bibliographical or theatrical problems. Again, this editor may have been someone from the playhouse, a clever compositor, or a professional corrector. It is unlikely to have been a scribe because the play has clearly been set from Q2, and would not have needed a complete copying out. The first option is also unlikely. Despite the many changes Q3 makes to Q2 (over 100), there are very few corrections to SPs, SDs, and other odd peculiarities of spelling and typography in Q2. For example, in Juliet's opening speech in 2.5 lines 2.5.16–17 are misassigned in Q2 to 'M.', which Q3 duplicates. This mistake may also indicate that the second option, the compositor, is also unlikely. Although I have not carried out a compositorial analysis there are several other duplications of erroneous layout that suggest a naive compositor. For example, at 5.2 Q2 mistakenly prints 5.2.23 (Exit. when Friar John leaves. Q3 slavishly reproduces this clear error, even adding a bracket to Friar Lawrence's 5.2.30 Exit. (2) (Exit. (3). Q3 is also set nearly entirely page-for-page, with Q3 duplicating catchword errors in Q2.

If the compositor of Q3 seems naively to have followed the printed copy of Q2, he must have been following a marked-up text because Q3 otherwise makes a large number of intelligent changes to Q2 and appears to have had access to Q1. In this regard, two or three changes seem significant. Q3 produces at 3.4.23 weele keepe, from weele make (1) and well, keepe (2). Q3 has 5.3.227 too or else, for or els (1) and too, else (2). And at 5.3.163 there is drinke all, and left (4) for drinke all and leave (1), drunk all, and left (2). Approximately 75 per cent of Q1 covers the same ground as Q2, and over half the lines in that 75 per cent are the same if not very similar (Irace). Twenty-five per cent of the text of Q2 has no counterpart in Q1. Q3 changes have been gathered into three categories: those which occur in text that is not found in Q1 (A), those which follow Q1 (B), those which occur where Q1 makes a change but does not make the same change (C).

*A)    Changes to Q2 in Text not Found in Q1*

Changes to Q2 in text not found in Q1 vary. There are significant word changes: 1.3.36 hylone (2) a lone (3); 1.4.80 Persons (2) parson's (3); 3.2.47 arting (2) darting (3); 4.1.116 walking (2) waking (3); 5.3.107 pallat (2) palace (3); 5.3.136 unthriftie (2) unluckie (3), and significant 'corrections': 2.5.11 Is there (2) Is three (3); 3.5.145 bride (2) Bridegroome (3); 4.1.110 is (2) in (3); 4.5.51 bedold (2) behold (3). There is also a large number of changes to punctuation (17+) which affect the significance of the text: 1.3.90 For fair without the fair, within to hide (2) For fair without, the fair within to hide (3); 3.5.17 on Wednesday next./ But soft,... (2) on Wednesday next, /But soft,... (3); 4.5.65 confusions care lives not (2) confusions, care lives not (3). Changes that affect meaning also occur in grammar (6), spelling (3), metre (5), and number (3).

*B)    Changes to Q2 which Follow Q1*

Similarly, changes where Q3 follows Q1 vary. Here Q3 coincides with Q1 in a smaller number of significant word changes (c. 5): 1.1.127 humour (2) honour (1/3); 1.4.57 ottamie (2) atomi (1) atomies (3); 2.3.22 stayes (2) slayes (1/3); 4.1.98 breast (2) breath (1/3); 5.3.209 My Liege (2) Dread Sovereign (1) Sovereign (3). Agreement is also present in changes to tense, punctuation and grammar (4–6 examples each) and a few instances of number and spelling. Punctuation that affects meaning is particularly evident: 1.2.45 one fire burns out, anothers burning (2) one fire burns out another's burning (1/3); 1.4.100 wind who wooes (2) wind,/ Which wooes (1) wind, who wooes (3); 3.5.171 smaller with your gossips go (2) smatter with your gossips, go (1/3); 5.3.12–13 with flowers thy bridal bed I strew/ O woe, thy canopy is dust and stones (2) with flowers thy bridal bed I strew,/ O woe, thy canopy is dust and stones (1/3).

*C)    Changes Coincident with, but Different from, Q1 Differences*

While there are approximately 45–50 changes to the 25 per cent of the text where there is no Q1 for Q2 (A), there are only between 55–60 changes to the 75 per cent of the text where Q1 does exist (B+C). In this latter number the breakdown is interesting. Roughly 40 per cent of the 55–60 changes are made to agree with Q1 (B), another 12 per cent are changes made to Q2 where Q1 agrees with Q2. The remainder, just under half, are changes made to Q2 at places where Q1 is different yet where Q3 does not agree with the change.

Most of these changes are clustered from Act 3 onward and include: 3.1.124 he gan (2) A live (1) he gon (3); 3.1.126 fier end (2) fier eyed (1) fier and (3); 3.5.25 How is't, my soul (2) What says my Love (1) How ist my soul (3); 3.5.171 Prudence smatter. (2) prudence smatter (1) Prudence, smatter (3); 3.5.180 liand (2) trainde (1) allied (3); 4.5.9 needs must (2) must (1) must needs (3); 5.3.204 it (2) it is (1) is (3); 5.3.500 at such rate (2) of such price (1) at that rate (3). However, many changes are to spelling: 1.4.39 dunn (2) done (1) dun (3); or to punctuation: 1.2.99 maide: (2) maid (1) maid, (3); or layout: 3.3.61 mad man (2) madmen (1) mad men (3); or number: 3.5.139 give you thanks (2) thankes ye (1) gives you thankes (3); or to combinations of these such as 4.1.75 death, himselfe (2) death it selfe (1) Death himself (3).

The coincidence of changes at these points (c. 30), despite their disagreement, renders the statistical likelihood of Q3 making changes at these points without consulting Q1 quite low. In other words a difference between Q1 and Q2 may prompt Q3 editor to consider a change. However it has to be said that the decisions made frequently seem open to straightforward corrections either of misunderstanding by Q2 or of the many typographical errors and the idiosyncratic grammar and spelling in that edition. In other words, if in its difference with Q1, Q2 makes a mistake or imposes an unusual style, it may in the process construct a reading that Q3 recognizes as needing correction even if it has not consulted Q1. At the same time, the sheer overall number of significant agreements, let alone the questionable disagreements, between Q3 and Q1, argue for substantial interaction – as does the difference in the number of changes between the 25 per cent of text for which there is no Q1 (45–50) and the number made for the remaining 75 per cent (55–60). At a conservative estimate that difference results in the statistical probability that Q3 will change Q2 twice as many times where Q1 is not there to corroborate, as when it is there.[4] Nevertheless, while the Q3 editor respects Q1, the number of changes that are different from Q1 (c. 35) indicate that he has a mind of his own. This is underlined by his treatment of 1.2.99 she shall scant show well that now shows best (1/2) she shall scant show well that now seems best (3).

## Quarto 4

Q4 seems to recognize the authority of the skill involved in editing Q3. It follows nearly all of Q3's changes, adding over 25 that agree with Q1 differences from Q3/2 (D), over 25 that do not agree (E), and over 25 unique to Q4 (F), with a thoroughgoing revision of SPs and SDs which indicate possible consultation of F. Again, Q4 never substantially changes Q3 if it has already made a change from Q2, and in only one or two places does Q4 change Q3 if Q1 agrees with Q3.

## D) *Changes to Q2/3 which Agree with Q1*

First, there are the changes Q4 makes to agree with Q1 where Q2 and Q3 agree. The most obvious agreements are at 2.2.188–91 and 2.3.1–4. 2.2.188–91 represents the lines which nearly duplicate those at 2.3.1–4, something that has worried editors ever since. They do not appear in Q1 or Q4, but do appear in Q2/3 and F. At the same time Q4 retains the duplication at 3.3.40–43 while Q1 cuts, and at 5.3.108 Q4 cuts a four-line duplication retained by Q2/3 and F, that does not exist in Q1. This pattern of allowing Q1 to advise but not dictate is found throughout the Q4 editorial changes. Just as Q3 with Q1 and Q2, Q4 appears to combine ideas from Q1 and Q3 in some places: 2.2.162–3 as mine,/With (1) then/With (2.3) then myne/With (4); 3.3.143 frownst upon (1) puts up (2.3) pouts upon (4); 4.5.129 and 4.5132 Pretie//Pretie too (1) Prates//Prates to 2) Pratest//Pratest to (3) Pratee//Pratee, to (4). However, most of the Q1/4 agreements are over significant words or phrases. They include: 1.1.26 sense (2/3) in sense (1/4); 1.1.200 A sick man in sadness makes … (2/3) Bid a sick man in sadness make … (1/4); 1.2.99 fly (2/3) it fly (1/4); 1.4.90 Elklocks (2/3) Elflocks (1/4); 2.1.12 her (2/3) heir (1/4); 2.1.38 Open, or (2/3) Open et cetera (1) Open & cetera (4); 2.2.43 Whats in a name (2/3) What's in a name? (1/4); 3.1.168 aged (2/3) agile (1/4); 3.1.109 devote (2/3) denote (1/4); 3.5.194 never (2/3) ever (1/4); 4.1.72 stay (2/3) slay (1/4); 4.1.83 chapels (2) chappels (3) chaples (1) chapless (4); and 5.1.76 pray (2/3) pay (1/4).

Like Q3, Q4 clearly respects Q1 and treats it as a reliable text. Nevertheless Q4 is also eager to make changes, and follows the Q3 pattern in making more changes when Q1 is not present to corroborate. It is of note that, in those places where Q1 differs from Q3 and Q4 does not follow it (E), there are between 8 to 10 examples where Q4 moves in the direction of the spirit of Q1. For example: 3.5.25 talke it is not (2/3) talke, tis not yet (1) talk, it is not (4); 3.5.130 show'ring in one little body? (2/3) show'ring? In one little body (1) show'ring: in one little body? (4); 3.5.151 proud (2/3) proud. (1) proud: (4).

## E) *Changes to Q2/3 which do not Agree with Q1*

The changes independent of both Q1 and Q3 made by Q4 focus on punctuation, with a few changes to spelling and words and a few other areas. Examples of changes in punctuation include: 2.1.7 passion, liver (1) passion lover (3) passion, lover, (4); 2.1.13 Abraham: Cupid (1/2/3) Abraham Cupid (4); 3.5.131 resemblest a (1) countefaits. A (2) counterfaits. A (3) counterfeits, a (4); 5.3.223 greatest (1,2,3) greatest, (4). Q4 also tends to add parentheses in addition to the few found in Q1 and Q3 at 1.2.3, 3.3.75, 3.3.76, 4.1.85. Changes in spelling include 4.1.63 umpeer (1,2,3) umpire (4); 4.2.14 self wild harlotrie (1) self willde harlotry (3) self willed harlotry (4).

Of the few words changed in this category is one at 2.2.167 My Neece (2/3) Madam (1) My Deere (4), both Q4 and Q1 not picking up the highly probable reference to 'nyas', a nestling in its aery, suggested by J. Dover Wilson and G. Duthie (1955) and part of the dense texture of falconry exactly at this point and part of the lighter texture throughout the play. There is also the still contentious 2.1.10 dove (1) day (2/3) die (4), which raises a piece of probable evidence for the Q4 editor either having been involved in the theatre or having attended a performance: spoken 'day' would have been shifting from 'die' (1400) to 'diay' (1600) to 'day' (seventeenth century), and 'die' from 'dee' (1400) to 'day' (1500) to 'die' (seventeenth century).[5] In other words 'day' and 'die' could easily be misheard, each for the other, but Q4 would have little reason to change the word if the editor had not 'heard' something different. A third change comes at 4.1.85 where Q3 (following Q2) leaves a gap, and Q1 has 'tomb' and Q4 has 'his shroud'. Q4 on the whole tries to correct for metre in innovative ways, and this is one example. By informative contrast, the Folio 'editor', who also pays attention to metre, adjusts for it largely by using apostrophes to indicate dropped vowels and by expanding for example 'isht' to 'ished'.

### F)    Unique Changes in Q4

The most radical changes in Q4 occur in the 25 per cent of the text where there is no Q1 corroboration, a pattern that follows the Q3 editing and which doubles the number of changes made there. The majority of the changes are to punctuation (10), spelling (7), metre (8) and words or phrases (9). Some punctuation changes make only a little difference to significance, for example 5.3.8 something (3/4) some thing (4). However, changes at 3.2.76 ravenous dovefeathered (2/3) ravenous dove, feathered (4); 3.3.21 death, mistermd, calling (2/3) death misterm'd, calling (4); 4.4.40 all life living (2/3) all, life, living (4) are substantive. Similarly the changes to spelling can reflect variant but meaningful shifts: 3.2.60 On (2/3) One (4); 3.3.79 errant (2/3) errand (4); and simple corrections can clarify: 5.3.252 hower (2/3) hour (4). Other spelling changes are more considerable: 2.6.34 sum up sum (2/3) sum up some (4); 3.2.81 bower (2/3) power (4). The metrical changes are usually careful: 3.2.19 new snow upon (2/3) snow upon (4); 3.2.109 murd'red (2/3) murdered (4); 3.5.82 [nothing] (2/3) him (4); 3.5.106 beseech (2/3) I beseech (4). Predictably the most clearly substantial are changes to words which include: 2.2.152 strife (2/3) sute (4); 3.2.13 maidenhoods (2/3) maidenheads (4); 3.2.21 I (2/3) hee (4); 3.5.126 Earth (2/3) Ayre (4); 4.1.100 Too many (2/3) too paly (4); 4.3.49 O I walke (2/3) Or if I wake (4); 4.4.20 Father (2/3) faith (4).

The most interesting changes are the subtle adjustments to punctuation that radically affect or effect significance including: 3.5.130, 2.2.43, 2.1.17, 2.1.13, 3.5.131, 3.2.76, 4.4.40. This category of change suggests an exceptionally attentive mind, dealing with ambiguity of significance that has engaged all editors ever since. Of course, the Q4 editor is not faultless. Mistakes are made (for example 5.3.215 monthes of outrage (1) mouth of outrage (2/3) moneth of out-rage (4), although this last may be 'moaneth' for Q4 elsewhere spells 'moans' as 'mones'). One spelling shift, 2.3.5 is (2/3) in (4), is uncharacteristically misjudged. And there are a few other examples, but very few. Apart from one or two cases, however, there is little evidence from the dialogue to suggest that Q4 editor is doing anything different to the Q3 text than the Q3 text did to Q2: both may have been highly skilled correctors or possibly the same one.

## Discussion

Not only did Windet have a corrector in his printing house, but Stansby also appears to have employed one (Bland 8–10). He ran a high-quality printing house (Plomer 137), and as the printer of Jonson's *Workes* probably would have had a reputation as one 'who on evidence of past production, [was] ready to respect an author's artistic aspirations' (Bracken 1988, 19). More to the point, such a person may have had respect for the complexity of a text. If a corrector had been employed on both Q3 and Q4, Q4 differs because it is also peculiarly attentive to the theatrical guidelines, the SDs, SPs, lineations and assignation of speech. Given that a printing house corrector may not have been as skilled in this field, Q4 may possibly have consulted F.

The two cited instances at lines 2.5.16–17 and 5.2.23 and 30 of slavish copying by Q3, are corrected in both F and in Q4. There are a number of other places where Q4 corrects 'Exit' to 'Exeunt', possibly from F (for example 2.1.42), or the shift in 3.3.71 They knocke (2/3) Knocke (4/F). Yet unlike F, Q4 clearly corrects misassigning: 1.4.23 Horatio (2/3/F) Mercutio (4); 3.1.

175–7 Capulet (2/3/F) Montague (4). At a number of points Q4 editor seems
to have had knowledge of the play in performance: 2.1.16 nay I'll conjure too
(assigned to Benvolio 1/2/3/F), (assigned to Mercutio 4). Q4 assigns 2.2.185 to
Juliet instead of Romeo (3/F), possibly because of the lineation in Q1. But the
solutions to assigning 3.5.172–3 to 'Father' and/or 'Nurse' are unique to Q4;
they make sense, and have been followed by many editors ever since. Q4 also
assigns 4.5.120 Then have at you with my wit, to Peter, again unique and
particularly significant because it makes sense to retain the assignation to '2
Musician' (1/2/3/F). Q4's 'unnecessary' change must have been prompted by
something, and may be the result of practical knowledge of production.

   Furthermore, another indication that the editor of Q4 may have had
theatrical experience is that Q4 completely recasts the incidental parts in Act
5: Q2/3 have Romeo entering with 'Peter', Q1/4 'with Balthazar', and F 'with
Peter'. Subsequent assignations run: 5.3.71 [unassigned] (2/3) Boy (1) Page
(4) Peter (F); Romeo's man is 'Man' throughout Q1–3 except l.272, and
'Balthazar' throughout Q4 but 'Boy' in F at l.272 (clearly incorrect). Paris
enters with a Page in all five editions, but 5.3.281–5: Boy (1/2/3/4) Page (F:
here clearly correct, yet the Q1/2/3/4 assignation is probably on the evidence
of the 5.3.180 SD to 'Whistle Boy' where 'Boy' is Paris' 'Page'). In other
words only Q4 makes it clear that Balthazar returns with Romeo from Mantua.
In fact in none of these instances where Q4 and F agree is there any strong
evidence that Q4 used F. Nor is it easy to claim that F used Q4, for it
incorporates none of the clear corrections.

   Q4 was dated at c. 1622 on the basis of ornament breakdown, but new
evidence from a survey of Stansby's use of this ornament indicates that the
edition could have been printed from 1616 onward, probably from 1618, and
probably no later than 1626.[6] Hence any relation between Q4 and F is radically
uncertain. Other circumstantial evidence for dating Q4 comes from the change
of SP at 4.5 of 'Peter' for 'Will Kemp', an SP retained by Q3 even though by
1609 Kemp had left the King's Men's company for many years (Gurr 157)
but then Q3 is similarly haphazard elsewhere (for example 1.4.23). Q4 firmly
deletes the actor's name presumably because it is no longer a selling point,
Kemp must have faded from people's minds. In addition, Q3 and Q4, like Q2
and Q1 but unlike F, retain 'sounds' or 'Zounds' (3.1.42, 3.1.91, and possibly
3.2.52) in three places. If printers are so reluctant to print 'zounds' in particular
following the Act of 1606, why are they reprinted in Q3 (1609) let alone Q4?
Is it because they are less formal texts that F? Or possibly because they are
both printed well before compositors began to take seriously the need to change
such words (Taylor 1993).

## Summary

As noted above Q4 pays quite careful attention to devices of layout that affect theatrical production. While not bothered by the different prefixes for either Capulet Father or Capulet Mother of 'Old Man' or 'Wife' and so on (Williams 1997), it corrects Q3's sloppy copying of Q2 in many of these areas, changing assignations and lineation, trying to make 'Exit' SDs correct in number, corrects names of characters, and attempts to make SDs more accurate. Given the attention to theatrical detail in Q4, including some decisions that indicate direct experience of knowledge of production such as the cited instance of possible 'mishearing', it seems likely that the Q4 was edited by someone who had at least seen the play. The attention to metre which is extensive and is frequently adjusted by changing spelling, grammar and punctuation, as well as by adding or deleting words (with or without corroboration from Q1), may reinforce the sense that this editor had auditory experience of the text, and had possibly seen both versions of it. One of the most satisfying explanations for the heavy reliance on Q1 by Q2/3/4 and F, is that this shorter version of the play was in simultaneous production with the longer.

Finally, and most intriguing, if the subtle changes made by Q4 to punctuation that radically affect significance indicate an exceptionally skilful corrector, working on Q3, why did he never make substantial changes to the 100+ changes already made? Is there a limit to correctibility? Probably not, since editors ever since have had no qualms about changing Q3. Was there a printing-house policy in Stansby's works that the immediately preceding printing should be followed, or that if the text had already been printed by Stansby's works it had to be followed? If so, why would Stansby's printing-house make even more corrections? Was it the same corrector, who felt that if he had already made a change he need not revisit it? It is highly likely that the Q4 editor had a marked up copy of Q2, used to produce Q3, in his hands. The only probable way Q4 could have avoided making the changes to the more than 100 places where Q3 had already done so, would be to have located them first. If he only had an unmarked copy of Q3 he would have had to go painstakingly through Q2 and Q3, noting the differences (which takes a long time). Was the prompt to print Q4 the receipt of another marked up copy from someone in the theatre, which was collated with Q3? Or had the corrector seen the play and annotated the script? Or was the corrector a theatre worker, working for Stansby, like Chettle for Danter?

What the Q4 text shows is that it is the result of an editor working just like a modern editor on the text itself, with the addition of a theatrical understanding.

We may have misjudged the role of the corrector in the printing-house: it may be far more extensive and engaged than we have previously thought. More to the point, it is clear that early seventeenth century editing also recognised the need to bring the theatre to the text. The tradition of textual editing has not yet properly addressed what that might mean, but Q4 shows that good practice goes back a long way.

## Notes

1 Methodological note: the essay makes hypotheses on the basis of observation of different kinds of change among the quartos, the frequency of that change, and in places its statistical significance. I have not logged every single change Q4 makes to Q3, or Q3 to Q2. 'Human error' makes it virtually impossible for me to have done so, even had computer collation been involved, which it has not. I have attempted to record every change that in my opinion might interest an editor, and have taken a wide view of what that might entail. For example, a contraction added to stabilize metre into a regular iambic pentameter is important because it reduces the possibility of significantly irregular speech. Where there are consistent patterns for contraction, as in F, this is especially worrying since compositorial or editorial style overrides any sense of textual particularity. Similarly, I approach punctuation, layout, grammar and spelling as potentially significant.
2 Evans's edition is the only one which collates Q3 and Q4 with any attention, and is the edition from which the line numbers of this essay are drawn. Jill Levenson's recent Oxford edition (1999) does not attend to either Q3 or Q4 in any detail.
3 I am grateful to Jonathan Sanderson, a doctoral student co-supervised by John Barnard and myself, for research on the publishing history which was funded by the Arden Shakespeare.
4 The ratio of the number of lines in Q2 alone, to those in Q2 and Q1 is roughly 1:3.5. If we hypothesize that the corrector-editor is not consulting Q1, then we would expect the changes to occur in the same ratio of 1:3.5. However, the changes are, respectively, 45 and 55 (conservatively), and a chi-square calculation renders the likelihood of the corrector-editor not consulting Q1 at well over 100:1; in other words, he probably did.
5 Dr Clive Upton suggested this possibility, drawing on Joseph Wright, §82 'day', §'73' die.
6 L. Hunter, forthcoming article.

## Bibliography

Arber, Edward (1967 [1875–94]), *A Transcript of the Registers of the Company of Stationers of London, 1554–1640 A.D.* 5v, 1875–94, reprint, Gloucester, MA: Peter Smith.
Bland, Mark (1998), 'William Stansby and the Production of The Works of Beniamin Jonson, 1615–16', *Library* 6th ser. 20, 1–33.
Bracken, James (1985), 'William Stansby's Early Career', *Studies in Bibliography* 38, 214–17.

Bracken, James (1988), 'Books from William Stansby's Printing House, and Jonson's Folio of 1616', *Library* 6th ser. 10, 18–29.

Evans, G.H. (1984), *Romeo and Juliet*, Cambridge: Cambridge University Press.

Greg, W.W. (1955), *The Shakespeare First Folio: Its Bibliographical and Textual History*, Oxford: Clarendon Press.

Gurr, A. (1987), *Playgoing in Shakespeare's London*, Cambridge: Cambridge University Press.

Honigmann, Ernst (1996), *The Texts of 'Othello' and Shakespearian Revision*, London: Routledge.

Irace, K.O. (1994), *Reforming the 'Bad' Quartos: Performance and Provenance of Six Shakespearean First Editions*, London: Associated University Presses.

Jackson, William (ed.) (1957), *Records of the Court of the Stationers' Company 1602–1640*, London: Bibliographical Society.

Johnson, Gerald (1985), 'Nicholas Ling, Publisher 1580–1607', *Studies in Bibliography* 38, 203–14.

Jowett, John (1998), 'Henry Chettle and the First Quarto of *Romeo and Juliet*', *Papers of the Bibliographical Society of America* 92:1 (March), 53–74.

Jowett, John (1987), *Romeo and Juliet*, in S. Wells et al.

McKerrow, R.B. (1910), *A Dictionary of Printers and Booksellers in England, Scotland, and Ireland, and of Foreign Printers of English Books 1557–1640*, London: Bibliographical Society.

Plomer, Henry R. (1915), *A Short History of English Printing, 1476-1900*, London: Kegan Paul.

Reid, S.W. (1982), 'The Editing of Folio *Romeo and Juliet*', *Studies in Bibliography* 35, 43–66.

Reid, S.W. (1983), 'McKerrow, Greg, and Quarto Copy for Folio *Romeo and Juliet*', *Library* 6th ser. 5, 118–25.

Taylor, G. (1993), ''Swounds Revisited: Theatrical, Editorial and Literary Expurgation', in Taylor and Jowett, 51–106.

Taylor, G. and J. Jowett (1993), *Shakespeare Reshaped 1606–1623*, Oxford: Clarendon Press.

Wells, S. and G. Taylor (gen. eds) (1986), *William Shakespeare, Complete Works*, Oxford: Clarendon Press.

Wells, S. and G. Taylor, with J. Jowett and W. Montgomery (1987), *William Shakespeare: A Textual Companion*, Oxford: Clarendon Press.

Williams, G.W. (1965), 'The Printer and Date of Romeo and Juliet Q4', *Studies in Bibliography* 18, 253–4.

Williams, G.W. (1997), 'Preface', in Williams (1997), xi–xxiv.

Williams, G.W. (ed.) (1997), *Shakespeare's Speech-Headings: Speaking the Speech in Shakespeare's Plays*, London: Associated University Presses.

Wilson, J. Dover and G. Duthie (eds) (1955), *Romeo and Juliet*, Cambridge: Cambridge University Press.

Wright, J. (1924), *An Elementary Historical New English Grammar*, Oxford: Oxford University Press.

Chapter Three

# Marvell's Coy Mistresses

Paul Hammond

The contemporary reputation of seventeenth-century poets depended much upon the mode of publication which was used for their work.[1] In Donne's lifetime, his *Songs and Sonets* circulated in manuscript amongst a relatively privileged readership: only after his death were the erotic poems penned by the Dean of St Paul's revealed in print to a wider public. Rochester's poetry was also passed around primarily in manuscript form, becoming increasingly degenerate (textually if not morally), and with his name also being attached to all manner of illegitimate offspring. His licentious life and ostensibly pious death ensured a ready market for the printed editions which appeared within months of his final illness in 1680. Marvell's case is strikingly different: apart from the political satires associated with his name, few of his poems were published in his lifetime in either manuscript or print; and some of them must have looked decidedly old-fashioned when the posthumous Folio collection of *Miscellaneous Poems. By Andrew Marvell, Esq; Late Member of the Honourable House of Commons* was published in the turbulent year of 1681, with the country gripped by the Exclusion Crisis.

Amongst the poems printed for the first time in this Folio was 'To his Coy Mistress',[2] but c. 1672 a shorter version of the poem had been copied into his manuscript collection of topical verse and prose by Sir William Haward, MP and Gentleman of the Privy Chamber to Charles II. This is now Bodleian Library MS Don. b. 8, and the poem is found on pages 283–4, without title or attribution.[3] In the following discussion the Folio printed text will be referred to as '*F*', and the Haward manuscript as '*H*'. The relationship between the two texts is puzzling, and raises a number of critical and editorial questions which this paper will attempt to address. The two versions are printed below in parallel columns, where for ease of comparison spacing has been introduced into the *H* text to keep the two texts aligned; there are no such gaps in the original. Substantive variants between the two texts are underlined.

F                                    H

### To his Coy Mistress.

| | |
|---|---|
| Had <u>we</u> but World enough, and Time, | Had <u>I</u> but world enough, & tyme, |
| This coyness <u>Lady</u> were no crime. | This Coynesse, <u>Madam</u>, were noe Crime. |
| <u>We would</u> sit down, and think which way | <u>I could</u> sitt downe, & thinke, which way |
| To walk, and pass our long Loves Day. | To walke, & passe our long-loues day. |
| <u>Thou</u> by the *Indian Ganges* side        5 | <u>You</u> by yᵉ Indian Ganges side        5 |
| <u>Should'st</u> Rubies <u>find</u>: I by the Tide | <u>Should</u> Rubyes <u>seeke</u>, I by the Tide |
| Of *Humber* would complain. I would | Of Humber would complaine, I wo'ud |
| Love you ten years before the Flood: | Loue you ten yeares before yᵉ Floud, |
| And you should if you please refuse | And you should, if you please, refuse, |
| Till the Conversion of the *Jews*.        10 | Till yᵉ Conuersion of the Jewes.        10 |
| My vegetable Love should grow | My vegetable Loue should grow |
| Vaster then Empires, <u>and</u> more slow. | Vaster, then Empires, <u>but</u> more slow. |
| <u>An</u> hundred years should go to praise | <u>One</u> hundred yeares should goe, to prayse |
| <u>Thine Eyes</u>, and on <u>thy</u> Forehead Gaze. | <u>Your Brow</u>, and on <u>your</u> forehead gaze; |
| Two hundred to adore <u>each Breast</u>:        15 | Two hundred to adore <u>your eyes</u>,        15 |
| But thirty thousand to <u>the rest</u>. | But thirty thousand to <u>your Thighes</u>. |
| An Age at least to every part, | An age att least to euery part, |
| And the last Age <u>should</u> show your Heart. | And the last Age <u>to</u> shew your heart. |
| For <u>Lady</u> you deserve this State; | For, <u>Madam</u>, you deserue this state, |
| Nor <u>would</u> I love at lower rate.        20 | Nor <u>can</u> I loue att lower Rate.        20 |
| But <u>at my back I alwaies</u> hear | But <u>harke, behind meethinkes I</u> heare |
| Times winged Charriot hurrying near: | Tymes winged Charriot hurrying neare, |
| And yonder all before us <u>lye</u> | And yonder all before vs <u>lyes</u> |
| Desarts of vast <u>Eternity</u>. | Desarts of vast <u>Eternityes</u>. |
| <u>Thy</u> Beauty <u>shall no more be found</u>;        25 | <u>Your</u> beauty <u>will stand neede of Salt</u>,        25 |
| <u>Nor</u>, in <u>thy</u> marble Vault, <u>shall sound</u> | <u>For</u> in <u>the hollow</u> Marble Vault |
| My <u>ecchoing Song: then</u> Worms <u>shall</u> try | <u>Will</u> my <u>Songs Eccho</u>, Wormes <u>must</u> try |
| <u>That</u> long preserv'd Virginity: | <u>Your</u> longe preseru'd Virginity. |
| <u>And your quaint Honour turn to durst;</u> | |
| <u>And into ashes all my Lust.</u>        30 | |
| <u>The Grave's a fine and private place,</u> | |
| <u>But none I think do there embrace.</u> | |
| Now <u>therefore, while</u> the | Now <u>then whil'st</u> yᵉ youthfull <u>Glue</u> |
| youthful <u>hew</u> | |
| <u>Sits</u> on <u>thy skin</u> like morning <u>glew</u>, | <u>Stickes</u> on <u>your cheeke</u>, like Morning |
| <u>And while thy willing Soul transpires</u> 35 |    Dew,        30 |
| <u>At every pore with instant Fires</u>, | |
| <u>Now let us sport us while we may;</u> | <u>Or</u> like <u>the</u> amorous <u>Bird</u> of prey, |
| <u>And now</u>, like am'rous <u>birds</u> of prey, | <u>Scorning to admitt delay</u>, |
| <u>Rather</u> at once our <u>Time</u> devour, | <u>Lett vs</u> att once our <u>Selues</u> deuoure, |

Than languish in his slow-chapt
  pow'r. 40
Let us roll all our Strength, and all
Our sweetness, up into one Ball:
And tear our Pleasures with rough strife,
Thorough the Iron gates of Life.
Thus, though we cannot make our Sun 45
Stand still, yet we will make him run.

Not linger in Tymes slow-Chop't power,

And synce Wee cannot make the Sun 35
Goe backe, nor stand, wee'l make him run.

In addition to these two texts, there is another copy of the poem, headed 'To a Coy Mistress', transcribed from *F* (as a note at the end states) in Leeds University Library MS Lt 61 fols 24ᵛ–25ᵛ, a personal verse miscellany compiled c. 1715 and owned by James Gollop. It follows *F* except for reading 'pleased' for 'please' (l. 9), a grammatical improvement; 'the' for 'thy' (l. 26); and 'Through' for 'Thorough' (l. 44); while in line 30 the epigram is refined as 'The Grave's a fine, a private place'. While this MS has no textual value, it usefully illustrates the combination of error and revision which tends to occur in the process of transcription. More significantly, there are manuscript alterations from c. 1700 in the Bodleian Library copy of *F* (MS Eng. Poet. d. 49; referred to hereafter as *T2*):[4] in line 24 'Desarts' has been changed to 'Deserts'; in line 33 'hew' has been changed to 'glew'; in line 34 'glew' has been changed to 'dew'; and in line 44 'gates' has been changed to 'grates'.[5]

The origin and authority of these various texts are unclear. Even their dates are doubtful: the publication of *F* in 1681 and the transcription of *H* around 1672 provide for each of those texts a *terminus ante quem*, but there is no evidence for their date of composition.[6] Nor is the hand responsible for *T2* easily datable. The prefatory note to the 1681 Folio, signed 'Mary Marvell', claims that 'all these Poems ... are Printed according to the exact Copies of my late dear Husband, under his own Hand-Writing' (sig. [A2ʳ]). Though one might be sceptical about the status of this supposed widow, it is difficult to dismiss out of hand the assertion that the copytext for the volume was Marvell's holograph, though that does not rule out unacknowledged editorial intervention, or compositorial error, affecting the text of *F*. Nevertheless, *F* does at least deserve *prima facie* respect. So too does the confident correcting hand *T2*, probably working from a manuscript source which he believed to be authoritative. What of *H*? Haward was a conscientious transcriber, but what is at issue here is not his own work so much as the status of the text which he received. There are several possibilities. It could represent (a) an early, rather rough draft of the poem, preceding the version found in *F*; (b) a later version than *F*'s text, perhaps adapted for a different milieu; (c) a version corrupted in transmission by copying; or (d) a version corrupted by oral transmission. It could also represent any combination of these: Hilton Kelliher suggested that it was both an early text and a memorial reconstruction (Kelliher 1970, 255). It could even be an early version, reworked independently of *F*, transmitted orally, and corrupted in transcription. Let us consider in turn the characteristics of *H* which might suggest each of these origins.

The idea that it may represent an early version of the poem, before it received the final polish represented by *F*, might be supported by a number of variants which suggest deliberate revision rather than accidental corruption. 'I' for 'we' (ll. 1, 3) deliberately focuses attention on the male speaker. The variant 'Madam' for 'Lady' (ll. 2, 19) shows a change of mind over the mode of address. The variant 'find'/'seeke' also points to revision. In all these instances, however, the direction of the change is debatable. Other variants may point to *H* representing an unrefined early draft: the more blatant reading 'eyes /... Thighes' for 'Breast /... rest' (ll. 15–16), and the strikingly direct comment, 'Your beauty will stand neede of Salt' (l. 25), both lack the subtlety of *F*. The absence from *H* of some of the epigrammatic lines for which the poem is best remembered (ll. 29–32 and 41–4) might also point to its being an early version, on the grounds that few attentive readers would omit or (if memorizing the poem) forget such verses.

But some of the evidence just cited could also be enlisted in support of the hypothesis that the poem was revised away from the *F* text, perhaps for readers of broader tastes: 'Thighes' is certainly more direct than 'the rest', and might indicate a target audience with a preference for the mode of Rochester over that of Herrick, whose poem 'Upon the Nipples of *Julia*'s Breast' is a possible source for that euphemism 'the rest'. 'Your beauty will stand neede of Salt' is similarly unsubtle, if not downright crude. The tone of *H* seems less refined than that of *F*, as if *H* represents a man striking a Don Juan pose to a male homosocial gathering rather than choosing the best strategy to appeal to a particular woman. The prominence of 'I' rather than 'we' supports such a scenario.

As for errors of transcription, 'would'/'could' (l. 3), 'would'/'can' (l. 20), and 'An'/'One' (l. 13) are typical of the almost indifferent variant which one regularly finds in seventeenth-century manuscript verse, though these variants could be generated in either written or oral transmission. The plural 'Eternityes' (*H* l. 24) is conceptually awkward, but to mistake 'e' and 'es' at the end of a word is an easy and common error of transcription. 'Nor' and 'For' (l. 26) could be mistaken for each other, and while they introduce statements of opposite effect, both ideas are plausible, *F* meaning: 'I shall not want to court

you when you are in your vault', or 'When you are in your vault you will not
be able to hear my love songs'; and *H* meaning: 'If you continue to resist, I
shall still be trying to court you when you are in your vault', or 'When you are
in your vault, you will hear my love songs echoing around you, and regret the
lost opportunity.' Again, though, *H* is cruder, so this variant may not be simple
error.

Other variants seem to point to lapses of memory rather than of
transcription. Complete couplets are missing from *H*, and couplets, as poor
Mr Brooke found when addressing the electors of Middlemarch, are liable to
slip from the memory under the influence of a glass or two of sherry. The
rephrasing of lines with a new syntactical structure and the approximate
rendition of striking images also points to memorial reconstruction (*H* ll. 26–
7, 31–4). We know that the memory is liable to recall the unusual image but
not its precise grammatical or rhetorical function: the mind behind the bad
(first) Quarto of *Hamlet* recalled the phrase 'The vndiscouered country', but
produced:

> The vndiscouered country, at whose sight
> The happy smile, and the accursed damn'd.
> (Shakespeare 1603, sig. D4ᵛ)

with its commonplace and ungrammatical second line, rather than:

> The vndiscouer'd country, from whose borne
> No trauiler returnes.
> (Shakespeare 1605, sig. G2ʳ⁻ᵛ)

which is the reading of the good (second) Quarto. And, to cite a Restoration
example, when Rochester's satire on Charles II circulated orally, being too
dangerous to be frequently transcribed, some couplets dropped out, others
were reordered, became triplets, or had their syntax rearranged (Rochester
1999, 85–90). In *H* there is surely a lapse of memory between its lines 30 and
31, where the joining of the two similes 'like Morning Dew, / Or Like the
amorous Bird' is grotesque. (It is just possible, however, that eye-skip could
have led a copyist to move from the first 'like' to the second 'like', if working
hastily and not reading the result.) The introduction of 'Thighes', 'Salt', and
the rhyme on 'Vault' is not beyond the ingenuity of someone patching up a
text from an imperfectly remembered version.

* * *

Weighing the textual variants in so short a poem cannot produce any certain conclusions, since several readings can be accounted for in more than one way. But it is possible to strengthen one of the hypotheses about the origin of *H* by considering some of the text's linguistic features. There are two such elements in *H* which suggest a different target audience from the audience envisaged for *F*, and perhaps a different date of origin. While *F* calls the coy mistress 'Lady', *H* calls her 'Madam'. The latter had become a standard polite form of address by the Restoration period, as Edward Phillips noted in 1696: '*Madam*, a Title of Honour, which is given as well in Writing as Speaking, to Women of Quality, as Princesses, Dutchesses, and others; but grown a little too common of late'.[7] Secondly, while *F* mixes 'you' and 'thou' forms, *H* uses only the 'you' form. 'In the course of the seventeenth century', writes Charles Barber, the *thou* forms fall into disuse, and by 1700 have disappeared from Standard English except as literary archaisms and in the special language used for liturgical purposes' (Barber 1997, 152–3; and see 156 for pronouns in Restoration comedy). If the *F* text were composed in the late 1640s or the 1650s, the mixture of 'you' and 'thou' forms would have been usual, for writers at that date might switch between them indifferently, or for grammatical ease. By the Restoration period, 'you' was standard polite usage, with 'thou' used to inferiors, to children, or 'when the emotional temperature rises'.

Etherege had a good ear for social nuances in language, and in *The Man of Mode* (1676) we find that the characters regularly address one another as 'you'. One exception is Sir Fopling Flutter, who, trying to ingratiate himself as an intimate friend of Dorimant, switches from using 'you' to Emilia to using 'thou' to Dorimant: 'Lady, your servant. – Dorimant, let me embrace thee.' Later, when Harriet turns aside to seek private support from her friend, she says, 'Dear Emilia, do thou advise me.' But moments of erotic intimacy do not seem to attract the 'thou' form, and when Dorimant and Bellinda discuss their mutual fidelity, they almost exclusively use 'you':

| | |
|---|---|
| *Bellinda.* | *You* have no more power to keep the secret than I had not to trust *you* with it. |
| *Dorimant.* | By all the joys I have had, and those *you* keep in store – |
| *Bellinda.* | – *You*'ll do for my sake what *you* never did before. |
| *Dorimant.* | By that truth *thou* hast spoken, a wife shall sooner betray herself to her husband. |
| *Bellinda.* | Yet I had rather *you* should be false in this than in another thing *you* promised me. |

(Etherege 1979, III.ii.133–4; V.ii. 38; IV.ii. 21–8; emphases added)

The opening and closing lines of this extract are in an idiom which soberly considers adult desire and sexual freedom; the characters use 'you'. The tone modulates into mock-seriousness in the rhyming couplet which the two characters construct, still using 'you'. Only in Dorimant's second line do we find 'thou', where he is using a now archaic biblical register to italicize wryly the seriousness of her promise. 'You' is the polite norm; 'thou' marks a move into a more intense register. Another character who uses 'thou' is Old Bellair, who says admiringly to Harriet, 'Adod, sirrah, I like thy wit well', and flirtatiously to Emilia, 'Go to, thou'rt a rogue' (III.i.170, V.ii.26); here 'thou' seems a generational marker, part of Old Bellair's antiquated idiolect. It may be that in 1672 (if the composition of *H* is close to its date of transcription) 'thou' would have seemed dated, out of place in a poem of libertine courtship.

The supposition is strengthened by a glance at Rochester's usage. His erotic poems use 'thou' when they are cast in a formal and somewhat archaic pastoral mode – 'Canst thou feele Love and yet noe pitty know?' ('Dialogue', l. 2) – or a religious idiom – 'If I by miracle can be / This livelong Minute true to Thee / Tis' all that Heaven allows' ('Love and Life', ll. 13–15). He uses 'you' when addressing a woman as an autonomous sexual partner – 'You Rivall Bottle must allow / I'll suffer Rivall Fopp' ('To A Lady, in A Letter', ll. 7–8) – or a long-suffering wife – 'I am by Fate slave to your Will' ('To his more than Meritorious Wife', l. 1). 'Thou' is used with affectionate contempt when addressing a male companion – 'Love a Woman! Th'rt an Ass' ('Love to a Woman', l. 1) – or, in mock heroic vein, a disobedient servant – in this case his own unruly penis: 'Base Recreant to thy Prince, thou durst not stand' ('The Imperfect Enjoyment', l. 61). There are significant nuances here. So in Marvell's poem the removal of 'thou' (and perhaps the substitution of 'Madam' for 'Lady'), along with the introduction of salt and thighs, suggest that the text has been slightly modernized, and angled towards the libertine taste and idiom of court or coffee-house wits.

\* \* \*

Though the origin of *H* is uncertain, there is one point in the poem where *H* may be able to clarify a crux,[8] the much-debated rhyme in lines 33–4, where the various witnesses read:

> Now therefore, while the youthful hew
> Sits on thy skin like morning glew,  (*F*)

Now therefore, while the youthful glew
Sits on thy skin like morning dew,   (*T2*)

Now then whil'st y[e] youthfull Glue
Stickes on your cheeke, like Morning Dew, (*H*)

*H* supports the correction made by *T2*. Since *H* and *T2* are almost certainly independent of each other, they are witnesses to the fact that 'glew/dew' was the rhyme in their common ancestor. While it is possible that this ancestor was itself corrupt at this point, it is also possible (and on the principle of *lectio difficilior* probable) that 'glew/dew' is the rhyme which stood in Marvell's original manuscript. If so, then 'hew/glew' is an alteration made by the editor or compositor of *F*. At this point in the argument, textual probabilities need to be supported by critical exegesis. What do the two pairs of rhymes mean? The originator of the 'hew/glew' rhyme seems to have imagined the mistress' youthful colour ('hew' being 'hue' in modern spelling) being like the rosy colour of the morning sky ('glew' being 'glow' in modern spelling).[9] The originator of the 'glew/dew' rhyme seems to have imagined the mistress's perspiration being like the morning dew. Here 'glew' may mean (a) 'glow', in the sense 'heat'[10] or even 'sweat';[11] and also (b) 'glow' in the associated metonymic sense 'ardour',[12] implicitly sexual ardour;[13] or (c) 'glue' in the sense 'sweat';[14] or (d) 'glue' in the sense 'gum', which was applied to a perfumed excretion.[15] The primary sense is probably either (a) or (c), 'sweat', each implying (b), 'ardour', with (d) 'perfume' as a punning additional conceit. The idea that the lady is perspiring with incipient erotic pleasure is extended in the following couplet: 'And while thy willing Soul transpires / At every pore with instant Fires' (ll. 36–7). Besides, the verb 'sits' seems more appropriate for moisture than for colour. Textually and rhetorically the reading of *T2* seems preferable to that of *F*, which is by comparison a commonplace image. The reading of *H* ('Glue') clearly takes 'glew' to mean 'glue' rather than 'glow', as its verb 'Stickes' confirms.

The editor of a single text of the poem based upon *F* has to choose between the *F* rhymes and the *T2* rhymes, since each presents a clear and coherent, but different, simile. The editor might reasonably choose *T2* ('glew/dew'): textually on the principle of *lectio difficilior* and the support of *H*, and critically on the basis of the rhetorical coherence of the passage and the productive Marvellian ambiguities which the reading offers.[16] This would assume that *F* on the one hand, and *T2* and *H* on the other, are witnesses to a common original which was corrupted and simplified into the *F* reading by someone other than

Marvell. But an editor might also choose $F$,[17] on the grounds that its reading could have been Marvell's own work, perhaps a revision made in order to remove an indecorous reference to the lady's perspiration. Whatever its status, the $F$ reading does seem to be a change: for the reading of $T2$ and $H$ to be a textual corruption, one would have to posit a common ancestor which had turned a simple reading into a difficult one before the stemma branched and the $H$ text was damaged and adapted, which is theoretically possible, but complex. What an editor should not do is to conflate $F$ and $T2$ as the Oxford editors did (Marvell 1971, i. 28), printing 'youthful hew / … like morning dew', which compares a colour with a liquid. This creates a reading for which there is no seventeenth-century evidence, and removes the one word ('glew') which all witnesses agree is one of the rhymes. The stemma looks something like this:

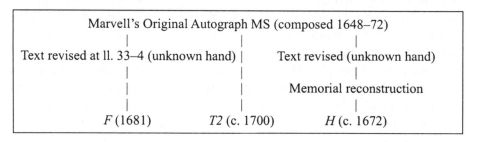

\* \* \*

Where does this leave us? It leaves us, I think, with two coy mistresses. The text in $F$ is presumably close to a Marvellian holograph, but will require emendation from $T2$ and $H$ at ll. 33–4 if we think that the 'hew/glew' rhyme was generated by a simplifying editor or printer; but $F$ can stand without emendation if we hold the poet himself responsible for the change. The text in $H$ is certainly corrupt (though at exactly which points is far from certain), having passed through scribal and probably also memorial transmission. It may represent an early version of the poem, though there seem to be no features which suggest this which cannot equally be explained by corruption, or by the hypothesis that an Interregnum poem was adapted for a Restoration audience with less refined sensibilities. It deserves to stand in its own right, perhaps as an example of a communally-crafted coffee-house text, but perhaps as an instance of Marvell himself trying to demonstrate his heterosexual credentials. For this text, with its raunchier style and its dramatization of the sexually demanding 'I', reached Haward in the very year, 1672, in which Marvell was being derided in print for his homosexual interests.[18]

## Notes

1  Beal (1987–93) catalogues the manuscript circulation of the principal writers. For the scribal culture see Love (1993), and for the interrelationship of manuscript and printed texts of Restoration literature see Hammond (1992) and Hammond (forthcoming).

2  The text used here is that of the copy in the Brotherton Collection, Leeds University Library. The British Library copy (C. 59. i. 8) and some pages from the annotated Bodleian Library copy MS Eng. Poet. d. 49 (which also has MS leaves supplementing the printed text) are reproduced in the Scolar Press facsimile (Marvell 1969), with a useful bibliographical note.

3  This text was first printed and discussed by Hilton Kelliher (Kelliher 1970), and a facsimile is provided in Kelliher (1978). See also Beal 1987–93, ii. 23. It is not always easy to tell majuscules from minuscules in Haward's hand.

4  Not an obvious *siglum*, but the one used in the Oxford edition (Marvell 1971), and retained here to facilitate cross-reference: for a discussion of *T2* see Marvell 1971, i. 227, 234–5, and Beal 1987–93, ii. 22–3.

5  For 'iron grates' cp. Phillips (1696): '*Grates*, a sort of Iron Lattices, and serving instead of Windows, in Prisons and Popish Cloysters' (sig. Aaa 3ʳ); not in the fourth (1678) edition; cp. 'Upon Appleton House', ll. 103–4. The image suggests that the ecstatic physical union of the lovers will let them escape from the prison-house of the body.

6  A *terminus a quo* for the *F* text is provided by the publication of Cowley's *The Mistress* (1647) and Herrick's *Hesperides* (1648), which contributed to Marvell's poem: see Marvell (1971) for the use of Cowley, and for Herrick see Hammond 1996, 114.

7  Phillips 1696, sig. Iiiᵛ; not in the fourth (1678) edition. Unfortunately, nowhere else in his verse does Marvell use either 'Lady' or 'Madam' as a vocative.

8  For an extensive (and somewhat opaque) discussion of this crux see Clayton (1972).

9  Cp. *Paradise Lost* viii. 612. The *OED* lists 'glew' and 'glewe' as seventeenth-century spellings of the verb 'glow'; I assume that the same spellings were available for the noun, though discussions of the crux have disputed this, and no example has been produced. Helge Kökeritz asserted (without citing evidence) that 'glew' must have been a northern dialect form of 'glow', which Marvell, as a Yorkshireman, would have known (quoted by George deF. Lord in Marvell 1984, 24).

10  *OED* 'glow *sb*. 1b', first example 1793; but 'glow *v*.[1] 5' has the same meaning from 1386.

11  Not in *OED*, but certainly a modern usage; how far back does it go?

12  *OED* 'glow *sb*. 3', first example 1748, but 'glow *v*.[1] 6' has the same meaning from 1649.

13  'A moist hand argues an amorous nature' (Tilley 1950, H 86); cp. *Othello* III. iv. 39, *Antony and Cleopatra* I. ii. 52–3.

14  This sense is not recorded in the *OED*, but Thomas Blount glosses 'glutinosity' as 'gluiness, clamminess', showing that 'glue' might be thought of as clamminess or moisture, not only as a sticky substance (Blount 1656, sig. S4ʳ). Nicholas Hookes plays comically on the two senses 'sweat' and 'glue' in his poem 'A Sacrifice to Amanda': 'I'd rather foot it twenty miles, / Then kisse a lasse whose moisture reeks, / Lest in her clammie glew-pie cheeks / I

leave my beard behinde' (from *Amanda* [1653], cited from the Chadwyck-Healey Literature Online database). The *OED* records 'glew' and 'glewe' as seventeenth-century spellings of the noun 'glue'.

15  *OED* 'glue *sb*. 3b', *OED* 'gum *sb*.² 2'; cp. *Paradise Lost* xi. 327.

16  Elizabeth Story Donno followed *H* in her Penguin edition (Marvell 1972, 51). However, her apparatus quotes the reading of *F* in modernized spelling as 'hue' and 'glue' which is misleading. She glosses 'glue' only by means of a quotation from William Baldwin (1547): 'Life is nothing else but as it were a glue, which in man fasteneth the soul and body together', which may resonate with other poems by Marvell but is insufficiently precise as an explanation of this particular image.

17  George deF. Lord followed *F* in his edition (Marvell 1984, 24).

18  For these attacks on Marvell see Hammond 1996, 115.

# Bibliography

Barber, Charles (1997), *Early Modern English*, 2nd edn, Edinburgh: Edinburgh University Press.

Beal, Peter (1987–93), *Index of English Literary Manuscripts: Volume II: 1625–1700*, 2 parts, London: Mansell.

Blount, Thomas (1656), *Glossographia*, London: Humphrey Moseley.

Clayton, Thomas (1972), '"Morning Glew" and Other Sweat Leaves in the Folio text of Andrew Marvell's Major Pre-Restoration Poems', *English Literary Renaissance* 2, 356–75.

Etherege, Sir George (1979), *The Man of Mode*, ed. John Barnard, London: Ernest Benn.

Hammond, Paul (1992), 'The Circulation of Dryden's Poetry', *Papers of the Bibliographical Society of America* 86, 379–409.

Hammond, Paul (1996), 'Marvell's Sexuality', *The Seventeenth Century* 11, 87–123.

Hammond, Paul (forthcoming), 'The Restoration Poetic and Dramatic Canon', in *History of the Book in Britain: Volume 4: 1557–1695*, ed. John Barnard and D.F. McKenzie, Cambridge: Cambridge University Press.

Kelliher, Hilton (1970), 'A New Text of Marvell's "To His Coy Mistress"', *Notes and Queries* 215, 254–6.

Kelliher, Hilton (1978), *Andrew Marvell: Poet & Politician 1621–78*, London: British Museum Publications.

Love, Harold (1993), *Scribal Publication in Seventeenth-Century England*, Oxford: Clarendon Press.

Marvell, Andrew (1681), *Miscellaneous Poems. By Andrew Marvell, Esq; Late Member of the Honourable House of Commons*, London: Robert Boulter.

Marvell, Andrew (1969), *Miscellaneous Poems 1681*, Menston: Scolar Press.

Marvell, Andrew (1971), *The Poems and Letters of Andrew Marvell*, ed. H.M. Margoliouth, 3rd edn rev. Pierre Legouis and E.E. Duncan-Jones, 2 vols, Oxford: Clarendon Press.

Marvell, Andrew (1972), *The Complete Poems*, ed. Elizabeth Story Donno. Harmondsworth: Penguin.

Marvell, Andrew (1984), *Complete Poetry*, ed. George deF. Lord, London: Everyman.

Phillips, Edward (1696), *The New World of English Words*, 5th edn, London: R. Bently.

Rochester, John Wilmot, 2nd Earl of (1999), *The Works of John Wilmot, Earl of Rochester*, ed. Harold Love, Oxford: Oxford University Press.

Shakespeare, William (1603), *The Tragicall Historie of Hamlet, Prince of Denmarke*, London: N.L. and Iohn Trundell.

Shakespeare, William (1605), *The Tragicall Historie of Hamlet, Prince of Denmarke*, London: N.L.

Tilley, Morris Palmer (1950), *A Dictionary of the Proverbs in England in the Sixteenth and Seventeenth Centuries*, Ann Arbor: University of Michigan Press.

# Chapter Four

# Congreve and the Integrity of the Text[1]

D.F. McKenzie

Song and dance were certainly among the many helps Congreve used in creating his characters. In *The Double Dealer* it's all too casual and undeveloped: some musicians who just happen to have been crossing the stage are diverted by Mellefont and asked to practise their new song as set by Purcell:

> Cynthia *frowns when-e'er I woo her,*
> *Yet she's vext if I give over;*
> *Much she fears I should undo her,*
> *But much more to lose her Lover:*
> *Thus, in doubting, she refuses;*
> *And not winning, thus she loses.*
>
> *Prithee* Cynthia *look behind you,*
> *Age and Wrinkles will o'ertake you;*
> *Then too late Desire will find you,*
> *When the Power must forsake you:*
> *Think, 0 think o'th' sad Condition,*
> *To be past, yet wish Fruition.*

Cynthia's there told to

> *Think, think o'th' sad Condition,*
> *To be past, yet wish Fruition.*

but it's all far too direct. Mellefont, not the truest or quickest wit in Congreve's pantheon, does nothing here to exploit it further and there's no response at all from Cynthia.

Congreve's integration of song, character, and action had been dramatically finer if morally coarser in *The Old Bachelor.* Take for example Heartwell's attempt to seduce Sylvia with song and dance. He's engaged a group of musicians to sing her an erotic song, and in the dialogue to which it gives rise Congreve brings out admirably both the degree of Heartwell's infatuation and Sylvia's practised ability to keep him at precisely the right distance. In its action, sense of character, inner dialogue, and concision, it's a fine example of the genre, and unlike many of its predecessors, it's even-handed in suggesting both the woman's and the man's disappointment. Again, it's Purcell:

> *As* Amoret *and* Thyrsis *lay*
> *Melting the Hours in gentle Play;*
> *Joining Faces, mingling Kisses,*
> *And exchanging harmless Blisses:*
> *He trembling cry'd, with eager haste,*
> *O let me feed as well as taste,*
> *I die, if I'm not wholly blest.*

> *The fearful nymph reply'd* – Forbear;
> I cannot, dare not, must not hear:
> Dearest Thyrsis, do not move me,
> Do not – do not – if you Love me.
> *O let me – still the Shepherd said;*
> *But while she fond Resistance made,*
> *The hasty Joy, in strugling fled.*

> *Vex'd at the Pleasure she had miss'd,*
> *She frown'd and blush'd, then sigh'd and kiss'd,*
> *And seem'd to moan, in sullen Cooing,*
> *The sad miscarriage of their Wooing:*
> *But vain alas! were all her Charms;*
> *For* Thyrsis *deaf to Loves allarms,*
> *Baffled and senseless, tir'd her Arms.*

> *After the Song, a Dance of Anticks*

In *The Way of the World* too there's a fine use of a song to point up the conflict between Marwood and Millamant. Millamant uses it to seal her victory over Marwood, one of the *'inferior Beauties'*, and to insult her *'Rival's Eyes'*. It's not clear from the text that it was sung off-stage but Mincing must leave to make the request and no one enters again until it's over. According to Curtis Price, 'Music played or sung "from within" is a common device to help create a humorous effect' (Price 25). If this were so here, and the facial expressions of the two actresses formed in effect an accompaniment to it, the song could reveal a great deal about the characters of both women. Still, the setting by John Eccles takes over five minutes and at that duration clearly implies a different idea of dramatic pacing from that we're used to. It's almost invariably cut in modern productions.

> *Love's but the Frailty of the Mind,*
> *When 'tis not with Ambition join'd;*
> *A sickly Flame, which if not fed expires;*
> *And feeding, wastes in Self-consuming Fires.*
>
> *'Tis not to wound a wanton Boy*
> *Or am'rous Youth, that gives the Joy;*
> *But 'tis the Glory to have pierc'd a Swain,*
> *For whom inferior Beauties sigh'd in vain.*
>
> *Then I alone the Conquest prize,*
> *When I insult a Rival's Eyes:*
> *If there's Delight in Love, 'tis when I see*
> *That Heart which others bleed for, bleed for me.*

For a third illustration let me take you back to a scene in *The Old Bachelor* where we find Congreve twice revising to get the balance right between Bellmour's dialogue, Araminta's perception of his meaning and the import of the song:

> *Thus to a ripe, consenting Maid,*
> *Poor, old, repenting* Delia *said,*
> *Would you long preserve your Lover?*
> *  Would you still his Goddess reign?*
> *Never let him all discover,*
> *  Never let him much obtain.*
>
> *Men will admire, adore and die,*
> *While wishing at your Feet they lye:*
> *But admitting their Embraces,*
> *  Wakes 'em from the Golden Dream;*
> *Nothing's new besides our Faces,*
> *  Every Woman is the same.*

Bellmour's innuendo in the speech which immediately precedes this song is that if he is to be tongue-tied, his other members must be free to express his passion:

> Ay, but if I'm Tongue-ty'd, I must have all my Actions free to – Quicken your Apprehension – and I-gad, let me tell you, my most prevailing Argument is express'd in dumb shew.

Congreve's first stab at this line was the mildly obscene wording 'my standing

Argument is depress'd in dumb Shew'. It's the reading all current editions of his comedies accept, in preference to what's thought to be Congreve's bowdlerization of it in his *Works* of 1710. In fact he first revised it during the opening season in 1694 by reading: 'My most *prevailing* Argument is depress'd in dumb shew' and then in 1710 settled for 'My most prevailing Argument is *express'd* in dumb shew'. Although it gets rid of the crude implications of 'standing' and 'depress'd', far from being a bowdlerization, this final version shifts the emphasis from Bellmour's physical collapse *after* making love to (if we must) his *expressive emission* while doing so. Because its implications are less obvious, Bellmour's wit is improved and (at the same time) Araminta's understanding of it, for she certainly finds in his words good cause 'to divert the Discourse' with a song.

Since I've now intruded a small editorial crux which shows Congreve at work improving dialogue, characterization, and the contextual point of the music, let me suggest some other physical features of his texts that seem to me to reinforce my comments about his respect for the individual and about various devices he used by which to heighten his readers' sense of a character.

Congreve made it quite clear in the preface to his *Works* of 1710 that that edition should supersede all other versions, especially the earliest Quartos of his plays. My own line of reasoning in agreeing with him is that in the 1690s there were no London printers prepared to take the trouble to adapt their stereotypical typography for plays to a style, and with a care, that would have better served Congreve's total commitment to neoclassical principles of scenic form. Only after Tonson set up John Watts as his printer, in 1707, were Tonson and Congreve able to show on the page one of the most dramatically significant features of Congreve's writing for the stage. When he uses the word 'scene' in his essay on humour and in his dedication to *Love for Love* of 1695, or when, in his *Amendments* of Collier of 1698, he locates a passage from his plays, he uses a system of numbering which only makes sense if the scenes are neoclassical ones.

When he came to edit his works in 1710, he was at last able to ensure that his plays were presented in their proper scenic form, presenting the units as distinct social groups and yet, by means of his *liaisons de scènes*, bringing a special art to those points of transition when a character arrived or left and thereby changed the human composition of the scene. But there was one feature for which he had to wait another ten years: centred speech prefixes. Because these each take a separate line, they're expensive of space and of course their extension of the text increases the cost of paper and printing. The three volumes of Congreve's *Works of* 1710 are not only handsome, they're efficient: the large type and short lines give the dialogue a marvellously immediate presence for the reader (Figures 1 and 2). But by the same token it would have been impossibly expensive, in that format and type, to add the further refinement of centred speech headings.

When the works were next reprinted, however, in 1719–20, Tonson and Congreve chose a smaller, duodecimo format and long primer type, and took the opportunity to introduce centred speech headings (Figure 3). You'd think perhaps all these might reduce the legibility of the text, but in fact the extra space around the characters' names, and their effect of separating out the lines of dialogue, more than compensate for the smaller page and type. To an eye familiar with its models, they created a text that was both more theatrically faithful and aesthetically pleasing. And it's a reasonable inference that Congreve specified it: of the many plays that Watts printed and the Tonsons published at this time, such a style is peculiar to his. The editions of 1725 and 1730 adopt it; and when Baskerville came to design his elegant three-volume edition of the plays and poems in 1761 he too accepted the scene divisions and centred speech headings of 1719–20. In that visual form, Congreve's works also claim a place alongside their prototypes, the fine seventeenth-century editions of Terence, Corneille, Racine and Molière, and implicitly affirm a value equal to theirs.

Those remarks are simply background to enable me to make my next point, that even as an editor Congreve still sought by such helps to give each of his characters as much presence as he could. Far from removing his texts further from the stage, as some have claimed, his typography heightened a reader's sense of the individual characters and gave them each a more distinctive voice on the page than the conventional abbreviated and sidelined forms in most English dramatic texts.

If we compare, for example, Millamant's exit and Mirabell's soliloquy on the sheet, we can see that in the Quarto (Figure 4) there's no visual space between the scenes, and Mirabell's isolated state, with Millamant gone, is obscured in a uniform page of type. As printed in *Works* (Figure 5), however, the visual space created by the scene division here is also the stage space through which Millamant passes as she separates herself from him, and it's the ever-lengthening space too over which Mirabell's words 'I have something more –' try to hold her back … until he is indeed alone. 'Gone.' And *his* – Mirabell's – aloneness, his solitary wonder, so expressively now signalled on the page, invests his thoughts, at least to my mind, with a special intimacy. Millamant has *gone* (the finality of her last words is even, you might say, elegantly underlined by the decorative types); but before she leaves, she offers him a *liaison:* 'and when you have done thinking of that, think of me'. And Mirabell obediently accepts it: 'Think of you! To think of a Whirlwind ....'

But that moment of parting has its counterpart in the reunion of Millamant and Mirabell. It's that wonderful point in the play when Sir Wilful has been making his addresses to Millamant, but could only show his ignorance when she invites him to cap her quotation from Suckling, suggesting that if he is to be a lover, he must show his *'Power and Art'*. Poor Sir Wilful is disgraced, makes a bashful exit, and returns to company more congenial to him. Millamant ends the scene with a reflection ('Ay, ay'), a laugh, and a line from Waller:

> *Like* Phoebus *sung the no less am'rous Boy.*

Again her momentary singleness is underlined by the decorative type at the scene end (Figure 3). It creates a spatial divide that it's the play's whole purpose to bridge in the union of Millamant and Mirabell. Yet once crossed, the same line becomes a flourish for the new stage world created by the entry of this new man, one with the Apollonian power and art to complete Millamant's love.

> *Like* Daphne *she, as Lovely and as Coy.*

There are other felicities here in the way the dialogue instantly plays with the myth of Daphne and Phoebus-Apollo. But my immediate concern is simply to reveal the effects of heightening the dramatic moment by these forms of division and unity and thereby of course deepening our knowledge of the characters and our feelings for them. Instead of a simple exit for Sir Wilful and an entry for Mirabell, as in the Quartos, we have also at the head of the new scene here, a statement of the twinned presence of Millamant and Mirabell in a pairing whose terms and permanence they're about to agree in the dialogue that follows.

Let me turn now to a moment in *Love for Love* where we can see a couple of other effects created by the manner in which the speech headings and scene change are marked in *Works* (Figure 7). Frail and Mrs Foresight have just been joined by Tattle and Miss Prue. The older women know perfectly well what Tattle ('sly Devil', 'cunning Cur') has in mind for the 'fresh harmless Creature', no less of course than to 'perswade her out of her Innocency'. While mouthing their protestations, they're permissive and worldly enough not to interfere. But their main concern is not to be implicated. So Congreve ends the scene with a proverb: 'I wash my Hands of it, I'm throughly Innocent.'

The scene-link here makes the women's physical departure a moral issue. Mrs Foresight's abdication is one with that of Pontius Pilate (then equated with Pope Innocent XII, elected 1691). Miss Prue (anagrammatically 'pure' of course, and the lamb left to the slaughter) bleatingly asks: 'What do they mean, do you know?' The *liaison* here lies in the allusion to Pilate and the implication of a sacrifice in a following scene; the centred speech prefixes heighten the identity and responsibility of those who leave Tattle and Prue alone; and the scene-head *shows* them to be so. It's not simply that the forms in *Works* are more dramatic than those of the Quarto (Figure 6): the important point is that these implications were written into the play as Congreve composed it but were muted or suppressed in its first printings, as they are in all the recent editions based upon them.

The forms we've been looking at in *Works* are not therefore revisions so much as the belated realization of subtle aids to characterization that were always there. But Congreve of course also revised his texts, and while there'll always be a place for editions of his plays from their earliest printed versions, documenting as they do a different historical moment and milieu, there is I believe a stronger case for respecting his adoption of readings that he himself thought improved his work.

Performance, of course, is such a flexible art that it's far from easy to decide which revisions take their authority from his extensive experience of the plays in rehearsal and production. He'd been intimately involved with Betterton's company, and in his dialogue and the actions it generated, he'd written with an exceptionally privileged and sympathetic eye and ear to the specific qualities of each of his actors. The changes he made in his language, scenic structure, and *depiction and judgement* of certain characters, demand the most careful consideration, for he brought to them a knowledge unrivalled by any editor or critic since.

## Note

1   In his Clark Lectures of 1997, D.F. McKenzie argues for 'Congreve's integrity as a writer – and as a man'. The second lecture, an edited extract of which appears in this chapter, discusses Congreve's construction of character through language and naming, before turning to the use of music and the *mise-en-page* of printed editions as evidence for the delicacy and precision of Congreve's dramatic judgement. We are very grateful to Christine Ferdinand for permission to publish this abbreviated version of the lecture, originally entitled '"A Dissection of Nature": Congreve's Characters'.

# Bibliography

Congreve, W. (1695), *Love for Love*, London: Jacob Tonson.
Congreve, W. (1700), *The Way of the World*, London: Jacob Tonson.
Congreve, W. (1710), *Works*, London: Jacob Tonson.
Congreve, W. (1719–20), *Works*, London: Jacob Tonson.
Price, C.A. (1979), *Music in the Restoration Theatre: With a Catalogue of Instrumental Music in the Plays 1665–1713*, Ann Arbor: UMI Research Press.

*Ang.* No, I have it; and I'll ufe it, as I would every thing that is an Enemy to *Valentine.* [*Tears the Paper.*

Sir *Samp.* How now!

*Val.* Ha!

*Ang.* Had I the World to give you, it cou'd not make me worthy of fo generous and faithful a Paffion: Here's my Hand, my Heart was always yours, and ftruggl'd very hard to make this utmoft Tryal of your Virtue. [*To Val.*

*Val.* Between Pleafure and Amazement, I am loft——But on my Knees I take the Bleffing.

Sir *Samp.* Oons, what is the meaning of this ?

*Ben.* Mefs, here's the Wind chang'd again. Father, you and I may make a Voyage together now.

*Ang.* Well, Sir *Sampfon,* fince I have plaid you a Trick, I'll advife you, how you may avoid fuch another. Learn to be a good Father, or you'll never get a fecond Wife. I always lov'd your Son, and hated your unforgiving Nature. I was re-folv'd to try him to the utmoft; I have try'd you too, and know you both. You have not more Faults than he has Virtues; and 'tis hardly more Pleafure to me, that I can make him and my felf happy, than that I can punifh you.

*Val.* If my happinefs cou'd receive Addition, this Kind fur-prize would make it double.

Sir *Samp.* Oons you're a *Crocodile,*

*Fore.* Really, Sir *Sampfon,* this is a fudden Eclipfe——

Sir *Samp.* You're an illiterate Fool, and I'm another, and the Stars are Lyars; and if I had breath enough, I'd curfe them and you, my felf and every Body—Oons, Cully'd, Bubbl'd, Jilted, Woman-bobb'd at laft—I have not Patience. [*Exit Sir Samp.*

*Tatt.* If the Gentleman is in this diforder for want of a Wife, I can fpare him mine. Oh are you there, Sir ? I'm indebted to you for my Happinefs. [*To Jere.*

*Jere.* Sir, I ask you Ten Thoufand Pardons, 'twas an errant miftake——You fee, Sir, my Mafter was never mad, nor any thing like it——Then how could it be otherwife ?

*Val. Tattle,* I thank you, you would have interpofed between me and Heav'n; but Providence laid Purgatory in your way— You have but Juftice.

*Scan.* I hear the Fiddles that Sir *Sampfon* provided for his own Wedding; methinks 'tis pity they fhould not be employ'd when
the

**Figure 1**    *Love for Love* (Quarto, 1695)

ftruggl'd very hard to make this utmoft Trial of your Vertue. [*To Val.*

*Val.* Between Pleafure and Amaze-ment, I am loft——But on my Knees I take the Bleffing.

Sir *Samp.* Oons, what is the Meaning of this ?

*Ben.* Mefs here's the Wind chang'd a-gain. Father, you and I may make a Voy-age together now.

*Ang.* Well, Sir *Sampfon,* fince I have plaid you a Trick, I'll advife you, how you may avoid fuch another. Learn to be a good Father, or you'll never get a fecond Wife. I always lov'd your Son, and ha-ted your unforgiving Nature. I was re-folv'd to try him to the utmoft; I have try'd you too, and know you both. You have not more Faults than he has Vir-tues ; and 'tis hardly more Pleafure to me, that I can make him and my felf happy, than that I can punifh you.

*Val.* If my Happinefs cou'd receive Addition, this kind Surprize wou'd make it double.

Sir *Samp.* Oons you're a *Crocodile.*

*Fore.* Really, Sir *Sampfon,* this is a fud-den Eclipfe.

Sir *Samp.* You're an illiterate old Fool, and I'm another.

*Tatt.*

**Figure 2**    *Love for Love* (*Works,* 1710)

Sir *WILFULL.*

Enough, enough, Coufin: Yes, yes, all a cafe——
When you're difpos'd. Now's as well as another time;
and another. time as well as now. All's one for that,—
Yes, yes, if your Concerns call you, there's no hafte; it
will keep cold, as. they. fay——Coufin, your Servant.—
I think this Door's lock'd.

*MILLAMANT.*

You may go this way. Sir.

Sir *WILFULL.*

Your Servant, then with your leave I'll return to my
Company.

*MILLAMANT.*

Ay, ay; ha. ha, ha.
*Like* Phœbus *fung the no lefs am'rous Boy.*

## SCENE V.

MILLAMANT, MIRABELL.

*MIRABELL.*

L*Ike* Daphne *fhe, as Lovely and as Coy.*
Do you lock your felf up from me, to make my
Search more curious? Or is this pretty Artifice contriv'd,
to fignifie that here the Chace muft end, and my Purfuit
be crown'd, for you can fly no. further?——

*MILLAMANT.*

Vanity! No————I'll fly and be follow'd to the laft
Moment, tho' I am upon the very Verge of Matrimo-
ny, I expect you fhould follicit me as much as if I were
wavering at the Grate of a Monaftery, with one Foot o-
ver the Threfhold. I'll be follicited to the very laft, nay
and afterwards.

*MIRABELL*

What, after the laft?

*MIL-*

*MILLAMANT.*

O, I fhould think I was poor and had nothing to be-
ftow, if I were reduc'd to an inglorious Eafe; and freed
from the agreeable Fatigues of Sollicitation.

*MIRABELL.*

But do not you know, that when Favours are con-
ferr'd upon inftant and tedious Sollicitation, that they di-
minifh in their Value, and that both the Giver lofes the
Grace, and the Receiver leffens his Pleafure?

*MILLAMANT.*

It may be in Things of common Application; but never fure in Love. O, I hate a Lover, that can dare to
think he draws a Moment's Air, independent on the
Bounty of his Miftrefs. There is not fo impudent a Thing
in Nature, as the fawcy Look of an affured Man, confident of Succefs. The Pedantick Arrogance of a very Huf-
band,- has not fo Pragmatical an Air. Ah! I'll never marry, unlefs I am firft made fure of my Will and Pleafure.

*MIRABELL.*

Would you have 'em both before Marriage? Or will
you be contented with the firft now, and ftay for the
other 'till after Grace?

*MILLAMANT.*

Ah don't be impertinent —— My dear Liberty, fhall I
leave thee? My faithful Solitude, my darling Contemplation, muft I bid you then Adieu? Ay-h adieu——My
Morning Thoughts, agreeable Wakings, indolent Slum-
bers, ye *douceurs,* ye *Sommeils du Matin,* adieu —— I can't
do't, 'tis more than impoffible——Pofitively *Mirabell,* I'll
lye a-bed in a Morning as long as I pleafe.

*MIRABELL.*

Then I'll get up in a Morning as early as I pleafe.

*MILLAMANT.*

Ah! Idle Creature, get up when you will—— And
d'ye hear, I won't be call'd Names after I'm marry'd; pofitively I won't be call'd Names.

*MIRABELL.*

Names!

*MIL-*

**Figure 3**   *Way of the World* (*Works,* 1719–20)

unlefs fhe fhou'd tell me her felf. Which of the two it
may have been, I will leave you to confider ; and when you
have done thinking of that ; think of me.          [*Exit.*

*Mira.* I have fomething more——Gone——Think of you!
To think of a Whirlwind, tho' 'twere in a Whirlwind, were
a Cafe of more fteady Contemplation ; a very tranquility of
Mind and Manfion.   A Fellow that lives in a Windmill, has
not a more whimfical Dwelling than the Heart of a Man that
is lodg'd in a Woman.  There is no Point of the Compafs to
which they cannot turn, and by which they are not turn'd ;
and by one as well as another ; for Motion not Method is their
Occupation.  To know this, and yet continue to be in Love,
is to be made wife from the Dictates of Reafon,  and yet perfevere to play the Fool by the force of Inftinct——O here
come my pair of Turtles——What, billing fo fweetly ! Is  WI. 666
not *Valentine*'s Day over with you yet?

             *Enter* Waitwell *and* Foible.

Sirrah, *Waitwell,* why fure you think you were married for
your own Recreation, and not for my Conveniency.

*Wait.* Your Pardon, Sir.  With Submiffion, we have indeed been folacing in lawful Delights; but ftill with an Eye
to Bufinefs, Sir.   I have inftructed her as well as I cou'd.  If
fhe can take your Directions as readily as my Inftructions,
Sir, your Affairs are in a profperous way.

*Mira.* Give you Joy, Mrs. *Foible.*

*Foib.* O las Sir, I'm fo afham'd——I'm afraid my Lady
has been in a thoufand Inquietudes for me.  But I proteft,
Sir, I made as much hafte as I could.

*Wait.* That fhe did indeed, Sir.  It was my Fault that
fhe did not make more.

*Mira.* That I believe.

[*Foib.* But I told my Lady as you inftructed me, Sir. That   WI. 667
I had a profpect of feeing Sir *Rowland* your Uncle ; and that
I wou'd put her Ladyfhip's Picture in my Pocket to fhew
him ; which I'll be fure to fay has made him fo enamour'd of
her Beauty , that he burns with Impatience to lie at her
Ladyfhip's Feet and worfhip the Original.

                                              *Mira.*

**Figure 4**    *Way of the World* (Quarto, 1700)

*The* W A Y *of the* W O R L D.    665

*Milla.* Without the help of the Devil,
you can't imagine ; unlefs fhe fhould tell
me her felf.  Which of the two it may
have been, I will leave you to confider ;
and when you have done thinking of that,
think of me.

           **SCENE VI.**

         MIRABELL *alone.*

*Mira.* I Have fomething more——Gone
——Think of you! To think of
a Whirlwind, tho' 'twere in a Whirlwind, were a Cafe of more fteady Contemplation ; a very Tranquility of Mind
and Manfion.  A Fellow that lives in a
Windmill, has not a more whimfical
Dwelling than the Heart of a Man that is
lodg'd in a Woman.  There is no Point
of the Compafs to which they cannot turn,
and by which they are not turn'd ; and by
one as well as another ; for Motion not
Method is their Occupation.  To know
this, and yet continue to be in Love, is
to be made wife from the Dictates of Reafon, and yet perfevere to play the Fool
by the force of Inftinct.——O here come
my Pair of Turtles,——What, billing fo
                                    fweetly!

**Figure 5**    *Way of the World* (*Works*, 1710)

to anfwer for, remember I wafh my hands of it, I'm throughly
Innocent.                          [*Exeunt* Mrs. Forefight *and* Frail.
· Mifs *Pru.* What makes 'em go away, Mr. *Tattle?*
What do they mean, do you know?
*Tatt.* Yes, my Dear——I think I can guefs——But hang
me if I know the reafon of it.
Mifs *Pru.* Come, muft not we go too?
*Tatt.* No, no, they don't mean that.
Mifs *Pru.* No! what then? what fhall you and I do together?
*Tatt.* I muft make Love to you, pretty Mifs; will you let me
make Love to you?
Mifs *Pru.* Yes, if you pleafe.
*Tatt.* Frank, I Gad, at leaft.  What a Pox do's Mrs. *Forefight*
mean by this Civility? is it to make a Fool of me? or do's fhe
leave us together out of good Morality, and do as fhe would be
done by——God I'll underftand it fo.             [*Afide.*
Mifs. *Pru.* Well; And how will you make Love to me——
Come, I long to have you begin;——muft I make Love too?
You muft tell me how.
*Tatt.* You muft let me fpeak Mifs, you muft not fpeak firft;
I muft afk you Queftions, and you muft anfwer.
Mifs *Pru.* What, is it like the Catechifme?——Come then
afk me.
*Tatt.* De'e you think you can Love me?
Mifs *Pru.* Yes.
*Tatt.* Pooh, Pox, you muft not fay yes already; I fhan't care
a Farthing for you then in a twinckling.
·Mifs *Pru.* What muft I fay then?
*Tatt.*Why you muft fay no, or you believe not, or you can't tell——
Mifs *Pru.* Why, muft I tell a Lie then?
*Tatt.* Yes, if you would be well bred.  All well-bred Per-
fons Lie——Befides, you are a Woman, You muft never fpeak
what you think: Your words muft contradict your thoughts;
but your actions may contradict your words.  So, when I afk
you, if you can Love me, you muft fay no, but you muft Love
me too——If I tell you you are Handfome, you muft deny it,
and fay I flatter you——But you muft think your felf more
Charming than I fpeak you:——And like me, for the Beauty which
I fay you have, as much as if I had it my felf——If I afk you to Kifs
me, you muft be angry, but you muft not refufe me. If I afk you
                                                          for

**Figure 6**    *Love for Love* (Quarto, 1695)

304    L O V E *for* L O V E.

Mrs. *F R A I L.*
Come, Faith let us be gone --If my Brother *Forefight*
fhou'd find us with them, he'd think fo, fure enough.
Mrs. *F O R E S I G H T.*
So he wou'd---but then leaving 'em together is as bad
———— And he's fuch a fly Devil, he'll never mifs an
Opportunity.
Mrs. *F R A I L.*
I don't care; I won't be feen in't.
Mrs. *F O R E S I G H T.*
Well, if you fhould, Mr. *Tattle*, you'll have a World
to anfwer for; remember I wafh my Hands of it, I'm
throughly Innocent.

S C E N E  XI.

T A T T L E, *Mifs* P R U E.

W HAT makes 'em go away, Mr. *Tattle?* What do
they mean, do you know?
T A T T L E.
Yes, my Dear————I think I can guefs—But hang
me if I know the Reafon of it.
Mifs P R U E.
Come, muft not we go too?
T A T T L E.
No, no, they don't mean that.
Mifs P R U E.
· No! What then? What fhall you and I do together?
T A T T L E.
I muft make love to you, pretty Mifs; will you let
me make Love to you?
Mifs P R U E.
· Yes, if you pleafe.

                                                    T A T T L E.

**Figure 7**    *Love for Love* (*Works*, 1719–20)

Chapter Five

# The Economics of the Eighteenth-Century Provincial Book Trade: The Case of Ward and Chandler

C.Y. Ferdinand

Early in 1744 the bookseller Richard Chandler, aged about thirty-one and on the verge of bankruptcy, blew out his brains. The following year his business partner Cæsar Ward, aged thirty-five, went bankrupt and was forced to sell his printing house in Coney Street, York.[1] As one of their competitors, the printer Thomas Gent, described it,

> but, alas! [Chandler's] thoughts soared too high, and sunk his fortunes so low, by the debts he had contracted, that rather than become a despicable object to the world, or bear the miseries of prison, he put a period to his life, by discharging a pistol to his head, as he lay reclined on his bed. As I knew the man formerly, I was very sorry to hear of his tragical suicide, an action that for awhile seemed to obumbrate the glories of Cæsar, who found such a deficiency in his partner's accounts, so great a want of money, and such awoful [sic] sight of flowing creditors, that made him succumb under the obligation to a statute of bankruptcy. (Gent 191–92)

At about the same time another bookseller, Benjamin Collins, aged thirty, was amassing a large book- and newspaper-based fortune in Salisbury. On the face of it, the York partnership was conducting a business that looked much like Collins's: both printed and sold books, both owned shares of books, both took on jobbing printing, both were based (at least in part) in the provinces, both participated in large book-trade networks, both ran newspapers. Yet when Collins died, he was worth between £85,000 and £100,000, whereas Chandler killed himself, and Cæsar Ward was still honourably attempting to pay off his creditors when he wrote his will ten years later.

Bankruptcy is a complicated affair, and we will never be able to recover all the facts surrounding Chandler's death and Ward's bankrupcty. But enough evidence survives of their careers, and of Benjamin Collins's and others in the book trade, to suggest some of the steps along the path that led to the downfall of the York partnership.

Cæsar Ward was born in London in 1710, son of Ann Ward and another Cæsar Ward, Citizen and Apothecary of London. His father died young, when Cæsar was only two years old. Cæsar Senior's own father George had died young too, by the time he was apprenticed in the Apothecary's Company.[2] Richard Chandler was born a few years later, probably in 1713. His father Robert, a perriwig-maker based in St Paul's Churchyard, was dead by the time Richard was apprenticed to the bookseller John Hooke in 1727 for a premium of £49 10*s* (McKenzie, no. 4131). Ward was probably the more advantageously placed, and for a larger premium of £80, to the bookseller-banker Robert Gosling, father of the more famous banker Sir Francis Gosling (Melton 60–77). This was in July 1725. One of Ward's fellow apprentices, in fact his co-temporary, was Francis Cogan. He was freed, after nearly twelve years of apprenticeship, the year before Caesar Ward; he too went into publishing, and by coincidence went broke the same year as Ward. But Cogan's is another story. Ward completed his apprenticeship, and was freed in 1732 (McKenzie, nos 3331, 3336). Robert Gosling's shop at the sign of the Mitre and Crown was variously described as over against or opposite St Dunstan's Church, or at the Middle Temple Gate, probably the same location, for Middle Temple Lane was across the street not far from the parish church.[3] John Hooke's shop, at the Fleur de Luce, was also described as over against St Dunstan's Church. At any rate, both masters had bookshops in the parish of St Dunstan in the West, near St Dunstan's, and it is not unreasonable to speculate that Ward and Chandler met while they were apprentices.

Richard Chandler's master died in September 1730, before Chandler could complete his apprenticeship. There is no record that he was turned over to another master, nor that he ever took up his freedom of the Stationers' Company by any other means. Nevertheless, with only about four and a half years in the trade, and most of that as an apprentice, Chandler could announce in May 1732 that he was taking over his former master's business at the sign of the Fleur de Luce, and moving to a location 'without Temple Bar', probably in the Strand.[4]

Four months later Cæsar Ward was freed, and about that time he, too, started up in business, taking over the shop formerly in the hands of the late James Lacy, another bookseller. This was at the sign of the Ship, then located between the Temple Gates at the end of Fleet Street. The Land Tax Assessment Books record Lacy at that address, paying a tax of 2*s*. 6*d*. on his personal estate through 1732. This is on the low side: the bookseller John Shuckburgh was paying 7*s*. 6*d*. at the same time, and Lacy's immediate neighbours were paying 10*s*. and 5*s*. The assessments for 1733 and 1734 record Cæsar Ward continuing the same payments of 2*s*. 6*d*. Some time before the assessor made his rounds in 1736 to collect the 1735 taxes, Richard Chandler joined Cæsar Ward, at least in the tax records. The Temple Gates shop was empty the following year, until another bookseller, George Hawkins, moved in.

One can get a sense of the networking possibilities the eighteenth century offered by following the tax collector around the Temple Bar end of Fleet Street in 1733. Book-trade colleagues included Robert Gosling; Philip Overton, the book and printseller; John Pemberton at the Golden Buck; Thomas Worrall at the Judge's Head; Lawton Gilliver next door at Homer's Head; John Senex the bookseller, engraver and globemaker; Thomas Wotton at the Three Daggers & Queen's Head; the printer Henry Lintot at the Cross Keys; John Coles, the stationer at the Sun & Mitre; John Shuckburgh; Thomas Woodward at the Half Moon; and Joel Stephens. John Nichols described the booksellers near Temple Bar as 'being proprietors of the copies of great part of the Law Books, and having more frequent opportunities than others of buying Libraries in that Science, can afford, and do sell them ... as cheap, if not cheaper, than others' (Nichols 3: 740). Benjamin Hoare & Partners and Sir Francis Child & Partners, the bankers, were also part of the neighbourhood.

Around 1733 Ward and Chandler added a second shop, in Scarborough, about which we know little except that it was described as at the corner of Long Room Street. The London premises were moved to the Strand, just outside Temple Bar, in 1736 – the church warden's account book for the new parish, St Clement Danes, records that the shop, previously occupied by someone called Warner Perry, was empty for the first two quarters of the year May 1736 to May 1737. The same account books show that Richard Chandler was the taxpayer there from late 1736 to sometime in 1742.[5] After that the shop was in the hands of William Sandby, who continued to act as agent for Ward and Chandler, and then for Ward alone until Ward's death in 1759. William was the brother of Ward's apprentice Edward Sandby.[6] Throughout these moves, the partners and their London agent retained the sign of the Ship.

Meanwhile Cæsar Ward had married Mary Kilsha (c.1715–36?) of Clothall, Hertfordshire, 29 February 1735/6. Soon after this he moved to York, but was evidently then married to a woman called Ann, so one can assume that Mary had died within the first year of marriage. Ward became a freeman of the city of York by purchase in 1736 (Collins). He took over a shop at the sign of the Printing Press in Coney Street, just opposite St Martin's Church. The printing office itself was in a building behind, formerly the Bagnio. Later the business was to move across the street to a house next to the George Inn, previously Kidd's Coffee-House: there, in a large room overlooking the river, the *York Courant* was printed (Davies 261). Ward was engaged in local politics and elected a common councillor for Bootham Ward in 1740 (after failing to be elected for Micklegate Ward the previous year); he declined the office of Chamberlain in 1741 by payment of fine; and he served on various city committees through the 1740s.

One can catch an early glimpse of Richard Chandler's somewhat impetuous business style in a note he sent to the antiquarian Thomas Birch (1705–66) in 1734, suggesting that 'My Friend Mr Gilbert Burnett having been pleased to order me toserve [sic] him with the Future Nos. of the General Dictionary desired me to wait on you who would inform me who had hitherto sent them that he might forbid them leaving more'.[7] He signs the note 'Rich Chandler & Co.', although Cæsar Ward was the senior partner. Here he is not only trying to take business from a competitor selling the *General Dictionary* in weekly parts, but is also attempting to establish a relationship with a historian, a contact that might prove useful for a publishing venture Chandler had in mind.

His dealings with Samuel Richardson some years later are even more telling. By 1741 Chandler would not have been thirty years old. Samuel Richardson (1689–1766) was well established, both as a printer and as the author of a recent successful first novel, *Pamela* (1740). Hoping that a sequel might enjoy similar success, Chandler engaged the journalist and playwright John Kelly (1680?–1751) for the project in 1741. This came as an unpleasant surprise to Richardson, who wrote to his brother-in-law, James Leake (another bookseller), describing Kelly as 'a Bookseller's Hackney, who never wrote any thing that was tolerably receiv'd, and had several of his Performances refused by the Stage'.[8] When it became clear that his plan was known, Chandler actually visited Richardson to explain that the project was begun on the rumour that the original author had no further plans for Pamela. This was only true, Richardson admitted, 'upon a Supposition, that no one would offer to meddle with it, in which Case I had resolved to do it myself, rather than my Plan should be basely ravished out of my Hands, and, probably my Characters depreciated and debased'. (Which of course is more or less what happened, when Henry Fielding pseudononymously created *Shamela* – Richardson always suspected Fielding, and never forgave him. Chandler of course was one of the gang of bookseller-partners in Fielding's the *Champion* [Battestin 259].)

Chandler probably only compounded the affront when he offered Richardson the opportunity to complete Kelly's work and publish it under his own name. When that was rebuffed, Chandler proposed to lose the money he had already paid Kelly and to start afresh with Richardson. This too was refused, and Richardson left the confrontation believing he had persuaded Chandler to publish Kelly's two sequel volumes as a new work, entirely separate from the original *Pamela*. This was not so. Instead Chandler and Company went ahead with publication of *Pamela's Conduct in High Life*, including an introduction that explains how this new information made its way to 'a Bookseller, who, I dare say very justly, bears the Character of a Man of great Probity'. Both sides became involved in unseemly advertising campaigns to promote their own 'authentic' versions of the life of Pamela-after-marriage, and there was much speculation about what experience either author could actually have had of *authentic* high life. Although the spurious volumes came out over the imprint of Ward and Chandler and three others, Chandler was clearly the prime instigator. Such bumptious behaviour was not going to endear Chandler to his book-trade associates.

There is no similar published account of Cæsar Ward, but there is a good word-portrait to be constructed from the letters he wrote to Charles Lyttelton (1714–1768), the antiquary and Bishop of Carlisle, after Chandler's death and his own bankruptcy.[9] This is when he and Francis Drake (1696–1771), the York historian were hard at work on their *Parliamentary or Consitutional History of England*, a title that was to be published by a London conger. Ward writes with pride 'of a Manuscript Acct. of all the most material Transactions of the two Parlts. of 4 Car. 1. An. 1628, & 9' presented to Ward by Sir John Napier about 1744 and of the pleasure of collating and compiling that with other accounts; another time he writes of 'My three Days Confinement in a Garret of Old Pamphlets last March, at St. James', [which] produc'd so many valuable Materials for our Work'; or he outlines an addition he is hiding from his co-author by omitting it from one set of proofs, explaining that it would balance a particular prejudice Drake held.[10] All in all, it is the description of a natural historian.

Much of the evidence for Ward and Chandler's activies lies in the books themselves of course. The *English Short Title Catalogue*, developed over the last twenty-five years and now stocked with literally millions of on-line records, can provide a near comprehensive list of existing works for any given pre-nineteenth-century English bookseller. As of 16 February 2000, the *ESTC* database contained approximately 105 titles or editions with Cæsar Ward and/ or Richard Chandler in the imprint up to 1744, when their bankruptcy became inevitable. Imprints can give us clues to when the Ward–Chandler partnership began and how it worked; they confirm the movements suggested by the archival evidence; they suggest links with the London congers and therefore strategies for spreading the financial risks of publishing; and they often reveal who printed the books for Ward and Chandler and their various colleagues.

Ward and Chandler concentrated on publishing and bookselling for the first few years, which is not surprising, for the two had after all been apprenticed to booksellers, not printers. It isn't until well after their York shop is set up that there is much evidence of printing, and then that was primarily newspaper and local jobbing printing under the charge of Cæsar Ward. The partners – themselves, or with congers – employed a number of London-based printers though, including Charles Jephson, Henry Kent, Henry Lintot, John Purser, Charles Ackers and William Bowyer. Fortunately the extant ledgers for both Ackers and Bowyer have been edited and published, and, for a number of titles, can provide information additional to the imprints on edition size, production costs, production time and paper quality (McKenzie and Ross; Maslen and Lancaster). Incidentally Ackers and Bowyer are never mentioned in Ward and Chandler imprints; the connection is evident only in the ledgers and a passing reference in one of Ward's letters.[11]

During the first year Ward and Chandler were in business, 1732, four of the five surviving imprints are Richard Chandler's. He appears in three of those with two other booksellers, Charles Corbett and John Wilford, almost as though he were casting about for a business partner. The one book printed solely for Chandler is a law book, the second edition of William Nelson's *The Laws of England Concerning the Game of Hunting*. The first volume in which Ward and Chandler's names are together is *The Flower-Garden Display'd*, a book of text and plates published by a conger that included three other London booksellers. The punctuation of this imprint suggests that Ward and Chandler were separate members of the conger, and not yet a partnership.

Ten imprints bear their names in 1733. Again they show that Richard Chandler was the more active of the two, but one imprint suggests that this was the year in which the partnership was formed and the shop in Scarborough acquired. Stephen Maxwell's *Eboracum: A Poem* was printed in York for the author, and sold by the author, John Hildyard, and Messieurs Chandler and Ward, Scarborough. They invested in their first periodical, *The Bee, or Universal Weekly Pamphlet*, as well as in a miscellaneous batch of books on law, gardening, theology and music. There was always to be a preponderance of law books, partly explained by their London shop's proximity to the law courts, partly by Ward's connection with Gosling, who owned shares in some of the law-book patents, partly by an effort to capitalize on the rise in the numbers of lawyers and a greater emphasis on their formal training.

Eighteenth-century imprints generally reflect the status of the booksellers listed, with those of greatest seniority placed first. The first two years of Ward–

Chandler activity suggest that Chandler was temporarily regarded as the senior of the two; that is his name is given before Ward's whenever they appear together. Despite his evident failure to secure freedom, perhaps Chandler's greater publishing activity gave him a higher profile that may have confused the trade. But by 1734 the order was permanently reversed to reflect Cæsar Ward's higher status as a Freeman (and son of a Freeman). One of the catalogues the partners issued later actually presents Ward's name in larger type than Chandler's.[12] The imprints also suggest a certain flexibility in the partnership, perhaps facilitated by the geographic distance that sometimes separated them. Occasionally one or the other would issue books under his own name.

The next few years see a healthy mix of publishing investments, including books aimed at their northern provincial market, and an increasing number of law books. There are only three titles in 1736, but that was the year the partners moved their London premises, Cæsar Ward married, evidently lost a wife, remarried, and moved to York. Numbers pick up again the next year, when there are twelve imprints, most of them suggesting Ward and Chandler's far-flung bookselling empire. The business seemed to be doing all right in the 1730s, even if it was unusually distributed in three different towns. Larger book-ventures were conservatively entered into with groups of other booksellers, as in Bayle's *General Dictionary* (1734–41) in ten volumes folio, or in second and third editions of *The Vocal Miscellany* (1734, 1738) in two-volume editions of 2,000 each (Maslen and Lancaster, no. 2110). The different local markets were acknowledged and some local printing jobs were secured; shares in copies were purchased at the London trade sales; and the partnership was edging towards newspaper ownership, which in the right circumstances could produce a steady and sustaining income. Some miscalculation is evident: for example Ward and Chandler published Karl Ludwig Pöllnitz's *Les Amusemens de Spa: Or the Gallantries of the Spaw in Germany* (1737) in a two-volume edition of 1,000, according to the Bowyer ledgers. Soon after, Bowyer was printing 750 title-pages to a so-called second edition, but this was in fact a reissue of most of the first (Maslen and Lancaster, nos 2319, 2466). The imprint to a Masonic volume in 1738 places Ward and Chandler amongst that brotherhood, and in 1739 they capitalized on the celebrity of Dick Turpin to print and publish at least five editions of an account of his trial and execution at York, probably one of their most successful ventures.

Perhaps success bred over-confidence. It is worth remembering Defoe's warning about this danger, that 'Nothing of its kind is more common than for the Tradesman, when he once finds himself grown rich, to have his Head full of great Designs and Undertakings' (Defoe 2: 102). In 1741 Ward and Chandler and Company began publishing John Kelly's spurious sequel to *Pamela*. About this time Chandler ventured alone into an ambitious project, the compilation and publication of *The History and Proceedings of the House of Commons from the Restoration to the Present Time*, which began publishing in 1741. The imprint to the first edition, first issue gives away nothing – it is simply 'printed in the year' – but the advertisements at the end of each volume are for books printed for Ward and Chandler. The sheets of the first twelve volumes were reissued the next year under Richard Chandler's imprint, and as if that were not clear enough, a further volume, published in 1743, has Chandler actually signing the verso of the title-page, testifying that this is his authentic copyright, entered into the Stationers' Company hall book, 'as my Sole Property'. By then Frederick had accepted a copy of the twelve-volume history, and Chandler could include his signed dedication to the Prince in volume 13. In retrospect it is ironic, or perhaps poignant, that in that same year Ward and Chandler published *The Law for and against Bankrupts*. Early the next year and with insolvency looming, Chandler decided to kill himself. Ward carried on through his own bankruptcy, and into a sort of recovery that included the compilation of his twenty-four-volume *Parliamentary History of England*. This was managed in such an altogether different style from Chandler's doomed project that even today the British Library records the work as an anonymous compilation.

There was of course a whole catalogue of disasters that could befall an eighteenth-century business, and there were relatively fewer safeguards then. Plomer's *Dictionaries of Booksellers and Printers* record book-trade calamity in all its variety. The volume that covers 1726 to 1775 notices robbery, extreme poverty, madness, nervous breakdown and punishment for libel. One bookseller, Alexander Cruden, was reputed to have left the book trade for moral instruction, because of his 'weak intellect'. Fires were very frequently mentioned. And many, like Cæsar Ward, were financially broken.

Thefts and the pillory were minor disasters that could, with luck and some assistance, be readily overcome. Many eighteenth-century booksellers seem to have made full recoveries after devastating fires, for lessons had been learned after the Great Fire, and fire insurance – formalized in the establishment of companies such as the Sun Fire Office in 1710 and the Royal Exchange in 1720 – had become readily available and relatively affordable (Dickson; Supple). So Stanley Crowder, who had Sun Fire insurance, was publishing *The Ladies Complete Pocket Book* in 1775, after a fire had completely destroyed his Paternoster Row premises a few years before.[13] Likewise Peter Elmsley, who insured his business in the Strand for £1,500. He carried on his trade for more than thirty years after fire swept through his warehouse and the adjoining offices of several other colleagues (Maxted 1992, 29). While we cannot now establish firm links between insurance and recovery, the suggestion is there.

Madness and bankruptcy, on the other hand, were crises that were very difficult, sometimes impossible, to overcome. Madness seems to have been rare, or at least rarely discussed, amongst the mid-eighteenth-century book trade. John Whiston is the best-known: he suffered a nervous breakdown in 1759, apparently as a result of a practical joke, left off business, and actually spent time in an asylum (Plomer 260). Thomas Worrall, who had been a neighbour of Ward and Chandler in Fleet Street in the 1730s, was another, who according to John Nichols, 'unfortunately laboured under a mental derangement, which terminated his life Sept. 17, 1767' (Nichols 3: 740–41).

Cæsar Ward was only one of many bankrupt booksellers, printers and publishers in the eighteenth century. Plomer describes twenty-one in his volume for 1726–75, while Ian Maxted adds another 130 or so to that number for the same period in his comprehensive survey of bankruptcy. If all of Maxted's paper stainers, engravers, parchment makers and papermakers – those on the fringes of the book trade rather than full participants – are removed, there still remain about eighty bankrupt booksellers, printers or publishers for this fifty-year period. This of course is an incomplete picture that has to be coloured in with all the other mid-eighteenth-century bankrupts, and set against a background of the prevailing economic conditions in England. While such a survey is beyond the scope of this chapter, it can be useful to know who else was going broke in the 1740s along with Richard Chandler and Cæsar Ward.

There are 131 certificates of bankruptcy recorded for the year 1745/6 in one of the Commissioners for Bankruptcy registers in the Public Record Office.[14] T.S. Ashton, in his *Economic History of England* in the eighteenth century, comes up with different figures, based on notices in *The London Gazette* and the *Gentleman's Magazine* (these were usually notices to creditors, or other announcements that would precede the actual certificate, which should account for the difference). So Ashton records 167 for 1746. What is more useful, though, is his table of bankruptcies 1732–1800, which suggests that the mid-1740s did not see any particular rise in insolvencies. Indeed these are some of the lowest figures Ashton records for these sixty-eight years. For example the 1780s and 1790s were particularly hard, with numbers ranging from a low of 381 in 1781 to 697 in 1788 and 1,256 in 1793. At any rate, three of our certified bankrupts in 1745 are booksellers: Cæsar Ward, plus Francis Cogan and Thomas Harris, both of London. William Raven of Holborn, who called himself stationer, dealer and chapman, was another. The four make up about 3 per cent of this sample. The rest are a mixed bag of trades, mostly of the middling sort. Bankruptcy might have been painful, humiliating, even devastating, but it is worth remembering that being a bankrupt was usually preferable to being an insolvent debtor. Until 1841 in the United States and 1869 in England, bankruptcy was an option open only to 'traders' who owed at least £100. The advantage was that a bankrupt trader could obtain an absolute discharge from his debts, usually after creditors were paid a dividend of what they were owed. Insolvent debtors were liable until their debts were paid off or forgiven, and since they were often placed in positions that made that impossible, insolvency could become a life sentence. There was some relief in the occasional Acts for Insolvent Debtors. This accounts for the large number of so-called chapmen in the 1745/6 list, for a chapman was someone whose business was buying and selling. A chapman was by definition a trader, who could therefore qualify for bankruptcy.

Contrasting the joint career of Ward and Chandler, the bankrupts, against Benjamin Collins's almost flawless rise to prosperity, suggests some of the larger mistakes the partnership could have made.[15] Benjamin Collins was always a serious businessman, generally keeping a low profile in Salisbury, unless he was moved to litigation.[16] The evidence suggests that Collins was anxious to observe etiquette in his dealings with his friends and colleagues. Richard Chandler's style was brasher, more flamboyant, and probably counter-productive in the end. Cæsar Ward showed himself to be an honest man, particularly in his attempts to pay off his creditors long after a certificate of bankrutpcy had been secured and dividends paid out. He was more honourable in his dealings than was Benjamin Collins, but that did not necessarily make him more effective. Certainly his eagerness to embrace the life of the scholar-historian does not suggest a man committed to business.

Collins diversified at the earliest opportunity, investing in real estate, East India stock and trade, and a plantation on Monserrat. He and his partner William Strahan put in a serious, if unsuccessful, bid for the Cambridge University printing rights in 1765. He sold patent medicines and even invented one, the Cordial Cephalic Snuff, that became so well known it appeared on stage, in the second act of *The Clandestine Marriage* (1766). He invested in provincial banking and in his later years he called himself 'Banker, Esquire'. There seemed to be little at which he could not make a profit. An indenture in the York City Archives for the lease and release of a new house between one Benjamin Grosvenor and Cæsar Ward, printer, suggests an element of modest prosperity, but for the most part Ward and Chandler stuck to the book and newspaper trades.[17]

Except for litigation, in which he was successful, Collins steered clear of the law. Cæsar Ward was not so fortunate. Just before his bankruptcy proceedings began, he was ordered on 5 April 1745 before the Bar of the House of Commons, where on his knees he was reprimanded by the Speaker and fined for printing proceedings of the House in the *York Courant* (*Journals* 854). On the 27 June 1745, he was registered legally bankrupt.[18] And of course, in a geographical sense, Ward and Chandler had always been surrounded by law in their London office.

The *London Chronicle*, a newspaper edited by Robert Dodsley and with contributors like Samuel Johnson, was another of Collins's inventions. He also founded a provincial newspaper, the *Salisbury Journal*, in a town that had been without its own newspaper for years. There was no local competition, except – as ever – from the London papers, and a fine equilibrium based on co-operation was maintained with other newspapers in the region for more than thirty years. When James Linden moved into the *Journal*'s catchment area with his *Hampshire Chronicle* in 1772, Collins probably assisted him to insolvency. Indeed Collins secretly bought a controlling share in the bankrupt *Hampshire Chronicle* and re-established it under his own management.[19] Collins was a powerful, controlling force in the Wessex book and newspaper trade, and took special pride in his newspapers, arranging that both the *Chronicle* and the *Journal* were painted into his portrait. (No portraits of Ward and Chandler have been discovered.) Ward and Chandler took over the *York Courant*, which had been established in 1725, from the bankrupt Alexander Staples in 1739. The *Courant* was York's second newspaper; the first, the *York Mercury* (established in 1719), had published concurrently for a few years, but had been run out of business in the early 1730s. According to Thomas Gent, the culprit here was Robert Ward, a coincidental surname, and almost certainly no relation to Cæsar (Gent 160, 163–4). During the parliamentary elections in 1741, another paper, the *York Gazetteer*, was set up in direct competition to the *York Courant*, which must at least have cut into the partners' profits (Wiles 510–18). The environment for newspapers was sometimes turbulent in York, and there probably wasn't much the two could do about it.

Once he had developed the newspaper into a mainstay of his business, Benjamin Collins did not look for flashy publication projects, nor did he seek out royal patrons. Instead he invested in steady-selling authors, like Oliver Goldsmith, Samuel Johnson and Tobias Smollett, and he found partners in like-minded booksellers. There were many publishing projects with London printers and booksellers, but one of his most successful involved a partnership with his friend John Newbery. The two invested in children's books that sold for a penny to as much as 6*d*. each, but they cost little to make and sold in the tens and sometimes hundreds of thousands. Collins claimed to have invented one of the best-selling, the *Royal Battledore*, which was a sort of paper hornbook. While Ward and Chandler began publishing in a fairly conservative way, they never found such a lucrative market niche. Managed differently, Chandler's *History* might have filled the bill. But there were evidently no other backers for Chandler's twelve- and then fourteen-volume venture, no conger to share the risks and profits. Neither Chandler nor his partner attempted to cushion the financial blow by taking up subscriptions in advance of publication, or by publishing in more manageable weekly or monthly parts. Instead, a large investment in paper, type, printing, marketing and distribution – or more likely the equivalent in credit arrangements – had to precede any returns. No matter what role Cæsar Ward actually played in the *History*, its failure inevitably affected him. Even though Chandler claimed sole credit for the multi-volume work, his suicide could do nothing to prevent his partner's bankruptcy (something a glance at their own publication of 1743, *The Law for and against Bankruptcy*, would have told him).

Ward and Chandler's account books are gone – all we have are the directions Cæsar Ward scribbled to his agent in the margins of the *York Courant*s he sent down to London – but, as the proceedings in another book-trade bankruptcy clearly demonstrate, investment in large multi-volume editions could be dangerously expensive, and could weaken or collapse a whole business structure. James Rivington's creditors tallied up the costs for publishing three editions of Tobias Smollett's *Complete History of England* at £22,228 16*s*. 0*d*.[20] This was a work that became more elaborate with each edition, beginning with four volumes in 1,000 copies published in 1757; to a second edition with seven volumes in 2,000 copies; and then eleven volumes to be published in numbers beginning in 1758. Rivington's bankruptcy halted this last edition, but only after 421,625 numbers had been printed and delivered, according to the still unpublished William Strahan ledgers in the British Library. Costs included thousands of pounds for illustration-work, over £1,500 paid to the author, as well as large bills for paper, printing and advertising.

Book-trade history is littered with similar examples, possibly beginning in the fifteenth century with Sweynheym and Pannartz, whose multi-volume edition of Nicholas of Lyra's *Postilla* very nearly brought the ruin of their business in 1472 (Hall 15). It was so bad that Giovanni Andrea Bussi, who wrote the preface to the fifth volume and hopefully directed it to the new Pope, noted that although the two German printers had been the first to introduce that useful art to Italy, they now found their workshop to be 'filled with printed quires, but empty of necessities' because of the forward expense of producing the *Postilla*. The Pope was then invited to take his pick of the unsold stock in return, it was suggested, for his financial assistance. Moses Pitt's road to ruin a couple of hundred years later was constructed of disastrous real-estate transactions and false dealings, but it began with a publishing venture that Michael Harris has described as utopian: the notorious and well-documented *English Atlas*, a multi-volume project well beyond Pitt's experience, equipment, expertise, premises and means (Harris 176–208). And today the delegates to Oxford University Press must sometimes wonder what return they will have on their huge investment in the *New Dictionary of National Biography*.

In the analysis, Michael Harris thought that some of Moses Pitt's problems lay in the late seventeenth-century's unregulated and informal financial institutions, and he looked forward to the greater security the next century would provide. While the rules did change, and banking became more organized in the eighteenth century, there still seemed to be plenty of room for financial failure. The details for each case will be different, but it seems likely that Ward and Chandler will prove to fit a broad pattern for book-trade insolvency, with the main points of stress lying in their inability to manipulate the local newspaper market and, more important, in their willingness to risk all in an expensive multi-volume publication.

## Notes

1   *Gentleman's Magazine* (June 1745); notice in the *York Courant* (25 June 1745): 'Having lately had the Misfortune to lose a very large Sum of Money by being engag'd with my Brother-in-Law, who died Insolvent, I have been oblig'd to sell the Printing-House …'.

2   London, Guildhall Library MS 8200/3: Society of Apothecaries, Court Minute Book, 1680–94.

3   The Land Tax Assessment Books for the Parish of St Dunstans in the West in the Ward of Farringdon Without for 1733 (Guildhall Library, MS 11,316/104). A number of tradesmen in the parish – the bankers Benjamin Hoare & Partners, as well as at least eight booksellers – described their business addresses as 'over against St Dunstan's', although it is clear that they were in different parts of Fleet Street nearby.

4   Fog's *Weekly Journal* (27 May 1732; in the British Library (BL), Burney Collection 291.b).

5   Overseers Accounts, 1734–1743, for the Parish of St Clement Danes, Royal Ward (Westminster Archives, B38–B41, microfilm reels 183–5).

6   William and Edward were sons of Josiah Sandby, clerk of the College of Worcester. William, apprenticed to Richard Manby in 1734, was freed 1741 (Mckenzie, no. 5148); Edward was apprenticed to Cæsar Ward in 1744 (Maxted 99).

7  Richard Chandler to the Revd Thomas Birch, 6 May 1734 (BL, Sloane MS 4302, fols 161–2).
8  Richardson to James Leake August 1741, Victoria & Albert Museum Library, Forster Collection XVI, I, fols 55–7; C, pp 42–5 (cited in Eaves and Kimpel 135).
9  Cæsar Ward to Charles Lyttelton, BL, Stowe MS 753, fols 113–14, 152–3, 191, 264–5, 273–4, 275, 278–9, 300–301; Stowe MS 754, fols 1, 10–11, 210–15. Ward's death is reported in Francis Drake to Charles Lyttelton, Stowe MS 754, fol. 39.
10  Ward to Lyttelton, 26 December 1750; 18 September 1754.
11  Ward to Lyttelton, 21 December 1754.
12  *A Catalogue of Books printed for, and sold by Cæsar Ward and Richard Chandler, Booksellers. At the Ship just without Temple-Bar, London, and at their Shops in Coney-Street, York, and the Corner of the Long-Room-Street, at Scarborough-Spaw* [1737?]. Copy at BL 11902.b.33.
13  Maxted records insurance of £2,000 on premises in Paternoster Row in 1782/3 (Maxted 1992, 23).
14  PRO, B6/1 (Certificates of Bankruptcy, 1733–51).
15  A full account of Benjamin Collins is to be found in C.Y. Ferdinand, *Benjamin Collins and the Provincial Newspaper Trade*.
16  For example *Collins* v. *Brewman* (PRO, CH12/1254/11), *Collins* v. *Faden* (CH12/104/32), and *Wilkes* v. *Collins* (E140/90–1).
17  York City Archives, E94/6.
18  Docket book, Commissioners of Bankruptcy Register (PRO B4/11, fol. 91, no. 2166).
19  *Wilkes* v. *Collins*, Exhibits (PRO, E140/90–1); Bills and Answers (E112/1959/147).
20  William Upcott Papers, BL Add. MS 38,730, discussed in Hernlund 77–122.

# Bibliography

Battestin, Martin C., with Ruthe R. Battestin (1989), *Henry Fielding: A Life*, London: Routledge.
Collins, Francis (ed.) (1900), *Register of the Freemen of the City of York – from the City Records*, Vol. 2: *1559–1759*, Durham: Andrews & Co.
Davies, Robert (1868), *A Memoir of the York Press, with Notice of Authors, Printers, and Stationers, in the Sixteenth, Seventeenth, and Eighteenth Centuries*, Westminster: Nichols and Sons.
Defoe, Daniel (1727–32), *The Complete English Tradesman*, 3rd edn, London: printed for C. Rivington.
Dickson, P.G.M. (1960), *The Sun Insurance Office 1710–1960*, London: Oxford University Press.
Eaves, T. Duncan and Ben D. Kimpel (1971), *Samuel Richardson: A Biography*, Oxford: Clarendon Press.
Ferdinand, C.Y. (1997), *Benjamin Collins and the Provincial Newspaper Trade in the Eighteenth Century*, Oxford: Oxford University Press.
Gent, Thomas (1832), *The Life of Mr. Thomas Gent, Printer, of York, Written by Himself*, London: printed for Thomas Thorpe.
Hall, Edwin (1991), *Sweynhaym & Pannartz and the Origins of Printing in Italy: German Technology and Italian Humanism in Renaissance Rome*, McMinnville, Oregon: Bird & Bull Press for Phillip J. Pirages.

Harris, Michael (1985), 'Moses Pitt and Insolvency in the London Booktrade in the Late-Seventeenth Century', *Economics of the British Booktrade 1605–1939*, eds Robin Myers and Michael Harris, 176–208, Cambridge and Alexandria, VA: Chadwyck-Healey.

Hernlund, Patricia (1994), 'Three Bankruptcies in the London Book Trade, 1746–61: Rivington, Knapton, and Osborn', *Writers, Books, and Trade: An Eighteenth-Century Miscellany for William B. Todd*, ed. O M Brack, Jr, New York: AMS Press.

*Journals of the House of Commons. From June the 25th, 1741 ... to September the 19th, 1745*, London: reprinted by Order of the House of Commons, 1803.

Maslen, Keith and John Lancaster (eds) (1991), *The Bowyer Ledgers: The Printing Accounts of William Bowyer Father and Son, reproduced on Microfiches, with a Checklist of Bowyer Printing 1699–1777, a Commentary, Indexes, and Appendixes*, London: Bibliographical Society.

Maxted, Ian (1985), *The British Book Trades, 1731–1806: A Checklist of Bankrupts*, Exeter Working Papers in British Book Trade History, 4, Exeter: J. Maxted.

Maxted, Ian (1992), *The British Book Trades 1775–1787: An Index to Insurance Policies*, Exeter: J. Maxted.

McKenzie, D.F. (ed.) (1978), *Stationers' Company Apprentices 1701–1800*, Oxford: Oxford Bibliographical Society.

McKenzie, D.F. and J.C. Ross (eds) (1968), *A Ledger of Charles Ackers, Printer of 'The London Magazine'*, Oxford: Oxford University Press, for the Oxford Bibliographical Society.

Melton, Frank (1985), 'Robert and Sir Francis Gosling: Eighteenth-Century Bankers and Stationers', *Economics of the British Booktrade 1605–1939*, eds Robin Myers and Michael Harris, 60–77, Cambridge and Alexandria, VA: Chadwyck-Healey.

Nichols, John (1812–15), *Literary Anecdotes of the Eighteenth Century*, 9 vols, London: Nichols.

Plomer, Henry R. (1932), *A Dictionary of the Printers and Booksellers Who Were at Work in England, Scotland and Ireland from 1726 to 1775*, London: Bibliographical Society.

Supple, Barry (1970), *The Royal Exchange Assurance: A History of British Insurance 1720–1970*, Cambridge: Cambridge University Press.

Wiles, R.M. (1965), *Freshest Advices: Early Provincial Newspapers in England*, Columbus: Ohio State University Press.

Chapter Six

# Thomas Gray, David Hume and John Home's *Douglas*

Roger Lonsdale

After the overnight popularity of his *Elegy in a Country Churchyard* (1751), the fastidious Thomas Gray did not find it easy to produce further poetry which would justify and sustain his new reputation. This is reflected in the known facts about the composition of the two poems which constitute his one major subsequent publication, the *Odes* (1757). Gray wrote all but the last seventeen lines of the first Pindaric ode, 'The Progress of Poesy', between September 1751 and July 1752, but then took two further years to complete it. Similarly Gray wrote lines 1–100 of 'The Bard' between March and August 1755, but the last forty-four lines had to await a sudden burst of creative energy in May 1757. The *Odes*, by most accounts a crucial early Romantic poetic document, were finally published on 8 August 1757.[1]

Gray gave his own explanation of what had inspired him to finish his second 'Odikle' in late May 1757, when sending lines 101–44 of 'The Bard' to William Mason, his friend and future biographer. This had been a recent concert given in Cambridge by the blind Welsh harper, John Parry:

> Mr Parry has been here, & scratch'd out such ravishing blind Harmony, such tunes of a thousand year old with names enough to choak you, as have set all this learned body a'dancing, & inspired them with due reverence for the Odikle, whenever it shall appear. Mr Parry (you must know) it was, that has put Odikle in motion again.

In 1775 Mason confirmed that Gray 'often declared' that 'hearing Parry play upon the Welch harp at a concert at Cambridge' had 'inspired him with the conclusion'.[2]

The numerous borrowings by Gray from earlier poets noted in my edition in 1969 included no very striking precedent for his Welsh Bard's spectacular and defiant suicide at the end of the poem. My present purpose is to investigate the plausibility of an apparently neglected suggestion by George Steevens, the Shakespeare scholar and friend of Samuel Johnson, in the article he contributed to Isaac Reed's *Biographia Dramatica* (1782) on John Home's once celebrated tragedy *Douglas*:

> Dr. Johnson blames Mr. Gray for concluding his celebrated ode with suicide, a circumstance borrowed perhaps from *Douglas*, in which Lady Randolph, otherwise a blameless character, precipitates herself, like the *Bard*, from a cliff into eternity. (2.93)

In his recent 'Life of Gray' (1781) Johnson had commented on 'The Bard': 'let it be observed that the ode might have been concluded with an action of better example: but suicide is always to be had without expence of thought'. This was consistent with Johnson's objections elsewhere, as in the 'Life of Pope', to 'the illaudable singularity of treating suicide with respect'.[3]

The basic facts are that the first London performance of *Douglas: A Tragedy* by the Scottish clergyman and dramatist John Home (1722–1808) took place at Covent Garden Theatre, with Peg Woffington in the central role of Lady Randolph, on 14 March 1757, only a few weeks before Gray was suddenly moved to finish 'The Bard'. There were further performances on 15, 17 and 19 March, and four more in April. The text of *Douglas* was published in London on 19 March 1757, the Edinburgh edition ten days later (*The London Stage 1660–1800* [1962] 585–95; Home 10–11).

As for the resemblance suggested by Steevens, it will be remembered that Gray's medieval Welsh Bard, situated 'On a rock, whose haughty brow / Frowns o'er old Conway's foaming flood' (ll. 15–16), ends his long prophecy of the fate awaiting the tyrannical Norman King Edward I and his descendants as follows:

> 'Be thine despair and sceptered care;
> To triumph, and to die, are mine.'
> He spoke, and headlong from the mountain's height
> Deep in the roaring tide he plunged to endless night. (141–4)

At the very end of John Home's *Douglas*, the suicide of the long-suffering Matilda, Lady Randolph, who has just learned of the violent death of her long lost and only recently identified son, is reported by her companion, Anna:

> She ran, she flew like light'ning up the hill,
> Nor halted till the precipice she gain'd,
> Beneath whose low'ring top the river falls

Ingulph'd in rifted rocks: thither she came,
As fearless as the eagle lights upon it,
And headlong down ...
O had you seen her last despairing look!
Upon the brink she stood, and cast her eyes
Down on the deep: then lifting up her head
And her white hands to heaven, seeming to say,
Why am I forc'd to this? she plung'd herself
Into the empty air.          (5.327–33, 337–42)[4]

While there may be only slight verbal resemblances between the two passages ('headlong', 'plunged'), both works end with spectacular suicides in precipitous landscapes. Although there is no evidence that Gray, normally resident in Cambridge, had actually attended a performance of *Douglas*, or even read the tragedy by the time he completed 'The Bard' late in May 1757, he was apparently in London on the day of the first performance at Covent Garden on 14 March. A letter of 3 March 1757 reveals that he was planning to travel to the capital two days later to stay with his friend Thomas Wharton. He was certainly in London on the 11th and expected still to be there on 14 March, since he offered to meet his old friend Horace Walpole on that day (*Corresp.* 2:496–7).

It will be necessary to return to Gray's journey to London on 5 March 1757, but it may first be asked whether he was likely to have had any particular interest in seeing *Douglas* during his visit, or, indeed, to have been aware of its imminent production. The well publicized performance at Covent Garden Theatre in March 1757 had in fact been preceded in Scotland by some three months of almost continuous controversy, together with bold claims for its high literary merit. To go back a little further, David Garrick had originally refused to accept *Douglas* for Drury Lane Theatre in July 1756, explaining at length to Lord Bute, John Home's patron, that the tragedy was 'radically defective, & in Every Act incapable of raising the Passions, or commanding Attention'.[5] After its London rejection, the successful performance of *Douglas* at the Canongate Theatre in Edinburgh on 14 December 1756 had rapidly become a matter of nationalistic triumph. The *Edinburgh Courant* of 18 December 1756 described it as 'one of the most perfect Works of Genius any Age has produced', and the *Scots Magazine* reported that 'there never was so great a run on a play in this country. Persons of all ranks and professions crowded to it'. According to a familiar anecdote, 'During the representation of *Douglas*, a young and sanguine North Briton, in the pit, exclaimed on a sudden, with an air of triumph, "Weel, lads; what think you of Wully Shakspeare now?".[6]

Fierce hostility, however, from the more conservative Presbyterian clergy soon followed, with heated objections to the fact that a clergyman should have written such a play and that other moderate clergymen had attended and admired it. For several months the controversy raged in Edinburgh (driving John Home himself out of the Church by June 1757), with published admonitions against the theatre by the Presbyteries of Edinburgh and Glasgow, attacks on the clergymen who supported Home, a protracted and prolific pamphlet war, and the eventual involvement of no less a figure than David Hume (Mossner 356–69).

David Hume, who had himself been under attack during 1756 for 'infidelity' by the General Assembly of the Church of Scotland (Mossner 344ff), provocatively intervened in the controversy on 7 February 1757 in the dedication (dated 3 January 1757) of his *Four Dissertations* to his friend John Home. Hume notoriously praised *Douglas* as

> one of the most interesting and pathetic pieces, that ever was exhibited in any theatre ... you possess the true theatric genius of *Shakespear* and *Otway*, refined from the unhappy barbarism of the one, and licentiousness of the other. (iv–vi)

Hume's dedication was to be widely reprinted in the London newspapers and journals, thus providing important advance publicity for the first London performance of the play at Covent Garden some five weeks later.[7]

Hume's *Four Dissertations* had in fact originally been planned, and indeed printed early in 1756, as *Five Dissertations*, before the philosopher, apparently under threat of prosecution, decided to omit an inflammatory essay 'Of Suicide' from the volume (Mossner 319–35). This must have been well known in some Edinburgh quarters in which copies of the suppressed text had evidently circulated. Indeed, some contributors to the heated pamphlet war over *Douglas* in the early months of 1757 gratefully seized the opportunity of linking David Hume's admiration for Home's controversial tragedy with the suppressed essay 'Of Suicide'. Thus, John Maclaurin's *Apology for the Writers against the Tragedy of Douglas* (Edinburgh, 1757) refers to Hume's 'celebrated dedication', and suggests that 'Lady *Randolph* dies like a virago who had carefully perused the late essay on SUICIDE' (6n, 13). *The Usefulness of the Edinburgh Theatre Seriously Considered* (Edinburgh 1757) made a similar thrust at Hume (while referring to Lady Randolph by her original name in the Edinburgh production):[8]

The public need not now lament the suppression of his celebrated essay on the *lawfulness of suicide:* This is more beautifully represented in the character of *Lady Barnet*, who throws herself over a rock with more than *Roman* courage. (5)

Lady Randolph's final suicide was in fact a recurrent topic in the controversy, whether or not David Hume was invoked. One of the charges against John Home's friend the Rev. Alexander Carlyle, was that as a clergyman he had attended 'a tragedy which tended to encourage the monstrous crime of suicide' (*Scots. Mag.* March 1757, 274). A defender of *Douglas* like Adam Ferguson, in *The Morality of Stage-Plays Seriously Considered* (Edinburgh 1757), might try to argue that her fate 'moves to compassion, and proves at last a warning against rash and fatal despair' (11). Sterner moralists, however, such as the author of *Some Serious Remarks on a Late Pamphlet* (Edinburgh 1757) despised so soft a view: 'at last her patience is worn out, she finds no Benefit in drawing nigh to the most High, Why should she wait upon God any longer? so she falls into Despair, runs mad, and kills herself ... an Instance of Despair and Self-Murder' (14).

According to *The Immorality of Stage-Plays in General, and of The Tragedy of Douglas, in Particular* (Edinburgh 1757), Lady Randolph's suicide was dangerous precisely because it was 'rather calculated to move pity towards the actor, than indignation at the crime'. As for *Douglas* as a whole, 'none can deny that intrigue, revenge, bloodshed, murder, yea suicide, blasphemy and impiety make up the great lines of it'. Home has 'crammed his tragedy with prayers, caused the same to be put up unto GOD, in pretence only, in the name of a person who, according to his own fable, had thrown herself over a precipice several centuries ago, and so is beyond the reach of prayer' (4–5, 19, 22). In the hostile account by 'A.B.' of Lady Randolph in *Douglas, a Tragedy, Weighed in the Balances, and found wanting* (Edinburgh 1757), she

is represented as guilty of suicide or self-murder ... a species of immorality so gross, so dangerous, and at the same time so irreparable, that I am quite at a loss for words to express the guilt and aggravation of it ... a sin of the deepest hue, a crime of the grossest nature. (33)

The Edinburgh controversy was followed with interest in the English press, especially as the play's London production drew near. In late February 1757 the *Gentleman's Magazine* reprinted the Presbytery of Glasgow's statement of support for the Edinburgh Presbytery's admonition on the evils of the theatre in general and *Douglas* in particular (89), giving a detailed account of 'The

Dramatic Story of DOUGLAS; a Tragedy' a month later (89, 124–7). On 12 March 1757, two days before the play's first performance, the *Public Advertiser* quoted David Hume's dedication in praise of *Douglas*, as did other papers and journals. In mid-March 1757, for example, Arthur Murphy in the *Literary Magazine* defended the theatre against the more extreme Edinburgh attacks, and reprinted both the Presbytery's admonition against *Douglas* and Hume's fulsome dedication to Home. Related articles (apparently also by Murphy) appeared in the *London Chronicle* on 24 February and 15 March 1757, the latter in particular sharing most of the *Literary Magazine's* materials (Murphy, 122–5).

Although a report from London in the *Edinburgh Evening Courant* of 26 March 1757 claimed that *Douglas* had 'brought greater Crowds to Covent Garden Theatre than have been there for many Years', including members of the Royal Family, critical opinion in London tended to agree that *Douglas* had failed to live up to the expectations raised by David Hume's claims. Such was the verdict of the *London Chronicle* of 24 March, and the *Critical Review* for March 1757 also dwelt on the play's faults precisely because of Hume's hyperbole. In May 1757 Oliver Goldsmith in the *Monthly Review* concluded that Hume's 'commendation' had 'sacrificed his taste to his friendship', and 'perhaps raised too much expectation in some, and excited a spirit of envy and critical prejudice in others'.[9]

As for Lady Randolph's self-inflicted fate, London comment was less heated than in Edinburgh, usually resting on aesthetic rather than religious grounds. Reviewing *Douglas* in the *Literary Magazine* in April 1757, Arthur Murphy summarized the plot at length and asked: 'Would it not have been better not to have made lady *Randolph* guilty of suicide, as she might have expired with grief over her dead son, and then the close would have been more pathetic'. Murphy nevertheless concluded that Home 'seems to have a correcter taste for the Dramatic art, than any writer that has appeared of late'.[10] The anonymous *Tragedy of Douglas Analysed* (1757) claimed that 'The strongest imagination cannot picture to itself any thing beyond Lady Randolph's affliction, which she consummates by throwing herself off a rock', while feeling bound to admit that there had been critical objections to 'the death of innocence' (11, 20). In the article already cited, the *Critical Review* of March 1757 stated more bluntly that the fate of the innocent Douglas and Lady Randolph 'is scarce reconcileable with poetical justice, which seems to have been violated by their deaths'.

Early in April 1757 John Hawkesworth's anonymous *A Letter to Mr. David Hume, On the Tragedy of Douglas* also touched on Lady Randolph's fate:

'why she should plunge from a precipice head-foremost into the sea, I cannot see any reason, nor for her, or her son's deaths' (15). Hawkesworth's main concern, however, was to reply to Hume's excessive praise of the tragedy and to defend David Garrick against 'all the foul-mouthed abuse that has been lavished on him' for originally rejecting *Douglas* in 1756. In refusing 'this *aurora borealis* of tragedy, that had so long corruscated over us from the North', Garrick had *not* deprived Drury Lane Theatre of 'the best play ever acted, not only on the *English* stage, but on any other, ancient or modern' (18). Hawkesworth mischievously suggested that the key to Lady Randolph's permanent melancholy was in fact her husband's low sex-drive: 'from ineffectual nights sprung the daily cause of her tears; and certainly a very material one. *Penelope*, it is true, mourned twenty years for *Ulysses*; but then she did not admit an *apathic* lover to tantalise her in bed' (Abbott 74–6).

With the promise that this narrative will soon return to Gray and 'The Bard', it is necessary to introduce next the formidable and industriously combative figure of William Warburton, clergyman and theologian (soon to become Bishop of Gloucester), formerly the friend, defender and editor of Alexander Pope. Writing to Hawkesworth in March 1757 about the pamphlet just quoted, Garrick mentioned Warburton's approval of these forthcoming 'Observations upon Douglas' and their attack on David Hume (Garrick 1963, 1:260). Intensely interested in, and invariably hostile to, Hume's literary activities, Warburton had evidently for some time been kept well informed about them in advance by Andrew Millar, the publisher he shared with Hume. Thus, in January 1757 Millar seems to have shown Garrick a letter in which Hume abused him for his rejection of *Douglas*. Garrick had in turn complained about this to Warburton, who replied on 25 January 1757: 'I think you very insolently treated by Hume, the Essay writer; nor do I see how Millar can be excused from impertinence in showing you the puppy's letter … I think you will honour him too much in returning any answer to it' (Garrick 1831–2, 1: 77–8). Garrick had nevertheless engaged Hawkesworth to make a public reply, evidently with Warburton's eventual approval.

Warburton himself, meanwhile, had his own game in view. Informed early in 1756 by Andrew Millar of David Hume's planned *Five Dissertations*, including the inflammatory 'Of Suicide', Warburton seems to have been primarily responsible for the threats of prosecution which led Hume to suppress it (Mossner 323–5). A year later, in February 1757, Warburton remained no less implacably hostile to the revised text of Hume's *Four Dissertations*, which Millar had again shown him in advance: 'I think a wickeder mind, and more obstinately bent on public mischief, I never knew'. Warburton was soon instigating his own disguised attack on one of the *Four Dissertations*, 'The Natural History of Religion' (Hurd 1809, 239–41; Mossner 323–7).

At this point we return at last to Thomas Gray's journey on 5 March 1757 from Cambridge to London, where he may or may not eventually have seen or at least read *Douglas*. His letter of 3 March reveals that he would be travelling to London with two Cambridge friends, Thomas Balguy (1716–95), Fellow of St John's College, and Richard Hurd (1720–1808), Fellow of Emmanuel (*Corresp.* 2:496). Since both Balguy and Hurd were in different ways aware of, or even involved in, William Warburton's long-running campaign against Hume, it seems reasonable to speculate that the imminent production of *Douglas*, David Hume's conspicuous admiration of it, and even the controversial subject of suicide, were likely to have entered the conversation of these travelling friends early in March 1757.

The earliest known reference to David Hume's suppression of 'Of Suicide' from his original *Five Dissertations* in fact occurs in a letter of 14 February 1756 from the ever-vigilant William Warburton to none other than the first of Gray's travelling companions, Thomas Balguy, whom Warburton had described to Hurd in November 1750 as 'a man of so uncommon merit and so close connexion with you'.[11] Richard Hurd, Gray's other companion on the journey to London, was by this time already working closely with William Warburton on *Remarks on Mr. David Hume's Essay on the Natural History of Religion: Addressed to the Rev. Dr. Warburton*. Hurd had been persuaded to compile this attack on the 'puny Dialectician from the North' and his 'futility, licence, and vanity' (2 and 8) from Warburton's own notes, and also to write an introduction which skilfully pretends to explain to Warburton what was essentially his own work (Watson 477–80; Mossner 325–8). The fact that, as we have seen, the compliant Andrew Millar had shown Hume's *Four Dissertations* to Warburton by early February 1757 enabled Hurd to publish the hostile *Remarks* in the following May.

This hardly amounts to clinching proof, of course, that Gray or his companions attended or even read *Douglas* in London in mid-March 1757, even if one may assume that they were aware of and interested in it.[12] It will become clear shortly that Gray at least was acutely aware of the tragedy. We can now return to his long-delayed completion of 'The Bard' in late May 1757, which he himself described as inspired by John Parry's recent Welsh harping in Cambridge. By 11 June Gray was able to send Mason the text of the whole poem, including a revised version of the ending, which had also apparently been seen by Thomas Wharton in London, and by Richard Hurd and Thomas Balguy in Cambridge, although 'both somehow dislike the conclusion of the Bard' (for example, the antithesis in ll. 141–2), and, indeed, preferred the earlier 'The Progress of Poesy'. Gray begged Mason: 'pray, think a little about this conclusion, for all depends upon it. the rest is of little consequence' (*Corresp.* 2:503–4, 1:434–7).

In the middle of his detailed discussion of 'The Bard' on 11 June, Gray suddenly told Mason that 'I have got the old Scotch ballad, on wch Douglas was founded. it is divine', quoting fifteen lines of it before returning to 'The Bard' (*Corresp.* 2:505). It is striking that no previous letter by Gray had so much as mentioned Home's *Douglas*, first performed in London the previous March, although he clearly assumes here that Mason knows all about the play, presumably from earlier (now missing) letters. It is as if, with part of his mind, Gray is belatedly acknowledging a connection of some kind between the completion of 'The Bard' and *Douglas*. As for the ballad, Gray had presumably obtained one of the two editions of *Gill Morice, an Ancient Scottish Poem*, published by Foulis at Glasgow in 1755, in which, with some resemblance to the catastrophe of *Douglas*, Lord Barnard murders Gill Morice, his wife's son, after mistaking him for her lover (see Groom 53). Several early critics, including David Hume himself, had detected in *Douglas* some debt to Voltaire's *Merope*, performed in Aaron Hill's translation at Drury Lane in April 1749. This might explain why John Home and others preferred to emphasise instead an old Scottish ballad as his true inspiration.[13] If Gray himself *were* in any way indebted to *Douglas*, his own professed fascination with its ballad source might seem to serve a similarly deflecting purpose.

When Horace Walpole published Gray's *Odes* at his Strawberry Hill Press on 8 August 1757, Hurd and Balguy were among the Cambridge friends to whom the poet asked for copies to be sent (*Corresp.* 2:509). Two days later he sent one to his friend Edward Bedingfield:

> You are desired to give me your *honest* opinion about the latter part of the Bard, wch you had not seen before, for I know it is weakly in several parts; but it is a mercy, that it ever came to an end at all … I know, I shall never be admired but in Scotland. by the way I am greatly struck with the Tragedy of Douglas, tho' it has infinite faults. the Author seems to have retrieved the true language of the Stage, wch had been lost for these hundred years; & there is one Scene (between Matilda & the old Peasant) so masterly, that it strikes me blind to all the defects in the world. (*Corresp.* 2:515)[14]

Here, at last, Gray's admiration for Home's *Douglas*, whether seen in live performance or merely read, is clear. His emphasis noticeably falls, however, not on Lady Randolph's final spectacular suicide, but on her encounter in Act

III with Old Norval, who protractedly reveals the identity of her long-lost son.[15] Once again, the completion of 'The Bard' may seem to have some submerged connection in Gray's mind with *Douglas*.

Gray was to return to the play once more in a letter to Edward Bedingfield of 31 October 1757, in which he mentions the ballad 'Gil Morice' to his friend for the first time:

> I have got the old Ballad on wch Douglas is founded. it is in my eyes a miracle not only of ancient simplicity, but of ancient art. the great rules of Aristotle & Horace are observed in it by a Writer, who perhaps had never heard their names. what I say, is a great compliment to the Genius of the Scotch, but a still greater to Horace & Aristotle. as to the Play, the single Scene of Matilda's interview with the old Peasant was the thing, that inchanted me.

While Gray continued to emphasize the Lady Randolph–Old Norval scene in *Douglas*, Bedingfield had evidently already raised the troublesome question of Lady Randolph's suicide at the end of the play, which must have been a sensitive issue for Gray in view of the similar ending of 'The Bard'. Gray's allusion to Bedingfield's religion (he was a Catholic) as 'you know what', and the somewhat troubled reflections which follow bring us as close as we will get to his views on this controversial subject, although there is no admission that his remarks had any direct bearing on his Bard's own suicide:

> pray keep your – you know what – from interfering with your judgement in poetry. nothing belongs to this, but what Men say, & what they do in different situations of life; not what they *ought* to say or do. I wish to God, that no good Man, or even no *Good Christian*, had ever known what despair was: but I fear they have too often been hurried to their own destruction. Providence may have interposed to prevent it, but whether it does *always* interpose, only that Providence can tell. however this is *gratis dictum*, for Matilda [Lady Randolph] is distracted, before she executes her purpose. (*Corresp.* 2:538–9).

What may one conclude from this unpredictably entangled context for George Steevens's original suggestion in 1782? Perhaps, at least, that the possibility that Gray was in some way indebted to *Douglas* is not without internal and external plausibility, that there is evidence that he could have seen Home's play in London in mid-March 1757, and that he was likely to have been acutely aware of it. There is definite evidence, though not before he finished 'The Bard', of his admiration for *Douglas* within a few weeks of its first performance, and of his tendency to associate it, if deviously, with the completion of 'The Bard', given that it crops up in that context in his letters three times in some four months in 1757. While one need not assume that Gray was literally indebted to Home for the idea of the Bard's final self-destruction, some barely admitted fascination with the controversial theme of suicide seems strangely to link 'The Bard' with David Hume and with *Douglas*, which (with or without the help of John Parry's harping) may have stimulated Gray to the long-delayed completion of the poem.

A few other loose ends may be tied up. Because of the celebrity of *Douglas* in 1757, Garrick was pressured into accepting *Agis*, Home's earlier tragedy, for Drury Lane in the following year. Gray was bitterly disappointed by it, deploring *Agis* in a letter of 8 March 1758 as 'all modern Greek; the story is an antique statue painted white and red, frized, and dressed in a negligée made by a Yorkshire mantua-maker' (*Corresp.* 2:565–6; Garrick 1963, 1:269–70, 281–2). Before long, however, Gray, John Home and David Hume were to be linked after a fashion once again. In 1760 Gray was fascinated by the publication of James Macpherson's *Fragments of Ancient Poetry* (1760), but suspicious of their authenticity. His enquiries in Scotland eventually elicited a long letter from David Hume (at that stage still convinced of their genuineness) to some intermediary, dated 16 August 1760, which explained John Home's crucial role in encouraging Macpherson to start 'translating' the 'wild poetry' of the Highlands and in gaining it publicity.[16]

One may wonder finally whether Gray and David Hume would have met in the newly opened British Museum, and taken the opportunity to talk over some of these still recent and complex matters during a coffee break. While working on his *History of England,* Hume applied to use the Reading Room, and was granted permission on 3 March 1759, which was renewed on 31 July and 6 November 1761 (Mossner 395). On 9 July 1759 Gray removed from Cambridge to take up residence in London to read at the Museum, and did not finally return to Cambridge until 19 November 1761 (*Corresp.* 2:624n). Perhaps the answer has to be negative. In spite of their shared admiration for *Douglas*, Gray had a low opinion of Hume, as he later told James Beattie on 2 July 1770:

> I have always thought David Hume a pernicious writer, and believe he has done as much mischief here as he has in his own country ... Is not that *naiveté* and good humour, which his admirers celebrate in him, owing to this, that he has continued all his days an infant, but one that unhappily has been taught to read and write? (*Corresp.* 3:1140)[17]

# Notes

1    Lonsdale 155–7, 177–9. This, my only serious attempt to reannotate a page or two of *The Poems of Gray, Collins and Goldsmith,* is respectfully offered by one of the original editors in the Longmans Annotated Poets series to its present General Editor, John Barnard.

2    *Gray* (1971) 2:501–2 (cited hereafter in the text as *Corresp.*); Gray (1775) 2:90. From 1749 to his death in 1782, John Parry was harper to Sir Watkin Williams Wynn II. He performed in London from the 1730s, living there continuously for long periods. Parry published *Antient British Music* (1742). Not long before Gray heard him in Cambridge (a concert of which no more seems to be known), Parry had played at benefit performances at Drury Lane Theatre on 31 March and 14 May 1757. For a recent account, see *A Biographical Dictionary of Actors, Actresses, Musicians [etc.] 1660–1800,* ed P.H. Highfill et al., XI (Carbondale, 1987), 214–16.

3    See Johnson, 3:440 and 226; and, for other objections to literary suicide, 101 and 396. Johnson had a low opinion of *Douglas* and its admirers, once taunting Thomas Sheridan, the theatre manager in Dublin, for giving John Home 'a gold medal for writing that foolish play', and defying him 'to shew ten good lines in it. He did not insist they should be together; but that there were not ten good lines in the whole play'. Boswell records Johnson speaking of 'Johnny Home, with his *earth gaping,* and his *destruction crying:* – Pooh!' (Boswell, *Life,* 5:361–2; cp. 2:320). For J.P. Collier's ascription of the article to Steevens, see D. MacMillan, 272.

4    According to Walpole, Gray himself originally wrote 'sunk' in the last line of 'The Bard', but revised it to 'plunge' on Garrick's suggestion: see *Corresp.* 1:437n.

5    Garrick (1963) 1:244–7; and 1:247–8, to John Hawkesworth, c.18 July 1756, whom Garrick had consulted about the play. For Bute's interest in *Douglas* as early as 20 September 1755, see Mackenzie (1822) 143–5. David Hume had already offered Home some objections to characterization in the play by late 1754, which would recur in many later critical discussions (Hume 1932, 1:215–16; see 1:452–3, for his further thoughts in 1764).

6    Gipson 43; *Scots Mag.,* 18 (1756) 624; *Biographia Dramatica,* rev. Stephen Jones (1812), I.i.360n. It is not clear whether this often-repeated anecdote refers to a performance in Edinburgh or London.

7    Hume more than once explained his reasons for supporting John Home in January–March 1757 (1932, 1:239–41, 245–6). Some of Home's supporters thought that he could only be damaged in Edinburgh by backing from such a source, which may explain why Hume noticeably distinguishes between their differences of 'abstract opinion' and 'speculative opinions' and their 'common passion for science and letters' (ii–iii). Hume in fact temporarily cancelled the dedication before telling Andrew Millar, to restore it, so that it is missing in some copies. It was often prefixed to later Irish editions of *Douglas.* For Hume's continuing interest in Home and his tragedy, see 1932, 1:246–7, 257, 260–61, 269, and 1954, 41–2 and 50 and nn.

8    Lady Randolph was originally Lady Barnet (see Lady Barnard in the ballad 'Gil Morice' below). According to Mackenzie (36 and 99), the change was made to obviate the 'bad effect' on an English audience of recalling 'the village near London'.

9    Gipson 21 and 205, quoting *Critical Review* 3 (March 1757) 258–68. For Goldsmith's review in *Monthly Review* 16 (May 1757) 426–9, see Goldsmith, 1:10–14.

10    Murphy discussed *Douglas* similarly in *London Chronicle* 24 March and 12 April 1757 (Murphy 128–36). It may be noted that when Murphy came to review Gray's Odes in the

*Literary Mag.* (September–October 1757) he had no problem with the end of 'The Bard': 'the bard's plunging from the rock, is a suitable catastrophe to a piece so full of the terrible graces' (Murphy 155).

11  Hurd 1809, 68; Mossner 323. Balguy's close friendship with Hurd is confirmed by the many other references to him in Hurd (1809) and Mason (1932).

12  A letter from Hurd to William Mason, 30 November 1757, implies a low opinion of Home's play. Hurd was sure that Mason's unpublished *Caractacus* 'will disgrace all the Athelstans and Douglases of our times, to that degree, that no man will bear to hear of them' (Mason 41). *Athelstan* (1756) was by John Brown.

13  See Gipson, 14, 47–8, 59–62, 202. The 'Advertisement' to *The Seven Champions of the Stage. In Imitation of GILL MORICE* [Edinburgh, 1758?], a contribution to the *Douglas* controversy, derisively described the ballad as 'that inestimable ancient song, which inspired the greatest genius that ever appeared in the world, with the most perfect work of genius produced in any age'. For the interest of Thomas Percy and William Shenstone in 'Gil Morice' a few months later, see Percy, 3, 7–8, 9. Percy eventually included it in *The Reliques of Antient English Poetry* (1765), 3:93–102, with a note: 'The foregoing ballad is said to have furnished the plot to the tragedy of DOUGLAS' (revised in *Reliques*, 3rd edn, 1775, 3:99, to 'This little pathetic tale suggested the plot of the tragedy of DOUGLAS').

14  Partly quoted in Gray 1775, 1:248.

15  Mackenzie, 92–3, also believed that this scene 'has no equal in modern, and scarcely a superior in ancient drama'. For Walter Scott's similar praise, see Gipson 180–81.

16  Hume 1932, 1:328–31; *Corresp.* 2:702, 704, 3:1227–9). William Collins had addressed his 'Ode on the Popular Superstitions of the Highlands of Scotland' to John Home, who had visited London in 1749/50 in an unsuccessful attempt to interest Garrick in *Agis* (Mackenzie 132–8; Lonsdale, 492). Collins's 'Ode' remained unpublished until 1788. In Lonsdale, 509n I noted a possible echo of it in *Douglas*: Home may well have told Collins about the 'kaelpie' ('Ode', ll. 99–120) and in turn refers to it himself in *Douglas*, 3.i.90: 'The angry spirit of the water shriek'd'. Although this line was often admired by early critics, John Hawkesworth, *A Letter to Mr. David Hume* (1757), 3, complained that its meaning was 'unknown to us *South Britons*' (10).

17  There is one remaining matter which would have been on Gray's mind for much of the period at the centre of this investigation. On 5 February 1757 his friend, Henry Tuthill (c. 1722–?) of Pembroke College, Cambridge, holder of several College offices since 1749, was deprived of his Fellowship for absence from the College and for falling 'under violent suspicion of having been guilty of great enormities'. One may merely speculate that these unspecified offences were homosexual in nature. Mason later tried to remove all references to Tuthill from Gray's papers, one reason why his letters are relatively sporadic in these crucial months. (For surviving allusions to Tuthill, see his letters to Wharton of 17 February and 17 April 1757, *Corresp.* 2:495 and 497.) Gray was greatly troubled by these events, but of his later editors and biographers only John Mitford, who claimed to know more about the 'circumstances' than he was prepared to reveal, emphasized the poet's 'pain and suffering'. Although the date of Henry Tuthill's death is unknown, Mitford told Alexander Dyce in January 1828 that he had committed suicide by drowning (*Corresp.* 2:495 and 497–8, and 3:1206–10).

## Bibliography

Abbott, John L. (1982), *John Hawkesworth: Eighteenth-Century Man of Letters*, Madison, WI: University of Wisconsin Press.

Garrick, David (1963), *The Letters of David Garrick*, eds D.M. Little and G.M. Kahrl, 3 vols, London: Oxford University Press.

Garrick, David (1831–32), *The Private Correspondence of David Garrick*, ed. James Boaden, 2 vols, London: Colburn and Bentley.

Gipson, Alice E. (1916), *John Home: A Study of his Life and Works*, New Haven.

Goldsmith, Oliver (1966), *Collected Works*, ed. Arthur Friedman, 5 vols, Oxford: Clarendon Press.

Gray, Thomas (1971 [1935]), *The Correspondence of Thomas Gray*, eds Paget Toynbee and Leonard Whibley, 3 vols, Oxford; corrected edn H.W. Starr, 3 vols, Oxford: Clarendon Press.

Gray, Thomas (1775), *The Poems of Mr. Gray, to which are prefixed Memoirs of his Life and Writings*, ed. William Mason, York.

Groom, Nick (1999), *The Making of Percy's Reliques*, Oxford: Clarendon Press.

Home, John (1972), *Douglas*, ed. Gerald D. Parker, Edinburgh: Oliver & Boyd.

Hume, David (1932), *The Letters of David Hume*, ed. J.Y.T. Greig, 2 vols, Oxford: Clarendon Press.

Hume, David (1954), *New Letters*, ed. Raymond Klibansky and Ernest. C. Mossner, Oxford: Clarendon Press.

Hurd, Richard (1809), *Letters from a Late Eminent Prelate to One of his Friends*, 2nd edn, London: Cadell and Davies.

Johnson, Samuel (1905), *Lives of the English Poets*, ed. George Birkbeck Hill, 3 vols, Oxford: Clarendon Press.

*The London Stage 1660–1800*, (1962), part 4, ed. G.W. Stone, Carbondale: Southern Illinois University Press.

Lonsdale, Roger (1969), *The Poems of Gray, Collins, and Goldsmith*, London and Harlow: Longman.

Mackenzie, Henry (1822), *An Account of the Life and Writings of John Home Esq.*, Edinburgh: Constable; London: Hurst, Robinson.

MacMillan, D. (1963), 'George Steeven's Contributions to *Biographia Dramatica*', in Carroll Camden (ed.), *Restoration and Eighteenth-Century Literature: Essays in Honour of Alan Dugald McKillop*, Chicago: University of Chicago Press.

Mason, William (1932), *The Correspondence of Richard Hurd and William Mason*, eds E.H. Pearce and L. Whibley, Cambridge: Cambridge University Press.

Mossner, Ernest C. (1980 [1954]), *The Life of David Hume*, 2nd edn, Edinburgh: Nelson.

Murphy, Arthur (1963), *New Essays by Arthur Murphy*, ed. Arthur Sherbo, East Lansing: Michigan State University Press.

Percy, Thomas (1977), *The Correspondence of Thomas Percy and William Shenstone*, ed. Cleanth Brooks, New Haven and London: Yale University Press.

Watson, J.S. (1863), *The Life of Bishop Warburton*, London: Longman.

Chapter Seven

# Texts in Conversation: Coleridge's *Sonnets from Various Authors* (1796)

David Fairer

In Autumn 1796, Samuel Taylor Coleridge put together a modest little pamphlet (so modest it has no title) which offers a case-history of how texts can gather new and even urgent meanings through the circumstances of their transmission. Hitherto largely ignored by Coleridge scholars, and never considered as a literary artefact, *Sonnets from Various Authors* (a title of convenience) is, I want to show, a carefully shaped collection with both a structured argument and a directed message. It is simultaneously a text and a context; it makes meaning in both space and time – through the particular contained circumstances of the sonnet form and of a few weeks during September–November 1796 – and under this joint spatial and temporal pressure it creates a Coleridgean text from the individual voices of others. The result is virtually a 'lost' Conversation Poem: a dramatic 'converse' meditating on themes of self and society, friendship and social action, and moving from single lonely thoughts to a more integrated sense of 'the one Life within us and abroad'.[1]

Coleridge wrote to Tom Poole on 7 November:

> I amused myself the other day (having some *paper* at the Printer's which I could employ no other way) in selecting 28 Sonnets, to bind up with Bowles's – I charge sixpence for them, and have sent you five to dispose of. – I have only printed two hundred, as my paper held out to no more; and dispose of them privately, just enough to pay the printing. (Griggs 252)

This little collection of sixteen pages, an octavo printed in half-sheets, consists of a first leaf containing a prefatory essay on the sonnet (signed 'Editor'), followed by fourteen pages of sonnets (printed two to a page); it has no title-page, just a short opening paragraph: 'I have selected the following SONNETS from various Authors for the purpose of binding them up with the Sonnets of the Rev. W.L. BOWLES'. This 'sheaf of sonnets', as it is sometimes known, consists of three by William Lisle Bowles, two by Charlotte Smith, one each by John Bampfylde, Thomas Warton, Sir Samuel Egerton Brydges, William

Sotheby, Thomas Russell, Thomas Dermody and Anna Seward, and four each by Coleridge himself, Robert Southey, Charles Lamb and Charles Lloyd. Not surprisingly, it is a scarce bibliographic item, and of the seven copies known three are indeed bound up with Bowles's sonnets as Coleridge hoped: Stella Thelwall's copy in the Victoria and Albert Museum and Sophia Pemberton's at Cornell are bound with the fourth edition of 1796, and in the Huntington Library Charles Lloyd's copy accompanies the third edition of 1794.[2]

So – seven years after the teenage Coleridge's first ecstatic encounter with Bowles's sonnets, memorably described in the opening chapter of *Biographia Literaria*, they are still a touchstone for his own work, a way of reaching out to his friends, and a gauge of his feelings for them. He recalls that during 1789–90, 'I made ... more than forty transcriptions, as the best presents I could offer to those, who had in any way won my regard' (Engell and Bate 15), and in the autumn of 1796 he is still wanting Bowles's sonnets to circulate, and is binding up himself and his friends with them. In this little collection, Coleridge and they are bound together, *contextus* (from *contexo*, 'to bind or weave together'), like the two pamphlets.

Why at this particular moment think of Bowles and the sonnet? The key is in Coleridge's prefatory essay on the sonnet form, which he defines as 'a small poem, in which some lonely feeling is developed'. He says:

> In a Sonnet then we require a development of some lonely feeling, by whatever cause it may have been excited; but those Sonnets appear to me the most exquisite, in which moral Sentiments, Affections, or Feelings, are deduced from, and associated with, the scenery of Nature. Such compositions ... create a sweet and indissoluble union between the intellectual and the material world.

The sonnet is consequently about finding 'union' from loneliness, and about drawing together the internal and external principles. The very confinement of the form makes it assimilable by the human spirit. At this moment for Coleridge the sonnet is intimately internalized, almost an organic part of ourselves: 'Easily remembered from their briefness ... these are the poems which we can "lay up in our heart, and our soul," and repeat them "when we walk by the way, and when we lie down and when we rise up."' In other words, they live with us and become part of our daily routine. In the hands of Bowles, the sonnet becomes for Coleridge the internal equivalent of settled domestic happiness: 'Hence, the Sonnets of BOWLES derive their marked superiority over all other Sonnets ... they domesticate with the heart, and become, as it were, a part of our identity'.

The period from late September to early November 1796 was a time when domestication was at the forefront of Coleridge's thoughts. Since the collapse of the *Watchman* in May, his prospects had swung giddily around to the dismay of his friends (Lamb called it his 'dancing demon'): to continue journalism in London with the *Morning Chronicle*? To become a dissenting minister? Engage himself as a private tutor? Translate Schiller? Open a day-school in Derby? Lamb wrote: 'I grieve from my very soul to observe you in your plans of life, veering about from this hope to the other, & settling no where … lies the fault, as I fear it does, in your own mind?' (Marrs 51). But Coleridge was – at this moment – attempting to settle. His son Hartley had been born on 19 September, and as he assembled his sequence of sonnets he was in Bristol sharing a bed with his new friend Charles Lloyd, now part of the family, all of them intending soon to settle (as he told Lloyd's father) to a life of 'rustic' retirement as Tom Poole's neighbours in or near Nether Stowey. Lloyd, subject to fits and shortly to suffer an emotional crisis, was ecstatic at his new domesticity with his brilliant tutor and friend, who was addressing poems to him, including 'To a Young Friend on his proposing to domesticate with the Author'.

In a very different vein, on 22 September, the 'domestic' became the terrifying focus for Charles Lamb's life, on that 'day of horrors' when all his prospects seemed to close down. Breaking the news of his mother's killing by his sister Mary, he wrote to Coleridge: 'You look after your family, – I have my reason and strength left to take care of mine' (Marrs 45). His letters to Coleridge in the following weeks convey a sense of someone managing under terrific spatial and mental pressure ('my mother a dead & murder'd corpse in the next room') – as he carefully plans out his family's domestic future and finds ways of 'managing my mind' (Marrs 48). Poetry, he declares, he is finished with forever. For Coleridge to turn back to the sonnet at this moment, and draw Lloyd, Lamb and himself together under the guiding spirit of Bowles, domesticating with the heart, becomes I think an understandable, even significant, gesture.

This pamphlet is indeed a 'turning back' to the sonnet. In his *Poems* published that spring, Coleridge had abjured the sonnet-form, retitling all his earlier sonnets 'effusions' and merging them under that title with the meditative-descriptive poem, Ossianic ballad, and ode. The preface to *Poems* shows a loss of confidence in his ability to write a true sonnet or even compare himself with Bowles:

> Of the following Poems a considerable number are styled 'Effusions' ... I might
> indeed have called the majority of them Sonnets – but they do not posses that
> *oneness* of thought which I deem indispensible in a Sonnet – and ... I was
> fearful that the title 'Sonnet' might have reminded my reader of the Poems of
> the Rev. W.L. Bowles – a comparison with whom would have sunk me below
> that mediocrity, on the surface of which I am at present enabled to float. (*Poems*
> ix–x)

By the autumn, with *Sonnets from Various Authors*, he is able not only to
reinstate the sonnet as a form, but interweave his and his friends' sonnets
amongst those of Bowles. The move from 'effusion' with its Latin sense (from
*effundo*) of 'pouring out', but also of immoderate (effusive) squandering and
slackening, back to the constraint of the sonnet, is marked in Coleridge's
prefatory essay by a new emphasis on the satisfying completion of an impulse
within prescribed bounds: '[The Sonnet] is limited to a *particular* number of
lines, in order that the reader's mind having expected the close at the place in
which he finds it, may rest satisfied.'

During those weeks when for Coleridge, Lloyd, and Lamb, life was
becoming more localized and contained, and expectations more focused, the
traditional 'narrow room' of the sonnet offered an appropriate form in which
external and internal pressures could find accommodation within prescribed
bounds. Through his Bowles-inspired anthology, Coleridge took the
opportunity of weaving together – contextualizing – select items of 'lonely
feeling' into a more communal mode, so as to bring individual voices into
dialogue. It is in this collective and friendly spirit that Coleridge selects and
arranges the twenty-eight sonnets. There is no space here to discuss each
sonnet or analyse the intricate verbal and thematic texture Coleridge achieves,
but some general idea can be given of the structure of the pamphlet, and how
he provides for Lloyd and Lamb both sympathetic echoes and instructive
accompaniments. Coleridge offers understanding and encouragement to his
friends, but also (as in life) a degree of frustration, in which the amicable
interweaving of texts, his garland of friendship (*antho*-logia) is finally broken,
and the poet turns to new horizons.

As editor, Coleridge has also designed his sequence bibliographically. He
is conscious of how sonnets are paired on the page, or grouped into four
across an opening, and he tries different combinations where appropriate:
alternation (*abab*) or enfolding (*abba*), much in the way a sonneteer would be
conscious of rhyme pattern. Indeed, the decisive break in Coleridge's sequence
comes at the page-turn after sonnet XIV, marking clearly the double-sonnet
structure of his collection, in two groups of fourteen.

The first page of text pairs Bowles's sonnet 'To a Friend' (an appropriate beginning) with one by Southey. Both use the image of life as a journey but offer contrasting perspectives on the road ahead. Bowles, in healing mode, stresses the difficulty ('our Road is lone and long', I.9) and offers a consoling respite; Southey, rather differently, looks down from a hilltop and urges us to continue on the downward path ('But cease fond heart in such sad thoughts to roam! / For surely thou ere long shalt reach thine home, / And pleasant is the way that lies before'. II.12–14). On this opening page, then, two sonnets establish the parameters between which the whole sequence moves: soothing sympathy and admonitory encouragement.

This prepares for the page-turn, where the reader immediately encounters, not Southey's 'pleasant' prospect, but two Charles Lloyd sonnets in which the Scottish landscape is uncomfortable, alienating, and full of neurotic suggestion. In the first, Lloyd negotiates a very different hill from Southey:

> Scotland! when thinking on each heathy hill
>   O'er whose bleak breast the billowy vapours sweep,
>   While sullen winds imprison'd murmur deep
> 'Mid their dim caves ... (III.1–4)

The paired Lloyd sonnets feature disturbing hidden places. The second, 'To Craig-Milton Castle', describes 'dark damp caverns' which ' breathe mysterious dread, / Haply still foul with tint of ancient crime', IV.5–6). Both are haunted landscapes ('I've trac'd thy torrents to their haunted source, / Whence down some huge rock with fantastic course, / Their sheeted whiteness pouring, they beguil'd / The meek dishearten'd one', III.6–9). In this context the 'bleak breast' (III.2) offers no maternal comfort, and where Southey had welcomed a cool, 'grateful' breeze, Lloyd feels it heavy and menacing:

> the flappings of the heavy bird
>   Imagin'd warnings fearfully impart,
> And that dull breeze below that feebly stirr'd,
>   Seem'd the deep breathing of an o'ercharg'd heart! (IV.9–12)

The nearest Lloyd comes to a sense of home is a distant glimpse of some crofters' cottages ('Thy white cots dimly seen yielding to me / Solace most sweet'. III.11–12). In pairing these sonnets Coleridge exploits their gloomy echoes and suggestions of hidden depths – as if to exemplify the character-sketch of Lloyd himself which he had sent Tom Poole on 24 September. He tells Poole of Lloyd's 'having been placed in situations, where for years together he met with no congenial minds' (Griggs 237). To offer Lloyd a 'congenial' context was therefore important for Coleridge, and to bring his friend's personal sonnets into sympathetic converse with others was, I would argue, one of the purposes of *Sonnets from Various Authors*. Writing to Poole, Coleridge stressed the importance for his friend's recovery of the right kind of intimacy: '[Lloyd] is assuredly a man of great Genius; but it must be in tete a tete with one whom he loves & esteems, that his colloquial powers open' (Griggs 236).

It is interesting therefore that Coleridge selected for the facing page, to fold down across Lloyd's two poems, the pairing of himself and Bowles. It is a double gesture – to print his own sonnet alongside Bowles's (no longer fearful of mediocrity), and also to bring them both tête-à-tête with Lloyd. With renewed confidence in himself and the sonnet-form, Coleridge places his newly completed sonnet 'To the River Otter' (V) beside Bowles's invocation of the healing powers of Harmony (VI) – two healing texts in colloquy with Lloyd's:

> Dear native Brook! wild Streamlet of the West!
>   How many various-fated Years have past,
>   What blissful and what anguish'd hours, since last
> I skimm'd the smooth thin stone along thy breast,
>   Numbering its light leaps! Yet so deep imprest
>   Sink the sweet scenes of Childhood, that mine eyes
> I never shut amid the sunny blaze,
>   But strait with all their tints thy waters rise,
> Thy crossing plank, thy margin's willowy maze,
>   And bedded sand that vein'd with various dies
> Gleam'd thro' thy bright transparence to the gaze.
>   Visions of Childhood! oft have ye beguil'd
> Lone Manhood's cares, yet waking fondest sighs,
>   Ah! that once more I were a careless Child! (V)

'I skimm'd the smooth thin stone along thy breast' – What a contrast with Lloyd's physically and emotionally resistant landscape of '*huge* rock' and '*bleak* breast'. Coleridge's maternal image encourages the child's playful energies, his dancing demon. And where Lloyd traced his torrents to their 'haunted source' in the 'sheeted whiteness' of a waterfall, Coleridge finds his native stream a colourful transparency, a bright clear medium. His sonnet's brilliant shift from surface to depth, from the 'light leaps' of his pebble to what is 'so deep imprest', was to leave its mark on Wordsworth's *Tintern Abbey*, but here it offers a reassuring return to the troubling depths of Lloyd's two sonnets, the 'dim caves' of 'mysterious dread'.

The accompanying Bowles sonnet ('O Harmony! thou tenderest Nurse of Pain!') reinforces this assurance with a note of poise and discretion, and as the reader moves from one sonnet to the next, Coleridge's 'Child' meets Bowles's 'Nurse', and with its more generalized language Bowles's sonnet acts as a kind of matrix for Coleridge's sharper images – the 'fairest tints' of its 'delightful dream' (VI.5,7) are waiting for Coleridge to realize them more specifically. But Bowles's poem also acts as a counterpoise to Lloyd's unsettled sonnets on the facing page. With its emphasis on the healing effect of harmony, Bowles's sonnet reconciles disparities and fuses alternatives – nowhere more subtly than in its third line ('Griefs which the *patient* spirit oft must feel' – my italics), which hovers between offering understanding to the *suffering* soul and exhorting spiritual *patience*. As the sequence proceeds, this almost imperceptible ambivalence widens out into a more marked duality of sympathy and admonition.

The page turns again, onto two allegorical sonnets by Bampfylde and Warton (VII–VIII) evoking the delights of Evening and of Health. Both celebrate purity and innocence, but in different ways: the first through worldly engagement and sociable mixing, the second in withdrawal to a cave. Together on the page they represent a choice between L'Allegro and Il Penseroso. The allegorical dualities continue on the facing page, with a sonnet by Brydges (IX)[3] featuring a pair of sleeping nymphs, Silence and Echo. As a hunting horn sounds Silence is terrified and disappears into the wood, but Echo is joyously liberated ('she takes her hasty way / Bounding from Rock to Rock, and Hill to Hill!', IX.11–12). These three sonnets converse with each other and in their allegorical figures posit a choice between activity and retreat.

Preparation has thus been made for the final sonnet of this opening , another text with an allegorical subject featuring a lost female companion, and a traumatic confrontation between the sociable and solitary impulses. This is Charles Lamb's disturbing sonnet, 'We were two pretty Babes', in which the speaker searches for his twin sister, Innocence:

> My lov'd Companion dropt a tear and fled,
> And hid in deepest shades her AWFUL head!
>     Beloved! who can tell me where thou art,
>   In what delicious Eden to be found,
>   That I may seek thee the wide world around! (X.10–14)

As in the previous sonnet, a little drama of separation is being acted out; but this echo of the allegory of Echo and Silence (10–11) only serves to raise questions of poetic decorum: Lamb's personified innocence as his lost sister touches a different register from Brydges' fanciful wit. His teasing figure is delightfully elusive and mocking, and his final note of mimic laughter seems an odd preparation for Lamb's miniature *Paradise Lost*. But the paired sonnets on the facing page (Bampfylde and Warton) also join in the conversation: their contrast of the sociable and solitary impulses helps us register the rather disturbing way Lamb sees adult sociability in terms of violation ('And my first Love for Man's society, / Defiling with the World my Virgin Heart', X.8–9).

But this is only the first of three successive pairings Lamb is given, taking us to the mid-point of the twenty-eight sonnets. His sonnet X ends plaintively ('Beloved! who can tell me where thou art?), and after the page-turn is William Sotheby's sympathetic echo: 'I knew a gentle maid: I ne'er shall view / Her like again' (XI.1–2). Sotheby's elusive figure, however, is two maids in one, combining the retired graces of Brydges' Silence ('in her silence dwelt / Expression', XI.9–10) with the vivacity of her sister Echo ('oft her mind by youth to rapture wrought / Struck forth wild wit and fancies ever new', XI.11–12), Il Penseroso with L'Allegro.

Sotheby's poem also acts as prelude to two more of Lamb's sonnets about a lost maid, 'Was it some sweet device' (XII) and 'When last I rov'd' (XIII). If the sonnet is a form 'in which some lonely feeling is developed', then in these poems Lamb is at his most lonely and lost. There is no escape from the repeated 'lonely glade' (XII.2,10), just a sigh ('Ah me!') and forlorn aimlessness. Avoiding 'converse', the speaker turns away from 'the little Cottage which she lov'd' (XIII.9) and is left 'self-wand'ring' through the woods.

On 9 June when Lamb wrote to Coleridge responding to his *Poems*, he singled out for praise 'that most exquisite & most Bowles-like of all, the 19th Effusion' (Marrs 20). It is this same poem that Coleridge now introduces in intimate converse with Lamb's. Its opening address to the heart appears to respond naturally to Lamb's line XIII.12 ('[It] spake to my Heart, and much my Heart was mov'd'). But Coleridge shifts in just three lines from sympathy to a sterner and more admonishing note:

> Thou bleedest, my poor HEART! and thy distress
> Reas'ning I ponder with a scornful smile
> And probe thy sore wound sternly… (XIV.1–3)

Coleridge thus has the last word in this first group of fourteen sonnets, and in this internal dialogue he is harsh and demanding of himself. Once more he takes risks with Lamb's sensitivities ('a maniac's hand', XIV.8); the purpose of his sonnet, however, is not to soothe, but to show Reason arguing with the emotions. The sestet's message is demanding – why, just when you need a vision of hope, do you discard it? Its bland whispers soothed the good times – why neglect it at a moment of crisis? You have to work hard to keep Hope alive:

> Thou should'st have lov'd it most, when most opprest,
> And nurs'd it with an agony of Care,
> Ev'n as a Mother her sweet infant heir,
> That wan and sickly droops upon her breast! (XIV.9–14)

The roles should be reversed: Hope is not the nurse – it must be nursed by you. In this favourite sonnet of Lamb's, Coleridge assumes the mantle of Bowles, but in doing so refocuses the maternal image into a more personally demanding one.

At this mid-point of the sequence, the page-turn is suitably dramatic as we enter the second set of fourteen sonnets. The message is a stark one, jolting us out of the introspective mode to recognize the misfortunes of others. Confronting the reader are four vignettes of social injustice: two Southey sonnets on a pregnant suicide (XV) and a Negro slave (XVI), followed by Coleridge's 'Sweet Mercy' (XVII) about a homeless old man, and Thomas Russell's sonnet on child beggars (XVIII). In these sonnets, 'domesticating with the heart' becomes a more capacious idea, and as Coleridge introduces the figure of 'the GALILÆAN mild, / Who met the Lazar turn'd from rich man's doors, / And call'd him Friend' (XVII.12–14), we are moved to that more radical idea for which Jesus provided the model: the *Friend of Humanity*. The celebration of personal friendship which this garland of sonnets in part represents, now begins to find a political dimension.

With this new context established, the next page-turn shows four sonnets grouped *abba*, repeating the pattern of the third opening, where Lamb's sonnets on his lost Anna (XII–XIII) were embraced by those of Sotheby and Coleridge (XI, XIV). At the centre now are Lloyd's feverish sonnets on his grandmother's death (XX–XXI) which are painful in their physical immediacy:

> (O my choak'd breast!) e'en on that shrunk cheek
> I saw one slow tear roll! My hand she took,
> Placing it on her heart: I heard her sigh,
> "Tis too, too much!" 'twas Love's last agony!
> I tore me from her! (XX.8–12)

Once more the poems are sensitively framed by Coleridge. Introducing them
is Southey's sonnet on Hope (XIX), which opens with a rainbow ('Mild arch
of promise!') and offers a death-scene of serene leave-taking for 'the realm
where sorrows cease' (XIX.14), and at their close is Charlotte Smith's sonnet
'To Tranquillity', whose figure of the watchful mother merges the image of
the deathbed (which holds such terrors for Lloyd) into that of the cradle:

> By the low cradles thou delight'st to sit
> Of sleeping infants – watching the soft breath
>    And bidding the sweet slumberers easy lie;
> Or sometimes hanging o'er the bed of death
>    Where the poor languid sufferer – hopes to die! (XXII.4–8)

Coleridge takes great care in this four-sonnet group to give Lloyd's frantic
words a supportive frame, embracing them reassuringly with sonnets on hope
and tranquillity, redirecting his disturbing visions in turn towards the rainbow
and the cradle. 'Charles Lloyd has been very ill' (he wrote to Tom Poole on
15 November), 'and his distemper … may with equal propriety be named
either Somnambulism, or frightful Reverie, or *Epilepsy from accumulated
feelings*' (Griggs 257). Coleridge brought in Dr Beddoes, and reported to
Lloyd's father that 'he *told* me, that your Son's cure must be effected by
Sympathy and Calmness' (Griggs 256).

The page turns again, and the final opening of four sonnets presents another
disturbed text carefully framed by sympathetic voices. Once again the
beneficiary is Lamb, who in sonnet XXV stands at midnight on the deck of a
ship contemplating suicide. Coleridge prepares for this very carefully with
two tranquil sea-pictures by Charlotte Smith (XXIII) and Thomas Dermody
(XXIV) featuring a calming moonlight. Smith offers the full strain of the
eighteenth-century melancholy sonnet, perfectly exemplifying that union 'in
which moral Sentiments, Affections, or Feelings, are deduced from, and
associated with, the scenery of Nature' (Preface). With Dermody's sonnet the
melancholy mood continues, as Tranquillity and Silence manage to keep the
ocean's more sublime features under control. With Lamb's sonnet XXV,
however, the Sublime is released with full force. The storm has now broken,
with the midnight wind scattering the ocean waves, and like a good Burkean,
Lamb experiences the contradictory *delight* of the sublime mode ('On wings
of winds comes wild-ey'd Phantasy, / And her dread visions give a rude
delight!' XXV.5–6). Lamb invokes the dark fantasies of a suicide gazing at
the flood:

> When wet and chilly on thy deck I stood
> Unbonnetted, and gaz'd upon the flood,
> And almost wish'd it were no crime to die!
>     How Reason reel'd! What gloomy transports rose!
>     Till the rude dashings rock'd them to repose. (XXV.10–14)

Lamb is held on the brink by the pivotal word 'rock'd' which in a dizzying way is poised between falling and slumbering. This is the dramatic climax of the sequence: Lamb on the edge.

Who better to step forward at the height of the storm than Bowles? He reaches out to Lamb's reeling visions, and talks him down. To do so, he has to go to the brink himself. But in this dramatic context it is Lamb to whom he is clearly talking:

> Thou whose stern spirit loves the awful storm
>     That borne on Terror's desolating wings
>     Shakes the deep forest, or remorseless flings
> The shiver'd surge, if bitter griefs deform
> Thy patient soul, O hie thee to the steep
>     That beetles o'er the rude and raving tide,
>     And when thou hear'st distress careering wide,
> Think in a world of woe what thousands weep. (XXVI.1–8)

The place of suicide becomes, for Bowles, a vantagepoint from which to contemplate human misery in general. This is not a time to become giddy, but to use Reason. We noticed how Coleridge placed alongside Lamb's sonnet XIII the sonnet of his own that was Lamb's favourite ('that most exquisite and most Bowles-like'). Here Coleridge is printing the original on which his own was based, with Bowles's message about remembering Hope at the darkest moment ('shroud thee in the mantle of distress / And tell thy poor heart – this is happiness!' XXVI.13–14).

Up to this point, with two sonnets remaining, the reader has followed a sequence which, I've tried to argue, creates a conversation out of individual voices. I have suggested that in returning to the sonnet in autumn 1796, and confidently measuring himself with Bowles, Coleridge used its ability to 'domesticate with the heart' to engage with, and guide, the voices of his friends Lloyd and Lamb, at a time when domestic intimacies and focused boundaries were offering hope to each of them.

Both Lloyd and Lamb used the sonnet as (in Lamb's phrase) 'a personal poem' (Marrs 21). Coleridge, however, sees dangers in this and works to steer their texts to a more extensive sympathy within a broader social or political context. Paul Magnuson (3–10) has stressed the importance of reading poems in their precise locations, and I have been trying to do this – both biographically and (perhaps more importantly) bibliographically. As editor, Coleridge is a subtle shaper and dramatizer of these texts; but the drama is happening across and between the pages. Within the frame he has supplied, Coleridge accommo-dates these units of thought and experience into his more ample scheme. The 'lonely feeling' at the heart of the sonnet-form meets the wider embrace of friendship and sociability. And Coleridge is always there drawing out meanings and ironies from individual poems – sympathizing, admonishing, encouraging.

There are, however, two sonnets remaining, and with the final page-turn Coleridge springs a surprise. Just when we think he is settling down, and drawing his friends into the social circle, we encounter Anna Seward's sonnet (XXVII) to Ingratitude ('Ingratitude, how deadly is thy smart / Proceeding from the form we fondly love!'). He invokes the betrayal of friendship by ingratitude, and in contradictory mood chooses to voice it in the words of a writer whose sonnets he had attacked in his preface as 'laborious trifles'. Through Seward we glimpse the inversion of the sympathetic social converse on which the sequence has been based, and as if to announce this *volte-face* the 'kindred prospect' (XXVI.9) promoted by Bowles in the previous sonnet now becomes 'kindred callousness' (XXVII.12).

And the last word, of course, must be Coleridge's. He had begun the pamphlet with Bowles's sonnet 'To a Friend', but he ends the sequence by turning away from Bowles, and his friends, to address the figure of Schiller and celebrate German romantic drama. He evokes the scene in Act IV of *The Robbers*, where a father emerges from an airless dungeon to discover that his son has betrayed him. Coleridge's sublime poet, with a Shakespearean 'fine frenzy', almost bursts the bounds of the sonnet and reaches for the loftier ode:

> Ah! Bard tremendous in sublimity!
>   Could I behold thee in thy loftier mood,
> Wand'ring at eve with finely frenzied eye
>   Beneath some vast old tempest-swinging wood!
>   Awhile with mute awe gazing I would brood,
> Then weep aloud in a wild extacy! (XXVIII.9–14)

To end his sequence thus, is in some ways an act of defiance, a turn away from the compact world of the sonnet to a greater challenge beyond, whether his friends liked it or not. Lamb did like it: 'Schiller might have written it', he said (Marrs 20). But John Thelwall did not, especially those last six lines.

Hence the note Coleridge added after this sonnet in the Victoria & Albert copy, the one he sent to Mrs Thelwall:

> I affirm, John Thelwall! that the six last lines of this Sonnet to Schiller are strong & fiery; and you are the only one who thinks otherwise. – There, a *spurt* of Author-like vanity for you!

After so amicably guiding the voices of Lamb and Lloyd through the sequence, Coleridge ends almost impatiently with a newly confident awareness of his own voice, and with a reminder that the sonnet can burst the bounds of the domestic and express the creative energies of the poet. If *Sonnets from Various Authors* represents Coleridge's least known Conversation Poem, it ends with an intimation of the world of *Kubla Khan*, opening out the previously contained textual dialogue to project a visionary desiring self. With the final page Coleridge is conscious of turning over a new leaf, and this awareness of his little book as a physical object suggests that he saw it as something more organic than an appendix. The care with which these twenty-eight sonnets have been chosen and ordered is evident in their physical arrangement. Verbal and thematic echoes find palpable expression as the various texts meet, touch and embrace. Bibliographical coding becomes a mode of communication, and individual 'lonely' meanings become more dynamic as they are released into something greater.

## Notes

1   'The Eolian Harp', 26.
2   V&A – Dyce 8° 1298 (Copy A); Cornell – Wordsworth PR 4161 B4 1796; Huntington – RB123964–5.
3   Coleridge wrongly attributes this sonnet to Henry Brooke (c. 1703–83). It was printed in Brydges's *Sonnets and Other Poems* (1785) and later editions.

## Bibliography

Engell, James, and W.J. Bate (eds) (1983), *Biographia Literaria*, Princeton: Princeton University Press.

Griggs, E.L. (ed.) (1956), *Collected Letters of Samuel Taylor Coleridge, volume 1 (1785– 1800)*, Oxford: Clarendon Press.

Magnuson, Paul (1998), *Reading Public Romanticism*, Princeton: Princeton University Press.

Marrs, Edwin W. (ed.) (1975), *The Letters of Charles and Mary Anne Lamb, volume 1 (1796– 1801)*, Ithaca and London: Cornell University Press.

## Chapter Eight

# Reading the Brontës Abroad:
# A Study in the Transmission of Victorian
# Novels in Continental Europe

Inga-Stina Ewbank

Authors die, but texts live on. The richer and denser the text the more likely that, in its language and country of origin, life will mean change: new generations will read it differently, and new texts will be generated from it. As a text moves into other languages and cultures, processes of transmission and translation will bring about such changes more or less immediately. This essay follows *Jane Eyre* through French- and German-language areas in the 1850s and early 1860s in order to address itself to the question: what did you read when, in the mid-nineteenth century, you read the Brontës abroad? How, and why, did the texts you read differ from those published in London?

*Jane Eyre* was first published in London, by Smith, Elder, in October 1847. Within four months the Leipzig firm of Tauchnitz had published an English-language edition for distribution across the Continent. Within eighteen months, an adapted version in French was running as a *feuilleton* in the Belgian *Revue de Paris*; in 1855 this was published as a single volume by the Paris firm of Hachette. The following year Hachette took over a more faithful French translation, initially published by D. Giraud in 1854; this *Jane Eyre* ran through seventeen further impressions by 1900. Meanwhile, German publishing houses in Berlin, Grimma and Stuttgart were vying with each other to supply translations: one appeared in 1848, two in 1850, and at least one other in the mid-1850s. By then the novel had also been adapted into a domestic-romantic play, *Die Waise aus Lowood*, first performed in Hamburg in June 1853 and soon playing on stages across Europe, in German or in translations as needed, retaining its extraordinary popularity until the end of the century. Partly in reaction against this vogue, a 'freely adapted' version of the novel in German was published in Vienna in 1862, turning *Jane Eyre* into a guide book to England and the English. This trajectory could of course be extended: with works as seminal as *Jane Eyre* has proved to be, literary relations, as Henry

James said of the human variety, 'stop nowhere'(James 5). But as given it forms an outline of features which conditioned the reading of English fiction on the Continent, at a time when the book trade was expanding, international copyright agreements were being negotiated, and you could read the Brontës almost anywhere in Europe.

Although the Smith, Elder editions could be had in selected bookshops in large centres such as Paris, by far the majority of copies of *Jane Eyre* in English read on the Continent bore the Tauchnitz imprint. In 1850 English was nowhere near the *lingua franca* it has now become, but readers included expatriates and travelling British nationals who were coming to depend on buying the cheap[1] and portable Tauchnitz editions – which, of course, they could not legally bring back into the United Kingdom or its colonies.

The title-page of the 1848 Tauchnitz *Jane Eyre: An Autobiography. Edited by Currer Bell* describes it as 'Copyright Edition for Continental Circulation'. When, in the year of Queen Victoria's accession, Christian Bernhard (later Baron von) Tauchnitz founded his firm, there was nothing to stop unauthorized publishing of English books on the Continent. Mounting pressure from authors and publishers finally resulted in an Act of 1844 which empowered the Queen in council to enter into agreement with foreign states for the exchange of privileges of copyright; and the first two of these agreements were signed with the German states of Prussia and Saxony in August 1846 (Nowell-Smith 1968, 41). Tauchnitz, who had begun publishing his 'Collection of British [later 'and American'] Authors' in 1841,[2] had anticipated what was coming, visited London in 1843, and made personal approaches to authors, offering a fee in return for the authority to publish their work on the Continent (Tauchnitz 1937a, b; 1962).[3]

In 1939 – by which time the firm of Tauchnitz had published over 40 million copies of altogether more than 5,000 titles (Todd 844) – *Jane Eyre* was listed as one of its '500 Best Titles' (Todd 46). In 1847–48 it may still have seemed something of a risk; but the response in England to the unknown Currer Bell must have prompted speedy publication, since the two-volume edition which Tauchnitz issued in February 1848 was composed of the text of the first (October 1847) Smith, Elder edition with the dedication to Thackeray and the preface of the second, only 'just published' on 22 January.[4] Following the success of *Jane Eyre*, Tauchnitz announced the publication of *Shirley* as simultaneous with that in London (26 October 1849), though in the end it appeared two weeks later; and the issue of *Villette* in 1853 was also less than a month after the London publication. Mrs Gaskell's *Life* stimulated a market for *The Professor*, published posthumously in London in June and in Leipzig in August, 1857. That Tauchnitz published a two-volume *Wuthering Heights and Agnes Gray* only in 1851, when he could use the second (1850) edition, with the 'Biographical Notice' by 'Currer Bell', suggests that he was investing in Emily and Anne Brontë as the sisters of Charlotte rather than in their own right. Anne's second novel, *The Tenant of Wildfell Hall*, never received the Tauchnitz imprint; but the rest of the Brontë works stayed in print until the recession of 1929–30, when lists were severely cut, leaving only the best-selling *Jane Eyre*.[5]

While the Tauchnitz volumes of *Jane Eyre* spread across the Continent, serving as the source text for translations,[6] a British copyright agreement with France was being negotiated. It was not concluded until 1852, but then it was the first to include consideration of translation rights (Nowell-Smith 1968, 32). Of the two early French translations of *Jane Eyre*, Forgues's was clearly not authorized, whereas Mme Lesbazeilles-Souvestre's proclaimed itself on the title-page 'Traduit avec l'autorisation de l'auteur'.[7] Both were published by the firm of Hachette, then in the process of establishing itself as the main disseminator of English literature in France. Louis Hachette's visit to the Great Exhibition in London in 1851 had opened his eyes to the marketing possibilities offered by the new railway system (Mistler 122–6). The result was the 'Bibliothèque des chemins de fer' series of books, launched in March 1853. Forgues's *Jane Eyre* appeared in this (1855). The 'Bibliothèque des meilleurs romans étrangers', in which novels by Thackeray, Mrs Gaskell and Lady Fullerton were soon to be had at one franc per volume, was originally meant to be only a subsection of the railway series but grew rapidly to become one of the most flourishing branches of Hachette's 'editions populaires' (Mistler 155). Mme Lesbazeilles-Souvestre's *Jane Eyre* appeared in this (1856). For many years the firm of Hachette had the sort of monopoly of railway bookstalls in France that W.H. Smith enjoyed in England[8] – stalls from which you could choose between a Tauchnitz *Jane Eyre* in English and a Hachette version in French.

The power of the translator over the text was a subject of concern to many of Charlotte Brontë's contemporaries.[9] Before the 1852 agreement took effect, authors had no control, and often no knowledge, of what was translated and how. In 1854 Thackeray is still full of unease as he writes to Amédée Pichot (a letter which seems never to have been completed or sent) about a translation of parts of *Vanity Fair* which he finds 'arranged':

> Which you gentlemen are perfectly authorized to do and which you especially
> (who know much more about our literature than English literary men themselves

do) do very well – but here is the difficulty with an author – I can't say that yours are faithful translations – that I would not prefer to have them *more* faithful. (Thackeray 411)

Louis Hachette must have seen that his rapport with famous authors depended to some extent on care for the quality of translations.[10] With the dead Brontë sisters there could be no rapport; but when in 1856 he arranged for the publication of all the novels of Dickens, he set up a team of translators under the direction of Paul Lorain, aided by a linguistic expert (Mistler 159–60). Dickens dined in Paris with 'the body of Translators' in April 1856 and met among them 'an extremely able old Savant who occasionally expressed himself in a foreign tongue which I supposed to be Russian ... but which my host told me when I came away, was English!' (Dickens 96). But when publication began with *Nicholas Nickleby*, translated by Paul Lorain himself, the first volume was prefaced with a translated Address, 'L'Auteur Anglais au Public Français', in which Dickens pays homage to Lorain as 'perfectly acquainted with both languages, and able, with rare felicity, to be perfectly faithful to the English text while rendering it in elegant and expressive French' (Dickens 262–3).

The criteria for translation which Dickens identifies are partly met and partly challenged by Paul-Emile Daurand Forgues in his *Jane Eyre ou Mémoires d'une Gouvernante de Currer Bell. Imités par Old-Nick*. A prolific translator, he was certainly acquainted with both languages.[11] Despite his diabolical pseudonym he was one of those 'gentlemen' who Thackeray thought 'know more about our literature than English literary men themselves do'. He certainly wrote elegant and expressive French, informed by a temperament which the Goncourts described oxymoronically as that of 'un méridional congelé, ayant quelque chose d'une glace frite' (D'Amat 100). Application of 'fried ice' to the text of *Jane Eyre* resulted in a slimmed-down 'imitation'. This may have to do with its origin as a serial story in a journal, published before the 1852 agreement; but the 1855 volume still runs only to 183 pages, as against the altogether more than 900 in the three volumes of the Smith, Elder 1847–48 editions. The plot outline remains, but the texture is thinned out; the childhood sections are vastly condensed; scenes that might be melodramatic and events that are merely symbolic disappear. Forgues has devised an entirely new structural framework in which the story is told to a female friend, 'ma chère Elisabeth', who knows much of it already. This brings with it a complete tonal change. Emotional engagement with the reader is relaxed, and the direct appeals to her or him are of course gone. The famous

'Reader, I married him' becomes a supererogatory 'Je ne vous dirai pas, car vous le savez de reste, que j'épousai M. Rochester' (181). The indelicate details of Rochester's relationship with little Adèle's mother can be omitted and the whole episode reported in a manner that makes it sound more like Flaubert than Charlotte Brontë:

> Je ne vous répéterai pas cette histoire, aprés tout assez vulgaire, d'un jeune et riche anglais séduit par une coquette mercenaire appertenante au corps de ballet de l'Opera. (41)

The reader of this *Jane Eyre*, then, met a story told concisely in a clear style, minute particulars of which reproduce Old Nick's overall attitude to Charlotte Brontë's text. Not afraid of recording Jane's emotions, he tends to put a cooling layer between experience and reader, as in Jane's agony at having (as she thinks) to leave Thornfield because Rochester is to marry Blanche Ingram:

> I see the necessity of departure; and it is like looking on the necessity of death. (C. Brontë 1969, 317)

> Je vois bien la nécessité du depart ... mais comme on voit la necessité de la mort ... sans pouvoir y accoutumer ma pensée. (81)

The added phrase – about 'not being able to get used to it' – shows Forgues doing what Thackeray called 'arranging' his source text. Similarly, while he is happy to record Jane's radical individualism, he reduces the ardour of its expression. Jane's simple punchline, 'equal, – as we are!' (318) becomes

> égaux, parfaitement égaux ... car là [i.e. au pieds du Seigneur] nous le serons ... et nous le sommes dejà, je le sens. (82)

Elegant French, but the force of a single passionate outcry in the original text has been weakened by repetition and afterthought, and the syntax explicates the logic which, in the original, is implicit in Jane's emotion.

In April 1855 the *Revue Britannique*, in its regular feature of 'Correspondence de Londres', carried the news of the death of Charlotte Brontë and followed it with a review of Forgues's *Jane Eyre*. Amédée Pichot, the founder editor of the *Revue* and one of Thackeray's literary gentlemen-translators, admits that the novel deserves being translated 'littéralement' but all the same feels that Old Nick has achieved something even better:

Currer Bell, en se relisant dans cette *imitation*, a dû éprouver la même sensation qui fait sourire en présence d'un miroir la beauté rustique qu'un caprice de grande dame a forcé de changer de costume avec elle. Une toilette de salon n'a jamais enlaidi la naïve villageoise. (Pichot 499)

It was perhaps as well that Charlotte Brontë (fond of the French language but not of French culture) did not live to meet this image of herself smiling at her new self as she 'rereads' her novel, since the mirror image is one which she repeatedly uses for exactly the opposite purpose: to make her plain heroines mortify themselves, but thereby also defiantly assert their identity, *vis-à-vis* some 'grande dame'. Jane Eyre is thus valued against Blanche Ingram, Lucy Snowe against Ginevra Fanshawe. Had she lived to read M. Pichot, she might well have quoted him Jane Eyre's response when Rochester wants to dress her in 'toilettes de salon': 'I shall not be your Jane Eyre any longer, but an ape in a harlequin's jacket, – a jay in borrowed plumes' (C. Brontë 1969, 326). Pichot's image, on the other hand, assumes the freedom of the translator to adapt a work to the culture of the target language. Thanks to M. Forgues, he writes,

le premier chef-d'oeuvre de Currer Bell est naturalisé désormais dans la langue des romans de Marivaux et prendra place à coté de *Mariane*. (Pichot 499)

No use crying 'not our Jane Eyre any longer' to the French reader who finds the novel another *Vie de Marianne* [12] – especially as that reader could, at least theoretically, point to a reverse kind of naturalization more than a century earlier, when Mary Collyer's translation, *The Virtuous Orphan or, The Life of Marianne*, cut Marivaux's text by a third and added material which so moralized and sentimentalized the heroine that she might well stand at the side of Richardson's *Pamela*.

The relative faithfulness of Mme Lesbazeilles-Souvestre's translation of *Jane Eyre* must have been one reason why, in 1856, Hachette acquired it and dropped Forgues's 'imitation', which was never reissued. *Jane Eyre ou Les memoires d'une Institutrice par Currer Bell* also had the advantage of being able to claim authorization 'de l'auteur'. Not that Hachette was as scrupulous as Tauchnitz in this respect. In 1858 he published Henriette Loreau's translation of *The Professor* (*Le Professeur*) 'avec l'authorisation de l'editeur'; but the following year he cashed in on the interest in Charlotte Brontë by publishing, in two volumes, *Shirley & Agnes Grey par Currer Bell*, translated by Ch. Romey and A. Rolet – for obvious reasons without any statement of authorization. He never found *Wuthering Heights* worth publishing,[13] nor *The Tenant of Wildfell Hall*.

Untypically, Mme Lesbazeilles-Souvestre was not a professional translator: this is her only published work, and – unlike Mme Henriette Loreau, who translated a number of novels by Dickens, Mrs Gaskell and others – she allowed her name to appear only as that of the wife of her husband and daughter of her father.[14] In reviews she is referred to only as 'la fille d'Émile Souvestre' (W.G. 167). Souvestre was a novelist, essayist and dramatist who would now be classed as minor, but who in his day had a major following throughout Europe.[15] Although his wife, Nanine, née Papot, herself wrote three novels and translated English fiction, their daughters seem to have bowed to paternal rule (Rimella 10). His son-in-law, Eugène Lesbazeilles, describes Souvestre as a man whose aim in life was to 'educate consciences and reform morals', and a novelist who 'renounced that which gives novels their most powerful appeal': 'il s'interdit sévèrement la peinture séduissante des passions qu'il réprouve' (Lesbazeilles vi). *Jane Eyre* could of course be seen as just such a 'peinture'. Although Forcade's influential review in the *Revue des Deux Mondes* had spoken of the novel as animated by 'l'inspiration mâle, saine, morale' (493), a reviewer of Mme Lesbazeille-Souvestre's translation could still insist that, because of 'la passion qui anime l'ouvrage tout entier', it was not a novel which a mother would give her daughter to read (W.G. 165). Noëmie Souvestre's mother did, however, and in a touching 'Avertissement' the daughter explains her motive in attempting a translation as a wish to share with others her admiration of *Jane Eyre*. But she is her father's daughter when she goes on to stress that what is 'éminent' about the novel, more eminent even than its art, is 'l'énergie morale dont ses pages sont empreintes' (C. Brontë 1856, i–ii). Yes, she writes, there is passion, but it is held in bounds by principles; there is instinct, but it is tamed by will.

Given these premises, it is not surprising that her translation, however apparently faithful compared to that of Forgues, manages in its own way to take the fire out of *Jane Eyre*. Quite literally so when the English text's 'A hand of fiery iron grasped my vitals' (C. Brontë 1969, 402) becomes 'une main de fer pesait sur moi' (316), thus losing both the 'vitals' and the fire – a recurrent image in the novel and one that uncannily links Jane with the madwoman in the attic. This is only one example of a style that would give the French reader little idea of how keenly both form and content of the original text depend on images which almost bodily draw the reader into Jane's passionate inner life. We cannot tell whether this is deliberate, self-imposed censorship or simply unconscious conditioning by fears, such as her father's, of being 'seduced' by the depiction of passion.[16] What must be deliberate is her consistent refusal – without the Forgues version's structural justification for this – to reproduce Charlotte Brontë's recurrent appeals to the individual reader. 'Reader, I married him' becomes here a factual 'J'ai enfin épousé M. Rochester'. The French reader is not invited, for example, into Jane's agony as she is tearing herself away from Rochester: 'Gentle reader, may you never feel what I then felt!' (C. Brontë 1969, 411). Here the 'Gentle reader' becomes 'Vous tous qui lirez ce livre'. The intimate engagement asked for by the style of the original is transformed into collective appeal and reasoned detachment. No doubt the very system of the language into which Mme Lesbazeilles-Souvestre is translating is also playing its part here. In her 'Avertissement' she refers to '[le] génie de notre langue' as something which her translation often challenges in pursuit of faithfulness, but it is difficult not to feel that even more often she has been relieved to be able to take refuge from Charlotte Brontë's idiosyncrasies in normalized French. Without falling back on clichés about the French language being more abstract, logical, and so on, than English, it may be worth remembering that, at much the same time as this, Victor Hugo praised his son for having made a 'clear' and 'faithful' translation of Shakespeare's 'cloudy' language – English being to French, according to him, like the night to the day, the moon to the sun (Hugo 330).

The 'genius' of the German language appears to be more accommodating to Charlotte Brontë's English, at least on the evidence of the translation of *Jane Eyre* by Christoph Friedrich Grieb, published by the Stuttgart firm of Franckh in 1850. Here – to use my earlier touchstones – Jane's words 'a hand of fiery iron grasped my vitals' become a literal 'eine glühende, eiserne Hand griff in meine innersten Lebenstheile' (II.148). In this text the reader is faithfully appealed to: 'Gentle reader' becomes 'Lieber Leser'; and 'Reader, I married him' becomes 'Leser! ich heirathete ihn' (II.342). His 'Leser' (presumably the masculine form includes the feminine 'Leserin') is addressed by the intimate 'Du', Mme Lesbazeilles-Souvestre's French reader, when at all, by the formal and polite 'vous'. Lexically Grieb is able to be remarkably faithful – so much so that in one instance he feels he has to resort to a footnote to explain a social detail in the source culture. Mrs Fairfax's kind concern on Jane's first arrival at Thornfield Hall on a cold evening, 'Leah, make a little hot negus and cut a sandwich or two' (115), becomes 'Leah, mach' ein wenig heissen Negus und bring' einige Sandwichs', with a note on 'Sandwichs' as '[k]altes, dünngeschnittenes Fleisch zwischen Brodschnitten' (cold, thinly sliced meat between slices of bread) (I.133). The German reader of the book is asked to be personally involved with the story but not to feel that the novel is 'naturalized'.

One could argue that the 'genius' of the language here overrides gender, as the male German translator seems more prepared than the female French to translate a woman's language faithfully. But Grieb's faithfulness is not so much a commitment to the particular text as a philological familiarity with the English language: his English–German/German–English *Wörterbuch* ran through at least a dozen editions between 1842 and 1907 (Schmuck and Gorzny, vol. 50, 208–9).There is nothing to suggest that he undertook the translation out of a special interest in 'Currer Bell', or as anything other than a professional commission. He translated a number of novels, from the French as well as the English, but no Brontë works other than *Jane Eyre*. His translations appear at an astonishing rate, with Charlotte Brontë's work sandwiched between Thackeray's – *Die Geschichte von Samuel Titmarsh* in 1850, *Das Jahrmarkt des Lebens* (*Vanity Fair*) in 1851 and *Die Geschichte von Henry Esmond* in 1853 – and at the same time with translations of the monthly numbers of *Bleak House*, 1852–54, running just behind their issue in England (March 1852–September 1853). All these were published by Franckh.

Grieb's was only one of several German translations of *Jane Eyre* in the first few years after the novel's appearance in English. In his pioneering study of the translation business (and it was a business) in Germany during the first half of the nineteenth century, Norbert Bachleitner shows the Franckh brothers to have been the leading practioners of what he terms the 'translation factory' system (Bachleitner 31). Together, the absence of consistent copyright legislation and the presence of a growing market for fiction had produced a state of fierce competition between different translations of the same works by English-language authors, such as Scott, Cooper, Dickens and Marryat. The result was often ill-paid hackwork, texts hastily and shoddily prepared. The 1846 copyright agreements between Britain and, respectively, Prussia and Saxony did not prevent the appearance of separate translations of *Jane Eyre* in each of these two states (see Bibliography). Nor could the agreements prevent the production of parallel translations in other German states. Into the early 1860s Franckh, in the kingdom of Württemberg, were still publishing competing translations of *Adam Bede*, *The Mill on the Floss* and *Silas Marner*. Only the Bern Convention of 1886, and a special convention in the same year between Britain and a unified Germany, put a final stop to this form of piratical publishing (Bachleitner 40).

Grieb's *Jane Eyre. Roman von Currer Bell* first appeared in eleven 'Bändchen' in 'Das belletristische Ausland: Kabinetsbibliothek der klassischen Romane aller Nationen', the flourishing series which Franckh had started in 1843, and which was to reach to 3,618 volumes by 1865 (Bachleitner 31). I have not been able to consult any of the competitors and so cannot tell whether it was the superior quality of the translation or (more likely) the business acumen of the firm of Franckh that prolonged the life of Grieb's translation (see Bibliography). A second edition, in two volumes and without the translator's name on the title-page, was published in 1864 (see Kayser, vol. 15, 79). Here the title of the novel had changed to *Jane Eyre, die Waise* [orphan] *von Lowood*. The highlighting of the heroine's orphanage suggests that by this time Charlotte Brontë's novel is firmly associated with Charlotte Birch-Pfeiffer's enormously popular dramatic adaptation, *Die Waise aus Lowood*. Judging by the number of further editions in the nineteenth century, Grieb's was the most frequently read translation of *Jane Eyre*. Put all the translations together, add the Tauchnitz issues, and it is still likely that, in German-language areas during the 1850s and 1860s, more people saw the play than read the text of the novel.[17]

In Vienna *Die Waise aus Lowood* opened at the Burgtheater in December 1853 and stayed in the repertoire until 1895, by which time it had had 102 performances (Burgtheater 113). Also in Vienna, in 1862 and with a second edition in 1867, the house of Pichler published a volume also entitled *Die Waise aus Lowood* but described on the title-page as 'Frei bearbeitet nach [freely adapted from] Dr Ch.F. Grieb's Uebersetzung von Jacob Spitzer'. The author was a Viennese pedagogue whose outspoken criticism of the Austrian educational system, both in the 'Märztage' of 1848 and later, had led, in 1855, to his suspension from state schools and to him taking a teaching post in a girls' school, the Hermannsche Töchterschule (Wurzbach 188–90). He was also the author of a large number of books for teachers and pupils at various levels, including some specifically aimed at girls' schools. His version of *Jane Eyre* does not openly declare itself as educationally programmatic but in its context – many of the young girls at the Töchterschule would go with their parents to the Burgtheater to see *Die Waise aus Lowood* and perhaps also be drawn to reading the book of the play – it is difficult not to see his text as an alternative *Waise*.[18]

In the history of drama, Charlotte Birch-Pfeiffer's twenty-four volumes of Collected Plays – originals and adaptations – are now demoted to 'Trivialdramatik' (Meske *passim*), but in the history of the Continental transmission of *Jane Eyre* the sheer magnitude of the phenomenon of *Die Waise aus Lowood* cannot be ignored, however skewed and ironical its relation to its source text. In 1848 radical Berlin students had sought to ban Birch-Pfeiffer's bourgeois plays from the stage; in the changed political climate of 1853 her version of the work which the *Quarterly Review* had denounced for revealing the same 'ungodly discontent' as the revolutionary movements of the age (Rigby 173–4) became a conservative box-office success. Her orphan is never seen at Lowood, since the first half of the play is set in the Reeds' house and the second in 'Lord' Rochester's; in both halves Jane is given self-assertive speeches, taken from the novel in quite faithful translation (see Birch-Pfeiffer 1892, 23–4, 103–4). But the point here is not 'ungodly discontent'. The action is played out on the level of domestic intrigue drama; and the point is that Jane unlearns hatred of the Reeds and learns trust in God, who is the real agent of the plot and in the final scene lands Jane in the arms of an un-blinded and un-mutilated Rochester (106–7). The madwoman in the attic is Adèle's mother but not Rochester's wife, and he is sinless and noble.

Morally far simpler and emotionally far less intense than the novel, the play would not have brought blushes to the cheeks of the young Viennese. This Jane does not declare her love, nor nearly make a bigamous marriage, nor threaten the foundations of a conservative society. But from Spitzer's viewpoint the play, as no more than a Cinderella story with a veneer of piety, could still be seen as potentially harmful to the pupils of his Töchterschule, promoting escapism rather than strengthening their moral and intellectual fibre. His version of *Jane Eyre* makes sense as an antidote to those of the two Charlottes. His Jane never asserts her own identity; she remains a true daughter to her pious dead parents and, in effect, also to her noble employer, Rochester; and her only desire is for learning facts – a role model for the pupils of Töchterschulen.

Fitness for its implicit purpose is, then, the context in which this version of *Jane Eyre* must be read. With Grieb's translation before him (as verbatim echoes show), Spitzer took from it the bare bones of the plot – a poor orphan, ill-treated by relations, is sent to school, becomes a governess, inherits a fortune, and marries her employer – and fleshed them out with factual material as cold and thinly-sliced as the meat in Grieb's definition of a sandwich. Like a real-life Gradgrind, Spitzer drains all the imagination, and with it all the inner life of the heroine as well as the romantic and Gothic elements, out of the novel. Instead of a love life – the marriage comes as an abrupt surprise in the last sentence – this Jane is given a socio-geographical life, or rather she becomes a peg to hang such information on. The opening sentence of the book asserts the industrial importance of Manchester and follows it with a detailed account of the machinery used in cotton spinning; and an invented parentage for Jane – her father wore himself out as a doctor to poor mill-workers – is used to provide readers with an outline of what they could otherwise find in Engels's *Die Lage der arbeitenden Klasse in England* (1845) or in the two German translations of *Mary Barton* which had appeared by 1852. Rochester's fortune is not colonial but based on ownership of factories; and, apart from his 'Schloss' of Thornfield, he has a magnificent mansion in

Salford with a view 'over the navigable Irwell' (131). There is of course no madwoman in the attic, but there is a fire which serves to send Rochester and Jane to London while the Schloss is being repaired, at which point the narrative point of view slides into that of a Baedeker and gives population statistics and the exact measurements of St Paul's, as well as full details of how the English middle and upper classes live, eat and sleep. It is altogether like being given the framework of a Victorian social novel without the fiction: the facts of life without the life.

From a literary point of view Spitzer's book – popular enough at the time, as the two editions indicate – is a bizarre and deservedly forgotten failure. In the British Library catalogue it is one of the works listed under the heading of '*Jane Eyre*'. At the end of my chosen trajectory it stands to point how a process of transmission, translation and adaptation may produce a cultural object subversive of the original source text. That text still lives, and will continue to generate new texts.

## Notes

1  The equivalent of 1*s*. 6*d*. per volume as against the customary 31*s*. 6*d*. for Smith, Elder's three volumes.

2  The first three books were Bulwer Lytton's *Pelham* and *Eugene Aram* (nos 1 and 4) and Dickens's *Pickwick* (nos 2–3). The two volumes of *Jane Eyre* were nos 145–6 in the Collection.

3  The letters of, for example, Dickens, Thackeray and George Eliot testify to the friendly relationships Tauchnitz built with his authors.

4  Unremarked by Todd, 45–6, the Tauchnitz 1848 volume reproduces the first edition's title-page 'Edited by Currer Bell' (changed by C.B. to 'By Currer Bell' in the second edition), and the text of the novel contains none of the errors introduced in the second edition (see collation in Brontë 1969, xvii–xviii).

5  The otherwise impeccable Todd errs in stating (710) that 'the Brontës' were eliminated 'entirely' from the list.

6  See, for example, Demidova 689–93, on the early transmission of *Jane Eyre* into Russia, where in 1849 Dostoevsky (in prison) read I.I. Vvedensky's translation which appeared serially in a magazine, *Otechestvennye zapiski*.

7  I have found no evidence to confirm this 'authorization'. Mme Lesbazeille-Souvestre is clearly not identical with the 'Mdlle B' whom C.B. refers to as having asked her consent to a French translation (which seems never to have materialized) and of whom she writes, tellingly, that 'whether competent or not, I presume she has a right to translate the book with or without my consent' (Smith 31).

8  The first W.H. Smith bookstall had opened at Euston station on 1 November 1848. By 1861 Hachette was being attacked for attempting to monopolize the selling of books in railway stations. See Chaix (1861), and Hachette (1861a and b).

9   C.B.'s only recorded reaction to translations of her work is to the passages from *Jane Eyre* quoted in Forcade's review which she found 'generally well rendered' (Smith 140). But see note 7, above.

10  Mainly, of course, it depended on financial transactions. With a tinge of moral blackmail, Hachette tried in December 1855 to offer Dickens, for exclusive rights to translate and publish his work, 500 francs for each novel published in England before the 1852 reciprocal copyright agreement and 1,000 francs for each published after it (see Mistler 156–8 and Dickens 39–40).

11  Among his translations are novels by Collins, Mrs Gaskell and Hawthorne, as well as *Uncle Tom's Cabin*. Apart from many articles on contemporary English and American writers, he wrote books on English culture: *La caricature en Angleterre* (1855) and *Originaux et beaux esprits de l'Angleterre contemporaine* (1860). While not alone among French translators in describing translations as 'imités', he seems to have favoured this approach to C.B.: his *Shirley… Imité de l'anglais par Old-Nick*, which had run as a *feuilleton* in *National* (1850), was published by Hachette in 1855 but seems to have been superseded by the 1859 Romey and Rolet *Shirley & Agnes Grey* (see above, p. 89).

12  Forcade (493) had already made the point that the plot of *Jane Eyre* – an orphan making good – reminded him of Marivaux's *Vie de Marianne*.

13  There was no French translation of *Wuthering Heights* before Wyzewa's *Un amant* in 1892.

14  From an incidental reference in Rimella 10, to M. Lesbazeilles's wife assisting her father with translations for his *Lectures journalières*, I deduce that her name was Noëmie.

15  *Brittany and La Vendée: tales and sketches … with a notice of the life and literary character of Emile Souvestre* appeared in Constable's 'Miscellany of Foreign Literature' (Edinburgh, 1855), and other works of Souvestre were translated into English in the 1850s. In February 1854 the young Ibsen, as stage-instructor at the Bergen Theatre, supervised a production of a Dano-Norwegian translation of Souvestre's play *Un paysan d'aujourd'hui*.

16  Hachette had faced the same fears, not unrelated to the reception of *Jane Eyre*, when in April 1852 he outlined his plan for a 'Bibliothèque des Chemins de Fer' to the railway companies. In the public interest, he would severely ban, he wrote, 'toutes les publications qui pourrait exciter ou entretenir les passions politiques, ainsi que tous les écrits contraire à la morale'. This, he goes on, is contrary to the practice in 'un pays voisin' (i.e. England) where young people, even young women, travel for the sole purpose of devouring novels which they would blush to read 'dans le foyer domestique' (Mistler 124).

17  In other areas, too: in Copenhagen, for example, the play remained in the repertoire of the Folketheater from 1859 to 1899. Translated and plagiarized versions were also performed in London (see Nudd).

18  I have discussed this more fully elsewhere: see Bibliography, Ewbank.

# Bibliography

Bachleitner, Norbert (1989), 'Übersetzungsfabriken: Das deutsche Übersetzungswesen in der ersten Hälfte des 19. Jahr-hunderts', *Internationales Archiv für Sozialgeschichte der deutschen Literatur*, 14, 1–49.

Barber, Giles (1961) ,'Galignani's and the Publication of English Books in France from 1800 to 1852', *Library*, 5th ser. 16, 267–86.

Birch-Pfeiffer, Charlotte (1863–80), *Gesammelte dramatische Werke*, 24 vols, Leipzig: Reclam.
Birch-Pfeiffer, Charlotte (1892), *Die Waise aus Lowood. Schauspiel … Mit freier Benutzung des Romans von Currer Bell*, Leipzig: Reclam.
Brontë, Anne [Acton Bell] (1859), *see* Brontë, Emily, 1847, 1850, 1851; and Brontë, Charlotte, 1859.
Brontë, Charlotte [Currer Bell] (1847), *Jane Eyre. An Autobiography*, 2nd edn, 1848, London: Smith, Elder.
Brontë, Charlotte (1848), *Jane Eyre: An Autobiography*, Leipzig: Tauchnitz.
Brontë, Charlotte (1969), *Jane Eyre*, ed. Jane Jack and Margaret Smith, Oxford: Clarendon Press.
Brontë, Charlotte –
French translations:
(1854), *Jane Eyre, ou Les Mémoires d'une Institutrice*, trans. Mme Lesbazeilles-Souvestre, Paris: D. Giraud.
(1855), *Jane Eyre, ou Mémoires d'une Gouvernante. Imités par Old-Nick*, Paris: Hachette (Bibliothèque des chemins de fer).
(1856), *Jane Eyre, ou Les Mémoires d'une Institutrice*, trans. Mme Lesbazeilles-Souvestre, Paris: Hachette (Bibliothèque des meilleurs romans étrangers).
German translations:
(1848), *Johanna Eyre. Roman*, trans. Ernst Susemihl, Berlin: Duncker & Humblot (Britannia: Englands vorzüglichste Romane und Novellen).
(1850), *Jane Eyre, Memoiren einer Gouvernante*, trans. Ludwig Fort, Grimma [Saxony]: Verlags-Comptoir (Europäische Bibliothek der neuen belletristischen Literatur).
(1850), *Jane Eyre. Roman*, trans. Chr. Fr. Grieb, Stuttgart: Franckh (Kabinetsbibliothek der klassischen Romane aller Nationen), 2nd edn, *Jane Eyre, Die Waise von Lowood*. Stuttgart: Franckh, n.d. [1864], new editions 1870, 1880, 1899, 1904.
(n.d.), *Jane Eyre oder die Waise aus Lowood*, trans. Aug. Heinrich, Wien: Hartleben (Neues belletristisches Lese-Cabinet der besten und interessantesten Romane aller Nationen in sorgfältiger Übersetzung) [betw. 1853 and 1858].
Translations of other Charlotte Brontë novels:
(1858), *Le Professeur*, trans. Henriette Loreau, Paris: Hachette.
(1859), *Shirley & Agnes Grey par Currer Bell*, trans. Ch. Romey and A. Rolet, Paris: Hachette.
Brontë, Emily [Ellis Bell] (1847), *Wuthering Heights*, London: Newby (2 vols, with Anne Brontë's *Agnes Grey* as vol. 3).
Brontë, Emily (1850), *Wuthering Heights and Agnes Grey. By Ellis and Acton Bell*, London: Smith, Elder.
Brontë, Emily (1851) *Wuthering Heights and Agnes Grey*. Leipzig: Tauchnitz.
Brontë, Emily –
Translations:
(1851), *Wutheringshöhe [Wuthering Heights]*, trans. anon., Grimma and Leipzig: Verlags-Comptoir.
(1892), *Un amant [Wuthering Heights]*, trans. Teodor de Wyzewa, Paris: Perrin.
Burgtheater (1951), *175 Jahre Burgtheater 1776–1951. Zusammen- gestellt und bearbeitet von der Direktion des Burgtheaters*, Wien.
Chaix, Napoléon (1861), *Réponse au mémoire de M. Hachette, Publié à l'occasion de l'Enquète faite par la Commission du Colportage sur les Bibliothèques des Chemins de Fer*, Paris: Imprimérie et Libraire Centrale des Chemins de Fer.

D'Amat, Roman (ed.) (1976), *Dictionnaire de Biographie Française*, vol. 14, Paris: Letouzey et Ané.

Demidova, O.R. (1994), 'The Reception of Charlotte Brontë's Work in Nineteenth-Century Russia', *MLR* 89, 689–98.

Dickens, Charles (1995), *The Letters of Charles Dickens*, vol. 8, ed. Graham Storey and Kathleen Tillotson, Oxford: Clarendon Press.

Ewbank, Inga-Stina (2000), 'Adapting *Jane Eyre*: Jacob Spitzer's *Die Waise aus Lowood*'. *Beiträge zur Rezeption der britischen und irischen Literatur des 19. Jahrhunderts im deutschsprachigen Raum*, ed. Norbert Bachleitner, Amsterdam and Atlanta, GA: Rodopi, 283–92.

Forcade, Eugène (1848), '*Jane Eyre. Autobiographie*', *Revue des Deux Mondes*, 24 (1 November), 471–94.

Forgues, Emile Daurand (1860), 'Le Roman de Femme en Angleterre', *Revue des Deux Mondes* (February), 797–831.

Hachette, Louis (1861a), *Examen de la Réponse de M. Napoléon Chaix*, Paris: Lahure.

Hachette, Louis (1861b), *La Question de Bibliothèques des Chemins de Fer*, Paris: Lahure.

Hes, Else (1914), *Charlotte Birch-Pfeiffer als Dramatikerin*, Stuttgart: Metzler.

Hugo, Victor (1969), 'Préface pour la nouvelle traduction de Shakespeare par François-Victor Hugo' (1864), *Oeuvres Complètes*, ed. Jean Massin, vol. 12/1, Paris: Club Français du Livre.

James, Henry (1962), *The Art of the Novel: Critical Prefaces*, ed. Richard P. Blackmur, New York: Scribner.

Kayser, Christian Gottlieb (1853–65), *Vollständiges Bücher-Lexicon*, vols 11–15, Leipzig: Weigel.

Keiderling, Thomas (2000), 'Leipzig als Vermittlungs- und Produktionszentrum englischsprachiger Literatur zwischen 1815 und 1914', *Beiträge zur Rezeption der britischen und irischen Literatur des 19. Jahrhunderts im deutschsprachigen Raum*, ed. Norbert Bachleitner, Amsterdam and Atlanta, GA: Rodopi, 3–76.

Lesbazeilles, Eugène (1857), *Notice sur la vie d'Emile Souvestre*, Paris: Michel Lévy.

Marivaux, Pierre Carlet de Chamblain de (1731–42), *La Vie de Marianne*, Paris: Prault.

Marivaux, Pierre Carlet de Chamblain de (1979), *The Virtuous Orphan or, The Life of Marianne, Countess of\*\*\*\*\**, trans. (i.e. adapted) Mary Collyer, London, 1735, 2nd edn 1743, reprinted New York: Garland.

Meske, Gunnar (1971), *Die Schicksalskomödie. Trivialdramatik um die Mitte des 19. Jahrhunderts am Beispiel der Erfolgsstücke von Charlotte Birch-Pfeiffer*, Diss., Universität Köln.

Mistler, Jean (1964), *La Libraire Hachette de 1826 à nos jours*, Paris: Hachette.

Nowell-Smith, Simon (1966), 'Firma Tauchnitz 1837–1900', *The Book Collector* 15, 423–36.

Nowell-Smith, Simon (1968), *International Copyright Law and the Publisher in the Reign of Queen Victoria*, Oxford: Clarendon Press.

Nudd, Donna Marie (1991), 'Bibliography of Film, Television and Stage Adaptations of Jane Eyre', *Brontë Society Transactions*, 20: 3, 169–72.

Pichot, Amédée (1855), '*Jane Eyre*', *Revue Britannique*, septième série (April), 499–500.

Rigby, Elizabeth (1848), '*Vanity Fair, Jane Eyre* and Governesses' Benevolent Institution Report for 1847', *Quarterly Review* 84 (December), 173–4.

Rimella, Erich (1928), *Emile Souvestre*, Göttingen: Inaugural-Dissertation.

Schmuck, Hilmar and Willi Gorzny (eds) (1980–85), *Gesamtverzeichnis des deutschsprachigen Schrifttums 1700–1910*, München: Saur.

Smith, Margaret (ed.) (2000), *The Letters of Charlotte Brontë*, vol. 2 (1848–51), Oxford: Clarendon Press.

Spitzer, Jacob (1862), *Die Waise aus Lowood. Frei bearbeitet nach Dr. Ch.F. Grieb's Uebersetzung*, 2nd edn 1867, Wien: Pichler.

Tauchnitz, Bernhard (1937a), *The Harvest, being the record of 100 years of publishing, 1837–1937, offered in gratitude to the friends of the firm by Bernhard Tauchnitz*, Leipzig: Tauchnitz.

Tauchnitz, Bernhard (1937b),*Centenary Catalogue 1837–1937*, Leipzig: Tauchnitz.

Tauchnitz, Bernhard (1962), *Festschrift zum 125jährigen Bestehen der Firma Bernhard Tauchnitz Verlag*, Stuttgart: Tauchnitz.

Thackeray, W.M. (1946), *Letters and Private Papers*, ed. Gordon Ray, vol. 3, Cambridge, MA: Harvard University Press.

Todd, William B. and Bowden, Ann (1988), *Tauchnitz International Editions in English 1841–1955. A Bibliographical History*, New York: Bibliographical Society of America.

W.G. (1858), '*Jane Eyre*, par Currer Bell. Traduit par Mme Lesbazeilles-Souvestre', *Revue Critique des Livres Nouveaux*, April, 165–68.

Wurzbach, Constant von (1878), *Biographisches Lexicon des Kaiserthums Oesterreich*, vol. 36, Wien: Hof- und Staatsdruckerei.

## Chapter Nine

# Sir Walter, Sex and the SoA

### Simon Eliot

Sir Walter Besant (1836–1901) was a popular novelist, historian of London and a prime mover in the creation in 1883 of the first successful professional organization for published writers in the UK, the Society of Authors (SoA). He was also a strikingly sociable man. In an age of innumerable dinners and banquets, soirées and 'at homes', he was in his element. But, for Besant, participation was never enough. His was not a passive sociability, but an active one. Like his role model, Dickens, he always needed to be doing something. This amounted at times almost to a manic defence in which endless occupation drives out anything – everything – that might possibly be worse. For Besant, sociability was both a pleasure and a duty, a defence and a call to arms.

He was, for instance, an enthusiastic Freemason, and identified its virtues thus:

> Properly carried out, the freemason has friends everywhere, and in the case of need, brethren of the same fraternity are bound by vow to assist him. Every lodge is a benefit club; the members are bound to each other by the vows and obligations of a medieval guild. (Besant 239)

This concept of what we might call 'defensive collegiality' is visible in almost all Besant-influenced organizations, and particularly in his charitable work, whether it was organizing employment bureaux for the newly emerging female secretarial class, or clubs for the workers of the East End of London. In the parish of St James's, Ratcliffe, for instance, they had:

> ... a girls' club numbering from forty to fifty. The girls came to the club every night; they talked, they sang, they danced, they learned needlework, they were on terms of friendliness and personal affection with the leaders; every night they had three hours' quiet, learning unconsciously lessons of self-respect and order. (Besant 251–2)

The same sort collective, protective support was to be offered to visiting Americans via the Atlantic Union which Besant helped set up in the late 1890s:

we in London engage ourselves to receive Americans and others, to show them collective and individual attention; we organise for them personally conducted walks and visits ... we shall hold receptions; we shall get up dinners, concerts, lectures; certain ladies will give garden parties and 'at homes' ... (Besant 272)

The SoA was merely the largest and most successful of Besant's defensive communities. Of the SoA he says variously:

Our office has become the recognized refuge for all who are in trouble. (Besant 237)

I should very much like to see established an institute akin to the Law Institute, but what I want, even more than the institute, is a Pension Fund. That, I see plainly, is above all to be desired. (Besant 238)

Given the importance of this defensive collegiality in the creation of the SoA, it is worth asking why Besant was so keen on it for himself and for others.

Few of Besant's personal papers survive, and those that do are, on the whole, rather unrevealing. Curiously enough, however, there is another source which one would not usually regard very highly but which, due to certain peculiar circumstances which gave rise to editorial oddities in its text, might well be more revealing than is usually the case. This is Besant's autobiography (uninspiringly entitled *Autobiography of Sir Walter Besant*), 'With a prefatory note by S. Squire Sprigge', which was published posthumously by Hutchinson in 1902. Sprigge had been one of the early secretaries of the SoA and was one of Besant's loyalist supporters.

Sprigge commented in the first paragraph of the prefatory note that:

An autobiography should be its own justification and its own interpretation. There should be no room for a preface and no need for any intermediary between the writer and the public to whom he has designed to appeal. (Besant vii)

Why then did Sprigge bother to add this apparently self-contradictory preface? Essentially because the *Autobiography* was regarded – by Besant's family, his literary executor and Sprigge himself – as being incomplete. Besant was engaged in writing it up until his death in June 1901, and at that point the volume was finished only in the sense that the first draft had been written up to and including the retrospective and contemplative final chapter. Besant's writing practice was, as Sprigge revealed, to allow for at least two stages of correction and amendment, the second being commonly greater than the first.

At the time of Besant's death some parts of the *Autobiography* had only gone through the first of these stages, as Sprigge admitted:

> But what he should include and what he should omit, what he should treat fully and what he should regard as episodes, had to be considered, and this was certainly not done by Besant in all places with his usual thorough care. If he had followed his invariable plan of composition, he would have made up his mind on many such points only when he came to the actual task of revising. This revision was wont to be done upon his manuscript roughly, and then very fully upon a type-written copy of that manuscript. The manuscript of the autobiography had not been type-written. The written manuscript was fully and freely corrected, and it may be taken for granted that the earlier portions of the work now appear much as they were intended to appear; but the later chapters would certainly have been amplified, and possibly modified in some directions. Such revision cannot be done now by any one, however sure we may feel that it would have been done by him. ... I would press that these points be remembered: that he died leaving the manuscript in what he would have considered an unfinished state; that it was his express desire that it should be published; and that any attempt to modify his work either by addition or subtraction, however honest in its intention to make a more accurate picture, would amount to a dangerous tampering with the original. (Besant ix–x)

What Sprigge seemed unaware of was that the lack of revision, particularly of the later parts of the book, allowed the *Autobiography* to be more revealing of certain passages in Besant's life than would have been the case had the author had an opportunity to muffle the experiences by judicious revision and rewriting.

Between 1851 and 1854 Besant was a boarding pupil at Stockwell Grammar, one of a number of schools associated with – or, as the jargon of the day had it, 'in connection with' – King's College, London University that were established in the 1830s in what were then rather remote and rural suburbs of the city. The school was a small one with no more than 120 pupils. On the whole Besant's memories of this time seem to have been happy ones: they included a collection of eccentric masters and many idyllic rambles in the surrounding countryside. In the summer of 1854 Besant finally left Stockwell as captain of the school and laden with academic prizes.

As Besant was intended for the Established Church, it seemed natural to enrol him at King's College which was then, and continued to be for some time after, a bastion of Anglican orthodoxy. After about a year in London he left for Christ's College, Cambridge. The year in London, however, had influenced him profoundly. From all that he wrote about this period, it is clear that it was a time of considerable unhappiness and ambivalence. It had presented Besant with a set of personal experiences that were to haunt him for the rest of his life.

Unusually, and significantly, this London period is dealt with twice in the *Autobiography*: once in its proper chronological position (as Chapter IV) and once again in the book's conclusion (Chapter XVI). If Sprigge is right, and there is no reason to doubt him, Chapter IV, being in the first half of the book, would have been subject to a higher level of revision than the conclusion. We would expect the second account of this period, therefore, to be rougher and more revealing than the first – and so it is. What is more surprising is that the narrative contained in Chapter IV is itself, despite the greater amount of revision, a confessional account which makes little attempt to hide the distress and desperation of the London experience.

In Chapter IV Besant described his time in London in the following way:

> My lodgings were in a place called Featherstone Buildings, Holborn.[1] I shared rooms with a brother, who was in the City. He had a good many friends in London, and was out nearly every evening. I had few, and remained left to my own devices; we had little in common, and went each his own way …
>
> I ought to have stayed at home in the evening and worked. Now Featherstone Buildings is a very quiet place; there is no thoroughfare; all the houses were then – and I dare say are still – let out in lodgings; our one sitting room, which was also my study, was the second floor front. In the evening the place was absolutely silent; the silence sometimes helped me in my work; sometimes it got on my nerves and became intolerable. I would then go out and wander about the streets for the sake of the animation, the crowds, and the lights; or I would go half-price – a shilling – to the pit of a theatre; or I would, also for a shilling, drop into a casino and sit in a corner and look on at the dancing. I was shy; I looked much younger than my age; I spoke to no one, and no one spoke to me. The thing was risky, but I came to no harm; nor did I ever think much about the character of the people who frequented the places. One of them was in Dean Street, Soho. It is now a school; it was then 'Caldwell's' – a dancing place frequented by shop-girls, dressmakers, and young fellows. I do not know what the reputation of the place was; no doubt it was pretty bad; but, so far as I remember, it was a quiet and well-conducted place. To this day I cannot think of those lonely evenings in my London lodging without a touch of the old terror. I see myself sitting at a table , books spread out before me. I get to work. Presently I sit up and look around. The silence is too much for me. I take my hat and go out. (Besant 70–72)

We should remind ourselves that Besant was of a scholarly disposition with a remarkable capacity for work and concentration yet, despite this, he seems to have been unable to defend himself against the *anomie* of his life in London. He is aware that alienation and loneliness forced him into frequenting places where the entertainment was, to say the least, morally risky.

London in the 1850s was a very different place from the late Victorian London that would have been familiar to most of the first readers of the *Autobiography*. To a large extent it would have been the 'unimproved' London that Dickens had known when, as a child, he had wandered its streets in the early 1820s. Its low-life, and its low-life entertainments, would have been more obvious, more extensive and more explicit than would have been tolerated once Victorianism proper had got into its stride. Besant does not admit to much in this passage, no more than to visiting Caldwell's, but his tone is defensive enough to suggest that he was aware of the moral and physical risks he ran during that desperate year in London.

So much for the account given in Chapter IV, the one that had almost certainly been subject to Besant's correction and amendment. What of the unvarnished second narrative, the one given in the conclusion of the *Autobiography*?

'Conclusion: The Conduct of Life and the Influence of Religion' suggests a calm, detached survey of life and the account of a measured, philosophical programme based on that survey. In part the chapter does deliver what we might expect of it but, being uncorrected, it also reveals a man who was far from detached, whose values had been forged in the heat of an experience, the intensity of which had not been diminished by the passage of time.

This experience was, of course, his year in London 1854–55. The second account repeats much of what he had written before (thus clearly proving its unrevised state) but it also goes significantly further:

> But there was the evening to get through. No one appeared to know how desperately miserable an evening all alone in lodgings may be. I have sat with my books before me while the silence grew more and more intolerable, rising up all round as a cloud hiding the rest of the world. When my nerves would stand it no longer, I have taken my hat and rushed out into the streets.
>
> The evening amusements of London were more varied, and far, far more coarse than they are now. As a young fellow of eighteen I ought not to have gone to them – that is quite certain. Yet what could be done when solitude became intolerable? There were the theatres at half-price – there were not so many theatres, and in a week or two one could get through them all. There were the dancing places of the more decorous sort, the Argyle Rooms, the Holborn Casino, 'Caldwell's', besides places whose reputation was such that one was afraid to venture within their walls. At the Holborn and the Argyle the ladies

were very beautifully dressed. I did not go there to dance or to make their acquaintance; I sat on the red velvet benches and listened to the music. At 'Caldwell's', on the other hand, where the girls were more simply attired, and where they liked to meet a young fellow who could dance, and could dance tolerably well, I did dance. Perhaps it was wrong; perhaps, however, it was not. I take no blame to myself on account of 'Caldwell's'. (Besant 275–6)

Despite Besant's claims that they were 'decorous' both the Argyll Rooms and the Holborn Casino had racy reputations. Of the Holborn, Kellow Chesney comments: 'It was frequented by a variety of young men – medical students, apprentice lawyers, young ships' officers, clerks, well-off young tradesmen – and by a large number of amateur and professional prostitutes. The floor, the band and the easy pick-ups were the great attractions' (Chesney 366).
    Besant continued:

There were places not quite so innocent whither my wandering footsteps led me. There were the Coal Hole, the Cider Cellars, Evans'. At these places there was singing; some of the songs were very beautiful and very well sung; part songs were given at Evans'; *poses plastiques* were offered for the corruption of youth at a place whose name I have forgotten; and at the Coal Hole or the Cider Cellars there was 'Baron' Nicholson and the 'judge and jury'. Such an exhibition would not be tolerated at the present day: I remember it as clever but inconceivably coarse.

The quality and content of the songs sung at such places can be assessed by the faint traces that they have left in the published record, for instance: *The Flash Chaunter, a ... collection of Gentlemen's songs, now singing at Offley's, Cider Cellars, Coal Hole, etc.*: [London?]: N. West, [1865?]; or *The Rambler's Flash Songster, nothing but out and outers ... now singing at Offley's, Cider Cellars, Coal Hole*, [London?]: N. West, [1865?]. Both are classified as 'P.C.' [Private Case] books by the British Library.
    Besant's summer rambles took him further afield:

In the summer one could go to Cremorne or to Highbury Barn: even, for curiosity, walk to the Eagle in the City Road. (Besant 277)

Kellow Chesney observes: 'Cremorne Gardens in Chelsea, which in the fifties were the last flourishing representative of the old-style London pleasure garden, attracted respectable citizens and smart whores alike' (Chesney 403). Apparently, Cremorne changed its character at night; as respectable citizens made their way home, discreet and well-dressed prostitutes moved in. It is

significant that Besant visited most of these places 'in the evening' just as
they would be in the process of transformation. Of the Eagle (immortalized in
'Pop goes the Weasel') Chesney says:

> The tremendous Eagle in the City Road Whitechapel, had grown from a pub to
> a music hall to a whole complex of diversions: there was a theatre in which
> opera could be staged and a garden with fountains, alcoves and boxes like a
> miniature Cremorne ... There was no lack of prostitutes and half-prostitutes at
> such places, and at times there were rough and rowdy scenes ...

Chesney adds, however, that such places were also like Cremorne in that they
attracted a mixture of the respectable and the not-so-respectable (Chesney
404).

Besant was horribly aware of the not-so-respectable:

> When I remember all these places and how, in order to escape the awful stillness
> of my lodgings, I would go out in the evening and prowl about looking in here
> and there, I wonder that some horrible obsession of the devil did not fall upon
> me, as it fell upon hundreds and thousands of young fellows like myself, turned
> into the streets because I could not bear to sit alone. Why, there were clerks and
> students all around me; every house in my street was filled with them; every
> man sat in his own dismal cell and listened to the silence till his nerves could
> stand it no longer. Then he went out into the street. If there are fifty devils in the
> streets today, there were five hundred then. It was not every one who at eighteen
> was so boyish in mind and manner and in appearance as I was; not every one
> who was short-sighted and shy; not every one who was able to sit among the
> rabble rout and listen to the music as if surrounded by nymphs and swains of
> the highest purity and virtue. (Besant 277)

Besant's description of the growing sense of oppression in his silent room
followed by the almost explosive rush into the streets is curiously close to an
experience described by a near-contemporary of his, George Gissing. Morley
Roberts, Gissing's friend and fellow student at Owens College, Manchester,
records Gissing's description of how he first discovered his second wife, Edith
Underwood. One Sunday, he observed, 'I could stand it no longer, so I rushed
out and spoke to the very first woman I came across' (Young xxxv). 'Stand it
no longer' and 'rushed out' are phrases common to both Gissing and Besant.
Frustration followed by desperation followed by violent action is the rhythm
of behaviour that characterized both events. Gissing, being the more explicit
of the two writers, shines a brighter torch on these obscuring phrases. The
event is significant for Gissing because, in the words of Arthur C. Young:

it is important to recognize that Gissing was simply in search of a sexual partner, not a wife, and that his fastidiousness ... would prevent him from accepting the advances of an obvious trollop while it would not hinder him from approaching a decent-looking working girl. (Young xxxv–xxxvi)

In other words, for Gissing the whole event is a description of sexual frustration and his attempt to relieve it. We could not expect such an overt declaration from Besant, but the similarity between his phrasing and that of Gissing's, and the description of street life that follows it in Besant's account, suggests that a parallel between the two experiences would not be a forced one.

Like many moralists before him and since, Besant adopts in the description of his London experience a curiously ambivalent position: he was in the world but not of it. Despite the ubiquity of temptation, we are to understand that his physical immaturity and myopia protected him (though not presumably from the obscene songs performed at the Coal Hole and the Cider Cellars). Despite claiming such differences between himself and all the others who were more vulnerable, he remembers his own motives for quitting his 'dismal cell' and confidently ascribes them to all the other young men who prowled about that corrupting city. Whatever else was on offer in that now historically remote city, whatever else he accidentally saw or experienced, Besant, we are assured, was only there for the music and the dancing. Just in case we have not quite grasped the point, Besant takes the reader aside to explain the matter historically:

> However, the thing to be remembered is that London was much coarser in its evening amusements then than now; that the outward show of morals was not insisted upon so much. London is bad enough now, but in most localities only after ten o'clock and before twelve, whereas in the fifties things went on all day long. (Besant 277–8)

From historical reflection, Besant then slips once again into his memories and, in doing so, reveals yet another layer of experience which he had not acknowledged in his earlier, revised reminiscences of that year in London.

> I remember that among the houses south of Waterloo Bridge there was a whole row where in the ground floor windows there was everyday an exhibition of girls dancing up and down, and inviting the young men to come in. And I remember that, apart from the 'judge and jury' business, the songs sung at some places were coarse beyond belief. And considering all these things, I cannot wonder that I went to them, having no one to warn or to restrain me, or to offer

any substitutes for the amusements which were gross enough, yet promised the
attractions of music and singing. (Besant 278)

We should not rush to accuse Besant of hypocrisy; it may well be that a
combination of his small stature (he was only 5 foot 6 inches tall), his naivety
and his myopia did allow him to frequent these places and remain, in his eyes
at least, untainted as though he were an Oliver Twist or, more accurately, a
Little Dorrit – an adult in an apparently child-like body. But if he did not fall,
and he was not pushed, he would still have been aware of what was going on
around him. He was eighteen years old; his later life would suggest that he
had a pretty normal heterosexual drive. He must have witnessed and been
subjected to sexual temptations from the most restrained invitation – 'May I
have the pleasure of paying my addresses to you?' was the conventional
opening line from a prostitute at a casino (Pearsall 337) – to the most explicit
soliciting of the dancing girls or their pimps in the unnamed road south of
Waterloo Bridge.[2]

The significance of these experiences for Besant can be measured by his
reaction to them. Whatever happened, or did not happen, it was a time that he
had to explore not once but twice in his *Autobiography*, and it was a time
whose recollection still pained him forty years and more after the event when
he was a father of four children, an established popular novelist and historian
who had been knighted for his charitable work. His discomfort was such that
his memory, normally so reliable and capacious, let him down. Here was a
man who was, in his sixties, to perambulate London recording and
remembering the city of the 1890s in a detail of which Stowe would be envious.
Yet in this earlier year in London, at a time (late adolescence) when experience
is often at its most vivid and the personality at its most impressionable, he
cannot remember details of experiences which are otherwise so intense for
him. When he finally brought himself to mention the *poses plastiques* he
adds hastily that it occurred 'at a place whose name I have forgotten' (Besant
276–7). Besant himself was aware of the poignant irony of all this. Here is an
historian of London who was going to write eloquently of the seventeenth-
and eighteenth-century city in his novels and popular histories. The 1850s
was the last decade in which many of the streets and buildings of the older
city survived in their unreconstructed state, or survived at all. It was still the
city of Hogarth, of Johnson, and of Dickens. In 1855 it could have been the
city of Besant. In a sense it was, but in such a way that he could not let
himself recover it. In Chapter IV of the *Autobiography* he articulated this sad
paradox:

When lectures were over I used generally to walk away by myself into the City. There was no reason for getting into the City; I knew nothing about its history; but it fascinated me, as it does to this day. Apart from all its historical associations, the City has still a strange and inexplicable charm for me. I like now, as I liked then, to wander about among its winding lanes and narrow streets; to stand before those old, neglected City churchyards; to look into the old inn yards, of which there remain but one or two. If I could only by some effort of the memory recall those streets and houses, which I suppose I saw while they were still standing, but have forgotten! I knew the City before they provided it with the new broad thoroughfares; before they pulled down so many of the City churches. I ought to remember the double quadrangle of Doctors' Commons – that quaint old college in the heart of the City; Gerard's Hall; St. Michael's subterranean Church; the buildings on the site of the Hanseatic Aula; St Paul's School; the Merchant Taylors' School; Whittington's Alms-House; and I know not what beside. Alas! I have long since forgotten them. In those days, however, I walked about these ancient monuments. (Besant 70)

Besant was able to let himself remember the next phase of his life in much greater detail. His ideal of college life was based partly on happier experiences in Cambridge for which he left King's College, London, in the autumn of 1855. At Christ's College he found a friendlier and more intellectually fulfilling academic tradition which did not have such an exclusive devotion to the training of would-be Anglican clergy. In Chapter V of the *Autobiography* he celebrates the advantages of a small Cambridge College: 'In the college of a hundred and fifty to two hundred men there is room for development of character; no one need be lost in the crowd' (Besant 80), and concludes the chapter by declaring:

What did Cambridge do for me? Well, it seems as if it did everything for me .... New habits of thought, new points of refinement, a wider mind, came out of this intimacy of so many different youths from different homes. If I may judge from myself, the effect of Cambridge upon the youth of the time was wholly and unreservedly beneficial. (Besant 97–8)

Speaking of the thousands of young men with whom Besant so closely identified, those whom he felt were driven out into the dangerous and tempting streets by the 'silence and loneliness' of their rooms, he declared:

If I were a rich man I would build colleges for these young fellows, where they could live together, and so keep out of mischief. (Besant 72)

Here we begin to get some idea of the source of the emotional force behind Besant's promotion of collegiality. For Besant, the city was a place of intense attractions and immediate dangers. A collective, protective social organization would make the former accessible while helping to neutralize the latter.

It should not surprise us that it is the sexual aspects of Besant's reminiscences of London that get pruned in the more respectable, better revised, earlier chapters. One would expect nothing else of a late Victorian autobiography. What is more puzzling is that Besant should have felt compelled to record these sexual observations in the first place, particularly as he might well have suspected that he would not get around to a final – and probably excising – revision. Another puzzle is that he should have spread these observations out, distributing them between an early chapter and the final one, like a man dividing his valuables and hiding caches of them in different places. Perhaps it is too much to claim that Besant was unconsciously intent on increasing the chances of the truth getting through, but the way in which he constructed his autobiography and distributed its revelations did mean that, if he died at any time before the *Autobiography* was fully and completely revised, then the record of his experience of social dislocation and sexual temptation would survive, at least in part, in its raw and unvarnished state.

This is particularly significant as it was his firm determination that the *Autobiography* should be published. Sprigge was very clear on this matter:

> Sir Walter Besant expressly meant his account of his life to be published …
> (Besant viii)

For Besant sexual temptation was simply a representative temptation. It may have been the most powerful, it was certainly the one to which he felt that he himself had been most subject, but it also stood for all the other sorts of moral and intellectual corruption to which a lonely, dislocated, uninformed (and therefore vulnerable) individual might be exposed.

Cambridge offered a vision of collegiality which, in a somewhat less eighteenth-century form, might provide the support and protection which Besant had so lacked in London. In this sense it could be argued that the creation of the SoA was motivated by a similar need to offer support and protection to that most vulnerable of creatures, the aspiring author. Thus the SoA, that profoundly significant institution in the professionalizing of authorship, had one of its roots buried deep in the dislocation and *anomie* of that extraordinary year Besant spent in London in the mid-1850s.

## Notes

1   Featherstone Buildings lay on the north side of Holburn just a quarter of a mile to the west
    of Furnivals Inn where Dickens had lived at the beginning of his writing career. There are
    a number of unforced parallels between the two writers. Besant was born at 3 St George's
    Square, Portsea, only a few streets away from the house in which Dickens had been born
    twenty-four years previously. Besant even managed to die on the same day of the year as
    Dickens: 9 June. One of the few things they did not share was genius.
2   'The neighbourhood of Waterloo was, among others, notorious for its child prostitutes-
    cum-beggars who whiningly plucked at the sleeves of passers-by, pleading for pennies in
    the same breath as they confided obscenities in the hope of titillating a potential client'
    (Harrison 226). 'Lambeth, Blackfriars, including Waterloo Road' was one of the designated
    areas in William Acton's survey of prostitution in London. In 1841 the area was the fourth-
    highest in terms of number of estimated brothels (Acton 275); by 1857, just a few years
    after Besant's experience of it, the area had gone up the ranks and was third-highest both in
    number of brothels (377) and estimated number of prostitutes (Acton 802). Another Walter,
    the author of *My Secret Life*, also observed Waterloo Road and the 'groups of half-naked
    women for hire in ground-floor windows' (Thomas 131).

## Bibliography

Acton, William (1870), *Prostitution*, London: John Churchill.
Besant, Walter (1902), *Autobiography of Sir Walter Besant*, London: Hutchinson & Co.
Chesney, Kellow (1972), *The Victorian Underworld*, Harmondsworth: Penguin.
Gissing, George (1961), *The Letters of George Gissing to Eduard Bertz*, ed. Arthur C. Young,
    London: Constable.
Harrison, Fraser (1979), *The Dark Angel: Aspects of Victorian Sexuality*, London: Fontana.
Pearsall, Ronald (1971), *The Worm in the Bud*, Harmondsworth: Penguin.
Thomas, Donald (1998), *The Victorian Underworld*, London: John Murray.

Chapter Ten

# Making (Pre-) History: Mycenae, Pausanias, Frazer

David Richards

Heinrich Schliemann, having amassed a considerable fortune selling supplies during the Crimean War, abandoned the grocery trade and turned his attention and his resources to his personal passion: the archaeology of the Trojan War. His ambition was to prove the historical veracity of the legendary tales of Paris and Agamemnon against the prevailing view that the Homeric epics were merely poetic traditions and fables. By 1873 he was convinced he had archaeological proof of the historical existence of one-half of the narrative when he discovered what he thought was the site of the city of Troy and the 'Treasure of Priam' at Hissarlik. Schliemann then moved his expedition to the site of the opposing combatants, the Greeks of Mycenae. In December 1876, he excavated the shaft-graves in the ruined city which contained, as he put it, an 'astonishing wealth of gold'. The gold grave masks, Baltic amber beads, the elevated status of the dead, their apparently hurried burial, all indicated to Schliemann that he had indeed discovered the Royal Tombs of the House of Atreus. Although Schliemann's crude methods of excavation were later to be questioned, as was his speculation about the mode of burial and the identities of the graves' occupants, he was never shaken in his conviction that he had, in the acropolis of a city deserted in 468 BC, discovered the remains of Cassandra and her twin children, of Elektra, of Eurymedon the charioteer, and of Agamemnon (Schuchhardt 5, 7, 135, 152, 161ff).[1]

Schliemann had not unearthed the House of Atreus entirely unaided, nor was his success greeted everywhere with warm enthusiasm. His guide had been Pausanias, a Lydian living during the reign of Marcus Aurelius, whose book of travels, the *Description of Greece* (c. AD 174–180), had led Schliemann to the burial site in the Mycenaean citadel. Schliemann's use of Pausanias was itself controversial. The leading classical scholar in Germany, Ulrich von Wilamowitz-Moellendorff,[2] began a 'vendetta', as Habicht and Ackerman describe it, against Pausanias, declaring him 'a lying knave or a confused fool'. In Wilamowitz's estimation, Pausanias invented what he saw or borrowed his 'descriptions' from the much earlier work of Polemo of Ilium. Wilamowitz may have had personal reasons to despise Pausanias. He had once been invited by a party of aristocratic Germans to conduct a tour of Greek monuments and he used Pausanias as a guide. The tour was a disaster, nothing seemed to be where Pausanias claimed it was, and Wilamowitz was humiliated in the eyes of his influential clients. Thereafter Wilamowitz directly, or indirectly through his coterie of academic disciples, returned repeatedly to the assault on Pausanias, questioning not only his accuracy, but also his honesty (Habicht and Ackerman 133–7). On the matter of the Mycenaean tombs, however, Schliemann had read Pausanias with more attention than Wilamowitz. Pausanias's claim that the tombs of Atreus were to be found 'by the walls' was taken by Wilamowitz to mean the cyclopean circuit wall of the city. Schliemann accurately interpreted the text to mean that the site was to be found by the walls of the citadel above the main city complex. To have Pausanias proved correct, and by a retired grocer and amateur classicist at that, was extraordinarily galling to the patrician Wilamowitz. To make matters worse for Wilamowitz and the German classicists under his influence, a series of archaeological digs were opened at sites throughout Greece, which followed Schliemann's successful use of Pausanias's *Description*. Within a period of twenty years, Pausanias led archaeologists to discoveries at Athens, Delphi, Cornith, Epidarus, Sparta, Mantinea, Thebes, Plataea and Messene. For Christian Habicht, the 'single page' on Mycenae in Pausanias's *Description* 'is the origin of what may be called professional archaeology' (Habicht 31–9 and 29).[3]

Habicht's declaration of an origin for professional archaeology in Schliemann's remarkable discoveries at Mycenae neglects earlier significant excavations – in Mesopotamia, at Rome and Pompeii, and in Egypt by Napoleonic expeditions. More precisely, Schliemann's Mycenaean excavations marked, not an 'origin' as such, but the commencement of a new mediation of knowledge of the ancient world, which forged a new set of negotiations and relationships with the past. The significance of the discovery at Mycenae lies in the effect it had in redefining questions about the status of the ancient textual legacy (both Homer and Pausanias) and its transmission to modernity, in transforming contemporary perceptions of the ancient Greek world, and further, of human cultural and civic origins, and in determining the nature of historical progress and social evolution. The ruins of Mycenae play a significant role in locating modernity in relation to the past (conceived as being transmitted in texts and artefacts as vessels of human disclosure). Yet the reverse is also true, for while the modern is seen as the product of a process which began in antiquity, modernity also projects itself onto the past, reproducing the present in Agamemnon's ruined city. Mycenae lies at the centre of a discourse where information about the past flows through texts and objects to the present, only to be returned – altered, and altering – to its point of origin.

In the first instance, however, the most pressing question which followed Schliemann's discoveries concerned the ownership of the ancient past. Schliemann was compelled to enter into often fraught negotiations with both the Turkish and Greek governments over the provenance of the objects he had found, and his detractors seized upon this as evidence of his impure, mercenary and unscholarly conduct. Increasingly his supporters and detractors divided along national lines, projecting, at the same time, their contemporary national antagonism onto the ancient past. While Schliemann enjoyed a certain notability in his native Germany, it was in England where he was treated as a celebrity. No less a figure than Gladstone wrote a preface to Schliemann's book on the Mycenae excavations, offering unequivocal support to his claim to have discovered the graves of Agamemnon and his companions in the face of German scepticism. And on visiting London after his successes at Mycenae, Schliemann wrote that 'I was received for seven weeks as if I had discovered a new part of the globe for England' (Schuchhardt 159). Schliemann's remark casts a revealing light on an international contest for sovereignty over the ancient past; a struggle which, as Schliemann saw, was mirrored also in the rivalry between powers for imperial dominion.

Not surprisingly, Schliemann's discovery attracted intense interest to Pausanias's text after 1,700 years of neglect, and some of the same contest for control is revealed in rival translations of the ancient text, in German, by Hitzig and Blümner (ten volumes, 1896–1910) and English, by James Frazer (six volumes, 1898). Just as Gladstone had championed Schliemann, so Frazer leapt to Pausanias's defence:

> Without [Pausanias] the ruins of Greece would for the most part be a labyrinth without a clue, a riddle without an answer. His book furnishes the clue to the labyrinth, the answer to many riddles. (Frazer 1898, vol. 1, xcvi)[4]

Frazer imagined that Pausanias could not have hoped that his book would be read long after the Roman Empire had passed away by 'the Britons in their distant isle, and by the inhabitants of a new world across the Atlantic', nor 'by the people whom he calls the most numerous and warlike barbarians in Europe [the Germans]'(Frazer 1900a, 38–9). In contradiction to Wilamowitz's portrait of mendacity, Frazer's Pausanias possessed all the Anglo-Saxon virtues. He is 'trustworthy', 'a man made of common stuff and cast in a common mould', a 'plain, free from embellishment, realistic, truthful, honest, fair-minded, credible, direct, modest, laborious, plodding man of plain good sense without either genius or imagination', whose thoughts are 'always manly and direct' (Frazer 1900a, 1, 69, 103–5, 108, 110).

These covert sub-texts of national differences extend beyond Frazer's defence of Pausanias's character as a classical source or archaeological guide. By the time Macmillan published his translation and commentary, Frazer had been at work on Pausanias for fourteen years and had forged a bond with Pausanias stronger than that of translator and commentator. Not content with the translation alone, Frazer also published in 1900 extracts from the introduction and commentary alongside his own travel writings on Greece, produced during a journey retracing Pausanias's steps which Frazer had made with the advance he received from Macmillan for the Pausanias edition. According to Frazer, Pausanias's *Description of Greece* is unfinished since it possesses neither a preface nor an epilogue, which his *Pausanias and other Greek Sketches* goes on to provide. Frazer provides an alter-text to Pausanias: a late Victorian mirror of a second-century travelogue.[5]

Although Pausanias had certainly travelled further and more hazardously than Frazer, both authors shared a singular passion: both had visited the Lake of Aricia where had lived 'the grim priest pacing sword in hand, the wonder of the Golden Bough' (Frazer 1900a, 16).[6] It was during the period of most intense work on Pausanias that Frazer transformed himself from a humble classical scholar to the internationally renowned anthropologist and author of *The Golden Bough*.[7] It was while he was working on Pausanias that he became influenced by William Robertson Smith, who inspired in Frazer an interest in primitive beliefs and customs. It was also at this point that Frazer read E.B. Tylor's *Primitive Culture* (1871), a text which was to have a decisive impact on the direction of his work and to change the way he viewed Pausanias and the world of the ancient Greeks (Downey 115). The six 'thick quarto volumes' of 3,000 pages, two-thirds of which consisted of Frazer's own commentary on the translated text, were produced during this formative period of Frazer's intellectual life (Ackerman 54–5). Yet although these contexts in the emergent discipline of anthropology inform both his own anthropological work and his interpretation of classical texts, his two disciplines – classics and anthropology – end in very different, indeed contradictory, conclusions.

Second-century Greece described in Pausanias exists, in Frazer's interpretation, in 'the Indian summer', 'the mellow autumn' of the 'Greek genius' (Frazer 1900a, 2). Pausanias's Greece is in decline, depopulated by 'civil brawls and wars'; the whole country could hardly 'put three thousand infantry on the field'. The once great city of Thebes lay deserted where 'only a single statue stood erect among the ruins of the ancient market-place' (Frazer 1900a, 3). Pausanias's descriptions are of 'shrunken or ruined cities, deserted villages, roofless temples, shrines without images'. Hordes of northern barbarians 'carried fire and sword into the heart of Greece', 'thinned its population, enfeebled its energies, and precipitated the decline of art' (Frazer 1900a, 4). Frazer's text returns repeatedly to these tropes of decline and extinction: the great precursor of which was the eclipse of the Mycenaean age. Mycenae, now a scene of 'desolate grandeur' 'more in keeping with the mist-wrapt stronghold of some old robber chief in Skye or Lochaber' (Frazer 1900a, 245) was once a 'luxurious semi-Oriental civilisation':

> [I]mposing fortifications, stately tombs, luxurious baths, magnificent palaces, their walls gay with bright frescoes or glittering with burnished bronze, their halls crowded with a profusion of precious objects of art and luxury, wrought by native craftsmen or brought by merchants from the bazaars of Egypt or Assyria; and in the midst of all a sultan, laden with golden jewellery, listening to minstrels singing the tale of Troy or the wanderings of Ulysses. (Frazer 1900a, 247)

Its end came, not as 'some writers' think in a sudden assault by its opponents, but in the gradual erosion of its power, by the repeated sapping of its strength by Dorian 'barbarians'. 'The typical Dorians were the Spartans, and no greater contrast can well be conceived' than that of Sparta's 'stern simplicity' and Mycenae:

> [An] open unfortified city with insignificant buildings, where art and poetry never flourished, where gold and silver were banned, and where even the kings prided themselves on the meanness of their attire. The Dorians, if we may judge of them by the purest specimens of the breed, were just as incapable of creating the art of Mycenae as the Turks were of building the Parthenon and St. Sophia. (Frazer 1900a, 247)

Mycenae's fall represents the master narrative of Greek history; a narrative repeated in the Greek settlements in Asia, on the 'beautiful island-studded coast, under the soft Ionian sky' of the 'new Greece', and, in Pausanias's time, under the yolk of the Romans. Mycenae's fate is the endlessly repeated history of the 'conflict between civilization and barbarism, the slow decline of the former and the gradual triumph of the latter'. Mycenae's ruins show the engine of history in action, a process of decline, conquest and colonization of civilization by barbarism:

It was thus that the Saxons step by step ousted the Britons, and the Danes obtained a footing in England; it was thus that the Turks slowly strangled the Byzantine empire. Events like the fall of Constantinople and the expulsion of the Moors from Granada are only the last scenes in tragedies which have been acting for centuries. (Frazer 1900a, 246)

Frazer is here engaged in a complex series of negotiations: with Pausanias's text, with Pausanias's Antonine historical context, with racial and cultural representations of difference, with a grand conjectural historical panorama, with imperial and colonial projects, and with his own evolutionary anthropology. Frazer's second expanded edition of *The Golden Bough*, which is exactly contemporaneous with *Pausanias and other Greek Sketches*, contained a major theoretical innovation which Frazer adapted from Comte, Renan and Mannhardt: that the evolution of human culture progressed inexorably through the ages of magic, religion and science from savagery, to barbarism, to civilization. Yet, the master example of Mycenae in *Greek Sketches* would seem to offer precisely the opposite conjectural historical paradigm to the evolutionary model which informs *The Golden Bough*: the history of culture is the history of descent into barbarism and the inescapable degeneration of civilization. Frazer writes, in this prospect of the decline and fall of antiquity, in a mood more reminiscent of the eighteenth-century universal history of Gibbon than the nineteenth-century cultural evolution of Tylor.

Similarly, Frazer's discourse on the nature of imperialism and colonialism, and his representation of racial and cultural differences, were in opposition to the underlying assumptions of the research methods he employed in gathering the copious amounts of information required to fill the numerous volumes of *The Golden Bough* and his other anthropological writings. From 1887, Frazer used every agency of the British imperial network to distribute a questionnaire to explorers, travellers, government officials, missionaries and merchants, in order to gather information on the peoples they encountered.[8] Frazer accomplished this accumulation of data with a sense of urgency as the evolutionary narrative of *The Golden Bough* predicted that the 'uncivilised or semi-civilised peoples' would be extinguished by the expansion of colonial civilization. Yet *Greek Sketches*, again coeval with the *Questions* project, assumed the opposite historical inevitability: it is barbarism which destroys civilization. Frazer's classical and anthropological works would seem to indicate a dilemma: if the historical logic of *Greek Sketches* was applied to the imperial conditions which determined the production of Frazer's anthropological writings, then one would have to conclude that Frazer saw the British imperial mission as one of those 'scenes in tragedies which have been acting for centuries' – the triumph of imperial barbarism over the civilizations of others, 'like the fall of Constantinople and the expulsion of the Moors from Granada'. Such a prospect would have been unthinkable for Frazer the evolutionary anthropologist, of course, but Frazer the classicist comes very close to articulating a critique of contemporary colonialism.

Frazer's theories of historical change and development are so radically different in his classical and anthropological writings that the ancient world for Frazer is often an inversion of the contemporary imperial world of his anthropological researches. Nowhere is this tension more apparent than in his treatments of Pausanias's own historical context. For Frazer, Pausanias inhabits a ruin, destroyed by barbarians and oppressed by the Roman imperial presence. Antonine Greece is 'injured by time or defeated by violence'. Greek art was a 'flower that could only bloom in freedom; in the air of slavery it drooped and faded'. The Greeks of Pausanias's time 'had forgotten what it was to be free' in the 'long twilight of decrepitude and decay'. 'No wonder that our traveller paused amid monuments which seemed, in the gathering night of barbarism, to catch and reflect some beams of the bright day that was over' (Frazer 1900a, 37–8, 39, 41, 52). Frazer's Pausanias emerges as an oppressed colonial subject witnessing the eclipse of a traditional culture under the tyranny of a foreign empire. Frazer never explicitly draws the analogy between second-century Greece and Victorian Britain's colonial subjects, but Pausanias's world exists as a powerful antithesis to the imperial discourse which Frazer's anthropology inhabits. The relationship between Frazer's classical scholarship and his anthropological works is essentially paradoxical, and *The Golden Bough* did not grow 'directly out of Pausanias', as Robert Ackerman has argued (Ackerman 58), except in a 'directly' inverted fashion. The Pausanias project, Frazer's life work until anthropology consumed him, and larger than both the first and second editions of *The Golden Bough* combined, is *The Golden Bough* from the native's point of view, in that it projects onto a second-century Greek the contemporary conditions of imperial domination.

Pausanias's identity as a 'native' is, however, a Frazerian construction, and is subject to paradoxical torsions similar to those which affect Frazer's classical scholarship and his anthropological works. 'The real interest of Pausanias', Frazer declares, does not lie with the people nor the country of his time, but with 'those monuments of the past' chosen to satisfy his 'antiquarian tastes' and his 'religious curiosity' (Frazer 1900a, 37–8, 39). Pausanias's interests are in very many respects identical to Frazer's, and as a 'historian of primitive religion' (Ackerman 128), they lead him to the ancient past of his own culture, the relics of the religious (rather than the civic) life of the fourth and fifth centuries BC. In this aspect, Pausanias emerges, at first, as a version of the gentleman antiquarian: amateur, leisured, reasonable, as if '[t]he way of life of a Greek or Roman citizen was not so very different from that of an eighteenth-century, middle class European' (Lévi-Strauss 392). But Pausanias changed shape in Frazer's representation of him, and Frazer's portrait of Pausanias's intellectual development bears a remarkable similarity to Frazer's own biographical transformation, from an antiquarian classicist in a distinctly eighteenth-century mould, to an evolutionary anthropologist. In commenting, for example, on Pausanias's description of the sceptre of Hephaestus, which was wielded by Agamemnon at Chaeronea, and, in Pausanias's time, was guarded by a priest who offered it sacrifices and 'fed [it] flesh and cakes', Frazer writes that:

> A ruder conception of religion than is revealed by this practice of adoring and feeding a staff it might be hard to discover amongst the lowest fetish-worshippers of Western Africa. And this practice was carried on in the native city and in the life-time of the enlightened Plutarch! Truly the extremes of human nature sometimes jostle each other in the street. (Frazer 1900a, 45–6)

Frazer probably had in mind the respect shown to ancestral *ikenga* staffs among the Igbo of Nigeria, which he had commented on in *The Golden Bough*. But in this gesture, Frazer ties classical scholarship to evolutionary anthropology – most notably the Tylorian theory of survivals – and he reads the ancient world of Pausanias's text through contemporary ethnography. The consequences are far-reaching for the perception and representation of the ancient world in the late nineteenth century. The movement from classical antiquarianism to savage ethnography reinvents the image of the Greek world as something infinitely more 'tribal' and uncouth than the received view of the 'Ionian white and gold' of ancient Greek culture, and Frazer, together with Jane Harrison, Gilbert Murray and A.B. Cook, was at the forefront in effecting this sea change. Frazer's Pausanias gives ancient Greece a contemporary African resonance.

Frazer repeatedly applauded Pausanias's 'anthropological' interpretations of the myths he recounts, to the point where the two seemed almost joined in their religious scepticism.

> [U]nder the fierce light of criticism the gods themselves seem on the point of melting away like mist before the sun, leaving behind them nothing but the clear hard face of nature, over which for a while the gorgeous pageantry of their

shifting iridescent shapes had floated in a golden haze. Had Pausanias followed up this line of thought he might, like Schiller, have seen as in a vision the bright procession of the gods winding up the long slopes of Olympus, sometimes pausing to look back sadly at a world where they were needed no more. (Frazer 1900a, 85–6)

Frazer employs Pausanias's scepticism of religious belief to express the covert sub-text of *The Golden Bough* and his other anthropological writings, and this is probably the closest Frazer ever came to articulating his own conviction that all religious truths 'melt away like mist before the sun' of rational interpretation informed by anthropological knowledge. By inference, Christianity is another such 'golden haze' which anthropology can show to have evolved from savage cults of resurrection and the immortality of the soul.

But Pausanias did not follow 'up this line of thought', he turned away from what Schiller and Frazer saw, and he recanted his scepticism. He had a 'change of heart in Arcadia' and the tales 'he had once ridiculed as absurd he now finds to be full of deep, if hidden, wisdom'. '[I]f he had a glimpse of the higher truth [by which Frazer meant atheism], it was only a flash-light that went out leaving him in darkness.' 'The scoffer had become devout' (Frazer 1900a, 86).

> The same antiquarian and religious tincture which appears in Pausanias's account of the Greek people colours his description of the country. The mountains which he climbs, the plains which he traverses ... the very flowers that spring beside his path hardly exist for him but as they are sacred to some god or tenanted by some spirit of the elements, or because they call up some memory of the past, some old romantic story of unhappy love or death. (Frazer 1900a, 31–2)

Written more than a decade before Lévy-Bruhl's conjectures on the nature of 'primitive mentalities', Frazer finally presents Pausanias as also possessing a 'savage mind'. Pausanias does not simply see objects as elements in a semiotics of differences; he perceives the world in terms of the ideal qualities and contents of objects. 'Civilised' rationality has little place in Pausanias's field of vision, for Pausanias is steeped in a magical, primitive perception, which opens a window for Frazer onto the mind of the savage.[9] Frazer will elaborate this theme, in the second edition of *The Golden Bough*, into an evolutionary theory, which will dominate his anthropological discourse and profoundly shape his representation of the 'savage' subject. Pausanias emerges from Frazer's account of him as an extraordinary hybrid: like Frazer, an 'historian of primitive religion', antiquarian and anthropologist, and a man utterly unlike Frazer, a religiously devout, even – in Frazer's anthropological lexicon – a 'primitive' believer.

Pausanias's hybrid identity combines 'the extremes of human nature', but the radically split subject that Frazer presents applies more readily to Frazer himself and the modes of representation he employed in both of his disciplines. The progressive evolutionary paradigms of Frazer's anthropology are thrown into disorder by the degenerative trajectory of the Mycenaean historical master narrative. History cannot be both Pausanias's Mycenae and *The Golden Bough*, yet the two strands form a helix of deep contradiction, which existed simultaneously in Frazer's writings. Similarly, the juxtaposition of classical and anthropological scholarship transforms the ancient Greek into the contemporary savage, but it also compels Frazer to admit another, alternative voice – Pausanias the native – into his anthropological conjectures. The scene of 'desolate grandeur' of Mycenae, and the ethnically cleansed landscapes of the Scottish Highlands or al-Andalus to which he compares it, are images of conquest and colonization, and Pausanias's ancient world forces Frazer to a recognition of an imperial regime which is utterly absent from his treatment of anthropological materials. Frazer projects these subversive secrets and disciplinary discords onto Pausanias himself, depicting the struggle between 'extremes of human nature' within him, and drawing the ancient other ever closer to the anthropological other. But those extremes belong more properly within Frazer, and it is only in the relative safety of his classical scholarship that Frazer can begin to explore the contents, the contradictions and the subversive significance of his anthropological researches.

The network of textual transmissions which constitute the discourse on Mycenae – from Homer to Pausanias, to Schliemann, who used the latter to find the former, to Frazer, in his three guises as classicist, anthropologist and travel writer – is characteristic of modernist representations of both the ancient and the primitive/colonized worlds. Frazer's often contradictory conceptions of the antique and the primitive represent a double myth of origins, twin *parousiae* of the sources of human culture, which played a central role in re-imagining the ancient and the colonized for painters, art historians, poets, novelists, essayists, anthropologists, psychoanalysts, political theorists and cultural critics. But the Frazerian construction of the ancient and the primitive as 'genesis' served to reinforce the modernist sense of a contemporary closure of history, their sense of an ending. The ancient past of Pausanias's world can only be 'recovered' in archaeological fragments, dispersed and distributed down through time in ever-diminishing particles: human genealogies are to be found, quite literally, in ruins. Any attempt to construct an origin is confronted by the ruined nature of its materials. Mycenae is a catastrophe of history and the spectre of these ruins haunt modernity. Ultimately, Mycenae's 'desolate grandeur' is not a symbol of patrimony, but an image of disinheritance.

## Notes

1   Schliemann also claimed to have discovered the grave of Atreus. Later archaeological analysis revealed that Schliemann had been mistaken in his identification of the burials at Mycenae and Hissarlik: excavations in Turkey uncovered multiple 'Troys', and the grave masks at Mycenae predated the putative chronology of the Homeric heroes.
2   Ulrich Friedrich Richard von Wilamowitz-Moellendorff (1848–1931), usually abbreviated to Wilamowitz, had a profound impact on Greek studies through his translations into German of Euripides, Callimachus and Pindar, and his literary criticism of Homer. He was also a great controversialist, most notably with Nietzsche over his *Birth of Tragedy* (1872).
3   Habicht writes, 'If just the one passage on Mycenae had survived from Pausanias' entire work, Pausanias could still claim a place in the annals of history' (31).
4   Also cited by Christian Habicht, *Pausanias' Guide to Ancient Greece*, 164.
5   It is also, in some respects, a rival to Pausanias's text, because as the Pausanias controversy lost its currency (and academic national rivalries were eclipsed by bloodier conflicts in the First World War), *Pausanias and other Greek Sketches*, was retitled for the second edition of 1917 and Pausanias's name was relegated to the subtitle, as the book became *Studies in Greek Scenery, Legend and History*.
6   Pausanias had travelled not only in Greece but to Syria, Jordan, Jerusalem, Antioch, Thebes and Byzantium. Frazer visited Aricia (Lake Nemi) in 1900.
7   The first edition of *The Golden Bough* was published in 1890, the second in 1900.
8   Frazer's *Questions on the Manners, Customs, Religion, Superstitions, etc. of Uncivilized or Semi-Civilized Peoples* began in 1887 as a privately published pamphlet of thirteen pages. The *Journal of the Anthropological Institute* published a supplement in 1889, which expanded the questionnaire. In 1907, Cambridge University Press undertook to print, free of charge to Frazer, a revised version, and Frazer radically overhauled and expanded the *Questions* of 1887 and the *JAI* supplement. The pamphlet more than doubled its length to fifty-one pages and from 213 questions to 507. Further reprintings by Cambridge University Press in 1910 and 1916 replicated this 1907 version. See Richards, chapter 5.
9   Wittgenstein's ironic remark on *The Golden Bough* captures the sense of 'difference' which underpins Frazer's treatment of Pausanias: 'Frazer is much more savage than most of his savages, for these savages will not be so far from any understanding of spiritual matters as an Englishman of the twentieth century. His explanations of the primitive observances are much cruder than the sense of the observances themselves' (Wittgenstein 102).

# Bibliography

Ackerman, Robert (1990), *J.G. Frazer: His Life and Work* (1987), Cambridge: Cambridge University Press, Canto edition.

Downey, R.A. (1970), *Frazer and the Golden Bough*, London: Gollancz.

Frazer, J.G. (1898), *Pausanias's Description of Greece*, 6 vols, London: Macmillan.

Frazer, J.G. (1900a), *Pausanias and other Greek Sketches*, London: Macmillan, reprinted as *Studies in Greek Scenery, Legend and History: Selected from his Commentary on Pausanias' 'Description of Greece'*, London: Macmillan, 1917.

Frazer, J.G. (1900b), *The Golden Bough*, 2nd edn, 3 vols, London: Macmillan.

Habicht, Christian (1985), *Pausanias' Guide to Ancient Greece*, Berkeley: University of California Press.

Lévi-Strauss, Claude (1975), *Tristes Tropiques* (1955), trans. John and Doreen Weightman. Harmondsworth: Penguin.

Lévy-Bruhl, Lucien (1985), *How Natives Think* [*Les fonctions mentales dans les societes inferieures*, 1910], trans. Lilian A. Clare, Princeton: Princeton University Press.

Ludwig, Emil (1931), *Schliemann of Troy: The Story of a Goldseeker*, London: Putnam.

Richards, David (1994), *Masks of Difference: Cultural Representations in Anthropology, Literature and Art*, Cambridge: Cambridge University Press.

Schuchhardt, C. (1891), *Schliemann's Excavations: An Archaeological and Historical Study*, trans. Eugénie Sellers, London: Macmillan.

Wittgenstein, Ludwig (1979), 'Remarks on Frazer's *The Golden Bough*', ed. R. Rhees, trans. A.C. Miles, Retford: Brynmill.

Chapter Eleven

# Editing Private Papers:
# Three Examples from Dreiser

James L.W. West III

Most scholarly editors, in their discussions of theory and procedure, have focused on public texts – poems, stories, novels, essays and drama scripts prepared by authors for print or performance. Less consideration has been given to the editing of private papers: letters, journals, diaries, fragments, trial drafts and aborted manuscripts. Questions of presentation and audience are foremost here; annotation and intention also figure in the mix. In this essay I shall discuss several difficulties that arose during the preparation of three editions of documents that survive in the papers of Theodore Dreiser. The editions, all published by the University of Pennsylvania Press, are Dreiser's *American Diaries*, his *Russian Diaries* and his autobiographical account *An Amateur Laborer*. These are private texts: either Dreiser did not write them for publication, or he set out to create them for print but at some point abandoned the effort. The decisions discussed here were made by the editors of the University of Pennsylvania Dreiser Edition. Some of these decisions worked out to the satisfaction of all parties; others did not, though it is hard now to see how the choices might have been made differently.

\* \* \*

The first set of decisions had to do with seven diaries that Dreiser kept during the first three decades of this century. These diaries were brought together and published in 1982 under the title *American Diaries, 1902–1926*. All seven diaries were kept by Dreiser in the United States, though in different locations: Philadelphia, Savannah, Greenwich Village, Indiana, the Jersey Shore, Hollywood and Florida. Dreiser was an intermittent diarist, typically keeping such journals in periods of unhappiness or travel or intense creativity. He saved these diaries, and they are important sources of information for anyone interested in his life and thought.

Dreiser was not a confessional diarist or a particularly meditative one; in most entries the style is workmanlike and the text often no more than a log of a day's activities. But some passages are memorable, and the effect of the whole accumulation of detail – as in his novels – is arresting and revealing. In these diaries one finds a record of how Dreiser lived his life: what he did, whom he saw, what women he was involved with, what he was writing, how he was pushing ahead in his literary career. And in one of them, the 1902–3 Philadelphia diary, he left us a harrowing record of a period of neurasthenia, or 'nerve sickness', that was pivotal in his life. It was obvious that these documents, all unpublished, should see print.

The question was whether to correct them for publication. Dreiser was a poor speller and grammarian; he knew this, and was sensitive about it, and employed personal editors and amanuenses throughout his life to help him put his public writings into respectable shape. These American diaries, by contrast, were private documents, not meant for publication; the prevailing orthodoxy in editorial circles is that such texts should be published with as little emendation as possible, in order to capture the flavour of the originals. The problem was that Dreiser had suffered during his career from a perception among critics that he was badly educated, clumsy and even oafish in literary style – that he was a rude talent who happened somehow to write three or four of the most powerful novels of his period. Would an edition of these diaries, preserving all of Dreiser's faults in grammar, spelling and style, reinforce this image? Would it give ammunition to those critics (still very much in operation) who would dismiss Dreiser's work as subliterate?

We had the example of F. Scott Fitzgerald's letters to contemplate. Fitzgerald, a Midwesterner like Dreiser, was an extremely erratic speller, and his grammar, like Dreiser's, was not always up to par. But Fitzgerald wrote wonderful letters: funny, revealing, newsy and full of fine turns of phrase and perceptive insights. In 1963 Andrew Turnbull, who had recently written a popular biography of Fitzgerald, edited *The Letters of F. Scott Fitzgerald*, a lengthy collection published by Charles Scribner's Sons. This was the first appearance in book form of any of Fitzgerald's correspondence; Turnbull and Scribners made the decision to clean up the texts, silently correcting Fitzgerald's misspellings and remedying his grammatical lapses. Fitzgerald, like Dreiser, had drawn criticism during his career for being undereducated and intellectually lightweight. His shortcomings in orthography and grammar seemed of a piece with that portrait. Turnbull and Scribners did not say so – indeed, there is no word at all in *Letters* about the editing of the texts – but apparently they decided to short-circuit such criticisms by fixing the mistakes in Fitzgerald's letters for him. Should we do the same for Dreiser in his diaries?

Our decision for the *American Diaries* was not to correct the texts. To do so, we believed, would alter the diaries in some fundamental way. Accordingly they were presented in a near-diplomatic transcription. Such misspellings as 'recieve', 'excitment', 'opourtunity', 'your' (for 'you're') and 'accross' were preserved, as were faulty agreements between subjects and verbs, misplaced or dangling modifiers, floating participles and errant pronoun references. Underlinings were printed as underscores rather than italics; odd spacing was reproduced as nearly as was possible in a printed medium. Some emendation was necessary: a few substantive changes were made to clarify confusing or nonsensical language, and periods were added where necessary, since Dreiser, in his haste, often omitted them from the ends of sentences. Place names were corrected when possible, because Dreiser often got them wrong, and erroneous dates for the entries were repaired, because Dreiser was sometimes inattentive about such details. To have left dates and place names uncorrected, we thought, would not preserve anything essential in the diaries and would surely confuse scholars and biographers. All emendations of these kinds were recorded in an apparatus.

One of the diaries (perhaps the most interesting of the seven) was kept by Dreiser in 1917 and 1918 while he was living the bohemian life in Greenwich Village. He was involved during this period with a woman named Estelle Bloom Kubitz, whom he calls 'Bert' or sometimes 'Gloom' in the diary. She functioned as his secretary and typist and was his lover as well. But Dreiser, who was unapologetic about his sexual 'varietism', was involved with other women during this period, and Estelle was unhappy about the situation, though she had the same privileges. As his secretary she had access to his papers and therefore, at some point, perhaps while he was away from New York, she made a typed transcription of this diary. It contains the names of Dreiser's lovers and details of his various sexual liaisons, along with much else. Estelle later turned this transcription over to H.L. Mencken, Dreiser's ally in the literary press, who was himself involved with her sister Marion. Mencken, as we know from his own letters and private diaries, was curious about Dreiser's sexual escapades; probably Estelle knew this and thought that the transcript would entertain him. He also functioned as a confidant for her, and she had confessed to him her frustration over Dreiser's womanizing. Perhaps she thought that the diary transcript would help Mencken sympathize with her, or at least that it would be documentary proof of her tales about Dreiser's wanderings. Whatever the case, Mencken saved the transcript and left it among the papers that he bequeathed to the New York Public Library. It is a happy circumstance that he did so because the original diary no longer survives. Estelle Kubitz's transcription is all that we have.

From an editor's standpoint, this transcription presents difficulties. Estelle was in the habit of correcting Dreiser's spelling and grammar as she typed his essays and novel chapters. She seems to have done the same as she transcribed this diary. Thus the surviving text of the Greenwich Village diary is more nearly correct and 'finished' than the texts of the other diaries. One might therefore argue that characteristic Dreiserian errors – misspellings and other blunders – should be reintroduced into the text of this particular diary, this to create an impression of 'authenticity'. No truly serious consideration was given to such a strategy; it would have involved much editorial intervention and would have been artificial. Still, the result is that the Greenwich Village diary, which falls third in the published volume, gives readers a text that is suddenly correct and polished, unlike the ones before and after it. Only if these readers have read the textual introduction before proceeding with the diaries will they understand what is happening.

One feature of these diaries required compromise. Especially when he travelled, Dreiser saved various items that he picked up along the way. Thus one often finds, interleaved in his diaries, much detritus – menus, photographs, ticket stubs, photographs and train schedules. Certainly these items contribute to the flavour and character of the original diaries, but practically we could not reproduce everything. We chose therefore to include facsimiles of the most important or visually interesting things and to omit the rest.

The result, I believe, was in most ways satisfactory. The *American Diaries* volume was published and was widely reviewed and discussed. A voice not available before – Dreiser's voice in the diaries, which is quite unlike his fictional voice – was now heard. The diaries generated a good bit of discussion of Dreiser and his career, and they were of great use to Richard Lingeman, whose two-volume biography of Dreiser, published in 1986 and 1990, has become standard. The renderings of the entries on the printed page do capture rather much of the flavour of the originals without seeming fussy or contrived. The edition sold nearly through its clothbound run and was reprinted in a scholarly paperback.

\* \* \*

The second of the Dreiser documents that deserved publication was a manuscript which he had entitled 'An Amateur Laborer'. This manuscript, which he produced in 1904, is related closely to the Philadelphia diary mentioned above, the journal in which he had kept a record of his period of depression. By 1904 Dreiser had recovered sufficiently well to think of putting these experiences into a nonfiction account, which he meant to publish. He began the manuscript – describing his nerve-sickness, tracing his mental decline and detailing his musings on suicide. He then told of his rescue by his songwriter brother Paul and recounted his activities at William Muldoon's sanitarium, a rehabilitation camp to which Paul sent him. Finally Dreiser narrated some of his subsequent experiences as a day-labourer on the New York Central Railroad. A doctor had prescribed outdoor labour to Dreiser as a cure for his depression, but he found himself inept and clumsy as a physical worker. Hence the title 'An Amateur Laborer'.

Dreiser never finished this book or published it in its entirety. He could not interest a publisher in the account; he produced twenty-five chapters in more or less finished form and left at least as much other fragmentary material with the manuscript – trial drafts of episodes that were meant for later chapters or sometimes only passages or sentences that he thought he might work into the narrative at some point. Dreiser did return to this material repeatedly during his later career. Some of it was used in his novel *The 'Genius'* (1915) and some in various other articles in newspapers and magazines. Other laboring experiences found their way into the sketches in *Twelve Men* (1919) or into short stories. These later reworkings, not surprisingly, depart considerably from the narratives that Dreiser had set down in the original 'Laborer' manuscript, as he thought back over the material and recast it for various purposes. The unpublished manuscript, written soon after the experiences on which it was based, was almost surely the most reliable of the accounts. Certainly it seemed to deserve publication.

This manuscript reveals a good deal about how Dreiser assembled a book, during this period at least. The surviving materials suggest that he worked first in fragments and short bursts, setting down incidents or remembered emotions in brief sections of holograph draft. Then he seems to have stitched these together into a narrative, providing a thematic or moral framework to accommodate them and making a fair copy as he went. The twenty-five complete chapters that survive are in relatively finished form, verbally and structurally. They appear to be fair copies, ready for a typist. The fragments, on the other hand, are the 'leading edge' of the manuscript – disordered and preliminary, as if Dreiser had yet to decide how to fit them into a narrative sequence.

How could a printed edition reflect these characteristics of the surviving manuscript? What distinctions could we make between finished and unfinished material? Our decision was to present the twenty-five completed chapters as 'public' texts, with spelling corrected and grammar faults remedied. This did not demand heavy emendation, but it did require some, and the texts lost something. They were certainly not rendered in such a way as to capture their flavour in manuscript. An argument could have been mounted to print them in diplomatic transcription, and such an argument would have carried a good deal of force. Whenever unfinished work is issued in 'public' form, it invites reviews and subsequent criticism which consider it as fully realized writing. This was clearly not the case with the first twenty-five chapters of 'An Amateur Laborer'. It is impossible to know what Dreiser would have done further to the texts of these chapters, had he completed the entire narrative, but he would surely have performed additional work on them. Still, in our judgment he had brought these units to a finished enough form to warrant their publication in corrected texts. After all, the converse is also true: if interesting but not fully completed material is published in diplomatic transcription, it is sometimes considered to be only of passing interest, wood shavings from the workshop floor.

The fragments, however, did qualify as wood shavings. A selection of these was made, and they were included in the rear of the published volume, but in 'private' texts, with misspellings and grammar faults and incomplete punctuation and other idiosyncrasies preserved. This strategy, we believed, would preserve their contrasting character, reflect Dreiser's composing methods and would prevent them from being considered or critiqued as fully finished work. The only disappointment here was that it was impossible to include all of the fragments. Many of them repeated one another; in a few cases we included two versions of the same incident for comparison, but in most cases we published only what appeared to be the fullest and latest draft of a passage. Other material was so fragmentary or brief as not to have much meaning when read alone. Thus the final volume, *An Amateur Laborer*, published in 1983, was an editorial confection. It presented a work in progress, showing the nearly finished chapters in public texts and the parts still under composition in private texts. The resulting book, if artificially constructed, still seemed to reflect the state of the surviving document. *An Amateur Laborer*, like *American Diaries*, was widely reviewed and discussed, sold through its hardback issue and went into a scholarly paperback.

* * *

The third of the documents, a diary kept by Dreiser during a trip to Soviet Russia in 1927 and 1928, was the most difficult to edit. Dreiser was invited by the Soviet government in October of 1927 to come to Moscow for a celebration of the tenth anniversary of the revolution. He was one among some 1,500 international celebrities – writers, artists, journalists, political figures and others – who were so invited. The Soviets hoped that good impressions of their experiment in government would be carried away and that the writers, in particular, would publish favourable accounts of what they had seen. Accordingly the hosts managed the tours carefully, showing only the most successful factories and farming collectives and exposing the visitors only to true believers in the Communist cause. Dreiser was naturally sceptical. He therefore asked that he be allowed to remain in the Soviet Union for a longer period, during which he meant to travel and see what he called 'the real, unofficial Russia'. His hosts were reluctantly obliging, and Dreiser ended up staying until January 1928, visiting Moscow, Leningrad, Kiev, Kharkov, Rostov, Baku, Sevastopol, Odessa and many other locations.

His secretary and companion on these travels was a young American woman named Ruth Epperson Kennell. She was a political pilgrim who had converted to Communism and now made her living by translating and editing English texts for the state publishing house. She and Dreiser were attracted to one another and fairly soon became lovers. She was indispensable to him in his travels, arranging for him to meet people who were not approved by his government hosts, dealing with language and money problems and taking notes on his conversations and on his visits to museums and historical sites.

Dreiser had begun his diary in longhand in New York on the day he received his invitation from the Soviet government. He had continued to make entries on the voyage to Europe and during stops in Paris and Berlin, on his way to Moscow. But the keeping of the diary became burdensome, so he asked Kennell to take over the labour for him. What is more, he made the unusual request that she keep it in his own voice, using the 'I' pronoun to mean him, not her. In effect he asked her to assume his identity in the diary. Initially Kennell found the task awkward but soon took to it, and much of the latter part of the diary was typed by her, in Dreiser's voice, on a portable typewriter that she carried on the journeys they took together. Some of the material was dictated to her by Dreiser; the rest she composed herself. Dreiser continued to make holograph entries from time to time, but the bulk of the diary, during the last six weeks of the journey, was kept by Kennell.

Dreiser had difficulty taking his diary out of the Soviet Union when he departed. Unbeknownst to him, Kennell had sent a carbon copy of the document to her superiors at VOKS, the government agency which handled cultural relations with foreign visitors. They were wary of the use he would make of the document after he returned to the United States. Eventually they did let Dreiser take the diary, however, and he had it with him in New York in February. Probably Kennell leaked the diary to protect herself: Dreiser was not entirely impressed by what he was seeing in the Soviet Union, and he had been obstreperous and aggressive in questioning some of the officials he had been allowed to see. What he wrote about the Soviet experiment, once he returned to the West, might not suit his hosts. Kennell must have felt it in her best interest to keep her superiors informed. The document that she sent to them survives today in the State Archives of the Russian Federation in Moscow. Kennell also kept a second, secret diary in which she recorded her own private thoughts about her work with Dreiser. This diary no longer appears to survive, but Kennell mentions it and draws upon it in her book *Theodore Dreiser and the Soviet Union*, published in 1969.

What were Dreiser's intentions for this diary? Possibly he thought of it only as an *aide-mémoire* for a book he meant to write about his journey, rather like the travel notes he had kept on the trips that he described in such volumes as *A Traveler at Forty* (1913) and *A Hoosier Holiday* (1915). But the character of this Russian diary is different from the jottings in those earlier journals. Dreiser sets down conversations in quoted dialogue and identifies references that would have been plain to him but would have needed explanation to a reader. After he returned to New York in early 1928 he spent a good bit of time with the diary, taking Kennell's sections, which she had given to him in loose typed sheets, emending and augmenting them in his own hand, cutting them up and pasting them on the leaves of the blue-bound diary that he had used for his holograph entries. It is quite possible, then, that Dreiser had plans to publish this document as a travel diary, a genre that was then popular. The surviving text shows indications of this intent, though Dreiser did not carry through on it. For some reason he abandoned his revising and never published the diary. Instead he took a short-cut, bringing together a series of articles that he had written for the *New York World*, revising and expanding them in places and publishing the result as *Dreiser Looks at Russia* (1928). This is one of Dreiser's weakest performances, a series of quickly written journalistic pieces which did little to advance his reputation. It is also the book for which he was accused of plagiarism by Dorothy Thompson, who believed that he had copied material from her own book *The New Russia* (see Lingeman, *An American Journey*, 315–17).

The accounts in the surviving Russian diary are much more revealing and vivid than those in *Dreiser Looks at Russia*. The diary includes colourful accounts of Dreiser's wanderings in Paris, where he met the young writer Ernest Hemingway, and it contains his observations on the 'large' personality, the figure who dominates his times by superior intellect and ambition. He had met a number of such men in Russia and had interviewed them: the cinema pioneer Sergei Eisenstein, the drama director Konstantin Stanislavsky, the political figures Anastas Molotov, Vladimir Mayakovsky, Karl Radek and Nikolai Bukharin, and the religious leader Archbishop Platon. The diary records his exchanges with them along with numerous other interviews with lesser figures – party bureaucrats, local priests and workers in factories and communes. Certainly, then, the diary deserved publication. It was, in fact, one of the last documents of its kind from the 1920s and 1930s to remain unpublished, and we were confident that it would find an audience and a continuing readership.

Is the Russian diary a public or private document? From the evidence on its pages, it appears to be halfway between. With his handwritten revisions and augmentations, and his cutting and pasting, Dreiser seems to have been bringing the diary toward publication in some form. Whether he would have rewritten Kennell's sections is unclear, but if he had not then the published diary would have had two very different textures and styles of prose. Perhaps he meant to have a rough copy made of the primary document, then to transform it all into his own language, but this cannot be known since he took his work no further.

It might conceivably be argued, then, that an editor should bring the text all the way into public form, carrying through on what seem to have been Dreiser's intentions. Such a course of action, however, would involve very heavy correction and emendation; it would still produce a document unfinished in organization and thought; and it would encourage the diary to be interpreted as fully realized work when plainly it is not. For these reasons it seemed improper to present the diary in public dress. The obvious course was to employ the same strategy used for the *American Diaries* and to publish this Russian diary as a private document.

Once that decision had been made, the problem was to differentiate Dreiser's parts of the diary, written in his own hand, from the parts typed by Kennell. Several possibilities were available. The first was to set all of the text in the same roman typeface but to screen or shade Dreiser's parts. This would make readily apparent what he had written and what she had typed, but it would also create headaches for typesetters and proofreaders and would produce a text which literally looked 'spotty' in the places in which Dreiser had only emended a word or phrase here and there.

A second possibility was to employ two typefaces, a 'script' face for Dreiser's parts and a 'typed' face for Kennell's. Compositors could indeed provide those faces, and two were selected for a sample, but parts of the book, especially toward the end of the diary, would be set almost exclusively in the typescript face. This would give the published volume the look of a 'typescript' book, such as those published by companies which specialize in secondary bibliographies and unrevised dissertations, and which often publish these books by shooting the image of the text directly from typescripts supplied to them by their authors. The volume we meant to publish, from the University of Pennsylvania Press, was projected to carry a fairly elevated retail price, too high for a 'typescript' book. And too, we thought of Dreiser's diary as an important document from a pivotal period of Soviet–American history; we hoped for attention and serious reviews. Books set in typescript usually do not receive such treatment. The idea of using a typescript face for Kennell's sections was scrapped.

We settled finally on italic and roman faces, italic for Dreiser and roman for Kennell. This seemed the most direct approach and promised the fewest difficulties for the compositors. We also decided to set the diaries in 'clear text', meaning that there would be no symbols or diacritical marks to indicate cancelled readings. Something was lost here, since it might be of interest to see what Kennell had first written and what Dreiser later substituted for it, but a careful trip through the text indicated that nothing significant would be sacrificed – only some changes in verb tense or pronoun reference. For the most part Dreiser had augmented her text, not changed it. A purist might object to our decision only to print final readings, but the gain in readability, we believed, would overbalance such criticisms.

Proofs were duly typeset, and the checking began. The only sour note, oddly, was the ampersand in the italic face we had chosen. Dreiser used an ampersand in his handwriting, but it was a quickly inscribed mark resembling a plus-sign. The ampersand in the italic face, by contrast, was an elaborate affair with swirls and curlicues. I should have noticed this problem on the typesetting sample, but I did not. The resulting text of Dreiser's handwritten entries is marred, as a result, by these ampersands. If the aim of the edition is to reproduce the flavour and look of Dreiser's text as nearly as is possible in a typeset medium, then we failed with the ampersand. It would have taken him five seconds apiece to inscribe ampersands of such calligraphic complexity in his diary; plainly he did not do this. He was jotting these entries down, recording his experiences and impressions with no thought of how the page would look. I asked whether all ampersands in the proofs might be changed to plus-marks, perhaps by a global command, but I learned that the plus-mark in this italic type face took up much less em-space than the ampersand, and that substitution of plus-marks throughout would cause the line endings to fall differently and make it necessary to create a new shooting copy for every page in the book, an expensive process. Thus we had to settle for the ampersands, but in my view they disfigure the text. The lesson I learned was to pay more attention to the preliminary dummies for future books, but it was too late for this one. On such small matters does an editor's satisfaction sometimes rest.

The ampersand was a minor irritation. A much larger problem was the title-page. How should it read? What should the title of the book be? And how should the byline read? These were important questions involving the nature of the collaboration between Dreiser and Kennell. The first page of the surviving document was headed 'Russian Diary'. Should the title-page of the published book then read '*Russian Diary*' and the byline 'by Theodore Dreiser'? Perhaps, but what of Kennell's contribution? Was she not the co-author? Should the byline read 'by Theodore Dreiser and Ruth Kennell'? Or perhaps 'by Theodore Dreiser with Ruth Kennell' – rather like a ghost-written book? Certainly Kennell had composed long sections of the diary in her own words, working from notes that she had taken, or from Dreiser's dictation, but she had done so in his employ (he paid her wages and expenses throughout) and at his direction. She had written in his voice, using his persona. Dreiser and Kennell had together created the physical text, but he possessed the results; he had cut and arranged and pasted her typescripts into the surviving diary; he owned the document and its abstract literary rights. Was this diary then a truly collaborative performance?

Such considerations, we knew, touched on current gender politics. If the diary were published under Dreiser's byline alone, then would we not be turning him into the kind of man who appropriates the ideas and labour of women in subordinate positions and presents them as his own? Perhaps, but he had done so before in his career, using the editorial talents of such women as Estelle Kubitz and (especially) Louise Campbell to help him put his fiction and other writing into shape for publication. Those writings had never been published under a dual byline and had never been considered to be true collaborations by Dreiser biographers and scholars.

Our decision was to use no byline and to entitle the book *Dreiser's Russian Diary*. The possessive word '*Dreiser's*' had several meanings in our minds.

This was a record of Dreiser's journey; it had value because he was who he was. He caused the record to be kept; it was an account of what had happened to him, not to Kennell. She wrote parts of it, but under his instructions and in his voice. And finally, he owned the resulting diary, the paper and ink and binding. The possessive form seemed appropriate. The book we would publish would be an edition of the surviving document, of 'Dreiser's Russian diary', which had rested unpublished among his papers for almost seventy years.

This was not an altogether satisfactory solution, but it seemed an acceptable compromise. I had hoped that the Library of Congress publication data on the copyright page might somehow reflect Kennell's role in the making of the diary, perhaps by listing her as a collaborator or assistant, but I learned that the Library of Congress has rules for the form of such data. One of these is that for a name to be listed in an authorial role, it must appear on the title-page. Dreiser's name would appear on the title-page because the book was to be published as '*Dreiser's Russian Diary*'. Kennell's name would not be there, so she could not be listed in the Library of Congress data.

By way of balancing the scales, Kennell was identified in the first paragraph of the preface as Dreiser's 'secretary and companion for the trip', who 'contributed significantly to the composition of the diary'. Her role in its making was described clearly in the introduction, written by my co-editor Thomas P. Riggio, and in the editorial principles section, composed by me. Riggio, in addition, emphasized the importance of Kennell to Dreiser as his first teacher about the realities of everyday life in the Soviet Union; she argued politics and social theory with him during his journeys and influenced him strongly in his final estimate of the Soviet experiment, a subject about which he was to write from time to time throughout the rest of his career. Still, her name was not on the title-page or copyright page. I wish it had been. It was impossible, though, to solve the question satisfactorily, and I cannot now see how things might have done differently without creating other distortions and problems.

\* \* \*

These three cases – from Dreiser's *American Diaries*, his *Russian Diary* and his manuscript for *An Amateur Laborer* – provide good examples of questions that often face editors of private documents. Usually such documents survive in only one copy; thus one avoids the difficulties created by multiple texts and versions. But private documents still present problems involving intention, authorship, arrangement and possible emendation. For a scholarly editor a private document is certainly not, as the saying goes, a piece of cake.

## Bibliography

Von Bardeleben, Renate (2000), 'Dreiser's Diaristic Mode', *Dreiser Studies* 31 (Spring), 26–42.

Dreiser, Theodore (1982), *American Diaries, 1902–1926*, eds Thomas P. Riggio, James L.W. West III and Neda M. Westlake, Philadelphia: University of Pennsylvania Press.

Dreiser, Theodore (1983), *An Amateur Laborer*, eds Richard W. Dowell, James L.W. West III and Neda M. Westlake, Philadelphia: University of Pennsylvania Press.

Dreiser, Theodore (1996), *Dreiser's Russian Diary*, eds Thomas P. Riggio and James L.W. West III, Philadelphia: University of Pennsylvania Press.

Fitzgerald, F. Scott (1963), *The Letters of F. Scott Fitzgerald*, ed. Andrew Turnbull, New York: Charles Scribner's Sons.

Kennell, Ruth Epperson (1969), *Theodore Dreiser and the Soviet Union, 1927–1945*, New York: International Publishers.

Lingeman, Richard (1986), *Theodore Dreiser: At the Gates of the City, 1871–1907*, New York: G.P. Putnam's Sons.

Lingeman, Richard (1990), *Theodore Dreiser: An American Journey, 1908–1945*, New York: G.P. Putnam's Sons.

## Chapter Twelve

# Coercive Suggestion: Rhetoric and Community in *Revaluation*

### Martin Dodsworth

### I

In somewhat grudging praise Rene Wellek described F.R. Leavis's *Revaluation: Tradition and Development in English Poetry* (1936) as being 'in a sketchy manner, the first consistent attempt I know of to write the history of English poetry from a twentieth-century point of view', and that might be reason enough to write about it here, as a form of transmission of texts in context. Leavis's iconic status for the post-war generation, exemplified best in Martin Green's study, *A Mirror for Anglo-Saxons* (1960), adds further justification, and Wellek's own misunderstanding of the style and intention of the book completes the case for an account of *Revaluation* in the light of its genesis and subsequent elaboration. Wellek says of it:

> the focus and tone of the chapters is rather various; the book, made-up of articles, though making a whole, shifts in its preoccupations; the chapter on Milton is an attack on his style and verse pursuing Eliot's objections, while the essay on Pope strikingly shows how Pope was inspired by an ideal of civilization in which Art and Nature should be reconnected and humane culture be 'kept appropriately aware of its derivation from and dependence on the culture of the soil ...' (242)

The implication is that, thanks to its first appearing as a succession of discrete articles, *Revaluation* is something of a mess. I am going to argue the stylistic integrity of the text and, in particular, the centrality of the chapter on Milton, which Wellek evidently finds eccentric. In order to do this I shall consider the development of *Revaluation* from the lectures which Leavis gave in 1932 to the finished book, since the context in which the book was originally published, that is, the journal *Scrutiny*, is what gives the style its peculiar inflection.

Wellek was evidently unaware of these lectures, which are mentioned by Ian MacKillop in his biography of Leavis:

he started 1932 with a set of lectures on quite new material, a survey of English
poetry from the metaphysical poets of the seventeenth century up to John Keats.
The series was called 'Tradition and Development in English Poetry (with texts)'
… Students were asked to bring Q's *Oxford Book of English Verse* and Grierson's
anthology of metaphysical poetry to the first lecture. The lectures given in those
two terms [sic] were the foundation of *Revaluation*. (135, 170)

That MacKillop is right is suggested by the fact that, in the first published
version of the chapter on Pope, Leavis amplifies a reference to Jonson by
citing the *Oxford Book*: 'Jonson (the Jonson represented in the *Oxford Book*
by Numbers 192 and 193)' (73). This reference, surely deriving from the
lectures where students would be book in hand, was subsequently edited out.
MacKillop's conjecture fits not only the subtitle of the book but also Leavis's
own statement in its 'Introduction' that:

> Though the chapters of this book were written as separate essays, the book was
> conceived first and the essays were conceived as part of it. The book was planned
> when I was writing my *New Bearings in English Poetry*, which offers an account
> of the situation as it appears today; indeed the planning of the one book was
> involved in the planning of the other. (1)

Perhaps the reference back to the time of *New Bearings* exaggerates a little –
there is no means of telling – but the story is a plausible one, given the excursion
into literary history in the first chapter of that book. On the other hand, *New
Bearings* was published early in 1932, so that the lectures themselves were
largely subsequent to the writing of it. What there can be no doubt about is the
planning of *Revaluation* as a whole prior to the writing of the articles. This
follows from the fact of the lecture series.

These articles, which all first appeared in *Scrutiny*, the journal of which,
since its third number at the end of 1932, Leavis had been an editor, indeed
the principal editor, did not appear in the same order as they do in the book.
Leavis began with Chapter 2, and followed it by Chapters 3, 5 and 6, only
then going back to publish the first version of Chapter 1, followed by Chapters
7 and 4. Chapter 2 is 'Milton's Verse'; Leavis began publishing his book with
the very chapter to which, in the passage quoted at the beginning of this essay,
Wellek seemed to take exception. The first four chapters published by Leavis
in *Scrutiny* all deal with single authors: Milton, Pope, Wordsworth and Shelley.
It rather looks as though Leavis put off writing the more general chapters as
long as he could. In the 'Introduction' to *Revaluation* he admits that 'The
consciousness that the period itself has had so much treatment in the last few

years inhibited the writing of the book.' Indeed, 'The first chapter was not written until *The Oxford Book of Seventeenth Century Verse* provided the occasion' (4). It is also apparent that the writing of the book kept pace with publication. If 'Milton's Verse' appeared in *Scrutiny* first, that was because it was the first of the original lectures that Leavis chose to write up.

In publishing the original versions of the chapters of *Revaluation* in *Scrutiny* Leavis did not describe them as parts of a work in progress. Or rather, the work in progress to which he attached them was not his own book. Four of the chapters, those on Pope, Wordsworth, Shelley and Keats, appear under the rubric of 'Revaluations', as in 'Revaluations (II): The Poetry of Pope'. This heading was first used for an article by W.A. Edwards in the June 1933 number of the journal (2.1): 'Revaluations (1): John Webster', a title which announced that *Scrutiny* was into the business of revaluing literature and expected to do more of it. It is, then, surprising that 'Milton's Verse', which appeared in the next number, was not designated an item in the series of 'Revaluations'. The reason may possibly lie in Leavis's feeling at this stage that his essay on Milton was exceptional and so should stand alone. If so, within three months he had changed his mind and identified his own work with the group project of revaluing. Between his piece on Pope and 'Revaluations (VI): Wordsworth', the next of the *Revaluation* chapters to appear, there intervened three other 'revaluations', of Burns, Hardy the novelist and Shakespeare's sonnets, by, respectively, John Speirs, Frank Chapman and L.C. Knights. Leavis's appropriation of his title, *Revaluation*, from the series in *Scrutiny* underlines his commitment to the values of that journal, which *Revaluation* in its book form must be seen as working to promote.

It is therefore not surprising that there is little significant difference between the journal form and book form of chapters. What *Revaluation* does is to add to what was published in *Scrutiny*; all the notes at chapter-ends, amounting to more than seventy pages of the book's 275, are new, with one exception. That is note C to Chapter 1, which appears as a footnote in the original journal publication ('English Poetry in the Seventeenth Century' 254–6). *Revaluation* adds significant new material in these notes, but does so whilst keeping faith with the journal, which has had the best of it, the chapters themselves.

Of course, Leavis took the opportunity offered by book publication to play with accidentals and to make necessary corrections. He changes 'Wit' ('The Poetry of Pope' 271, 280) to the less reverential, and more conventional, 'wit', for example (*Revaluation* 72, 73, 86). Mindful of rivals reluctant to forgive scholarly faults, he corrects, in the chapter on Keats, '*Ode to Autumn*' ('Keats' 393, 400) to 'Ode *To Autumn*' (*Revaluation* 264, 272).

He was also obliged to take account of some criticism. In 'Milton's Verse' he had used Allen Tate as something of a whipping-boy, and Tate had objected. The objection is duly noted in a footnote:

> It is fair to add that Mr. Tate objects to the representation of him given here, and that he does not, I gather, now hold the position with regard to Milton set forth in the essay referred to. (42n)

Nor is this all. Leavis removes the snide remark with which the piece had ended in *Scrutiny*: 'Mr. Allen Tate thinks that "there is no abler critic in English than Mr. Montgomery Belgion" (*The New Republic*, March 16, 1932)' (Leavis 1933a, 136). What he preserves from *Scrutiny* is the placement of his own work in a context defined by Tate and the *New Republic*, a context of his own time. Another writer to extract a footnote from Leavis was Empson. In the piece on Wordsworth, Leavis animadverts on a remark by him about 'the mountains as a totem or father-substitute'; this evidently led to an attempt to defend himself by Empson and the addition of a footnote in the book: 'Mr. Empson has replied that there is, he thinks, both the father and the mother in Wordsworth's Nature' (160n). Again, the reference to Empson is not removed; it stays as part of the context in which the book's judgements are to be understood.

Apart from this work of correction, minor and, more or less, major, *Revaluation* also engages in some amplification, not so much of Leavis's own words, but in quotations. They seem to be extended for two reasons: to make explicit what in the journal publication might be merely implied, and to allow the text to run more easily. An example of the first kind of amplification would be the moment in 'Milton's Verse' where, in *Scrutiny*, Leavis alludes to the song in *Comus* by citing its first four words only: 'Sweet Echo, sweetest Nymph ...' ('Milton's Verse' 134); in the book, the first six lines of the song are given, presumably for the benefit of those without *The Oxford Book* to hand. As for the second, there is an example in the same chapter, where *Revaluation* extends a quotation from *Lycidas* (lines 152–8) by a further four lines (159–62) to add the alternative left uncomfortably hanging in the original version: 'Whether ... Or whether ...' (*Revaluation* 56). This is to suppose that Leavis was not simply restoring what had been cut in his manuscript for journal publication, which, given the tendency to fill up each number of *Scrutiny* with a continuous sequence of articles rather than to begin each article on a new page, seems a reasonable supposition. The only exception may be with the last chapter to be published in the journal. 'English Poetry in the

Eighteenth Century', *aliter* 'The Augustan Tradition'. Towards the end of this, *Revaluation* adds almost seventy lines of text on Crabbe, mostly quotation. Were they added after the *Scrutiny* version went to press, or were they, for some reason not readily to be found, cut from it? The number of *Scrutiny* is dated 'June, 1936' and presumably went to press sometime in late April or May. The first review, by Edwin Muir, of *Revaluation* appeared in the *Scotsman* for 15 October 1936 (McKenzie and Allum 58). There might have been time for some second thought before the book went to press. Certainly, the speed with which book publication followed the appearance of the last instalment in *Scrutiny* suggests that the book was accepted by Chatto on the basis of what had already appeared rather than on sight of the completed manuscript. Since they had published *New Bearings*, and since I.M. Parsons, their editor, had read English at Cambridge and had fallen under Leavis's spell there (MacKillop 109), this is not surprising, but suggests that, just as the author wanted his book to be seen as a *Scrutiny* product, his publishers were happy to accept it as such.

Although he was writing chapters for his next book, Leavis took care to give his *Scrutiny* pieces an air of immediacy. The Pope piece, for example, came out under the 'Revaluations' rubric, but this was not just a flag of convenience; Leavis refers to it in his text: 'the heading "Revaluation", Pope's achievement being so varied, is over-ambitious', a phrasing which has to be rehandled in the book ('The Poetry of Pope' 268; *Revaluation* 69). It is probably the appearance of the Wordsworth essay under the same heading that led to its ending with two paragraphs on the poet's decline which the more economical *Revaluation* omits. Wordsworth's last forty years offering a chance for revaluation, *Scrutiny* readers were entitled to hear whether Leavis felt they merited that; the book's eschewal of any claim to comprehensiveness (2) meant that the question need not there be pursued. Leavis fosters a sense of closeness with his *Scrutiny* readers, referring back to previous numbers (*'English Poetry and the English Language*, reviewed in the last *Scrutiny'* ('Shelley' 162)) and genially assuming that they will have kept up with what has been going on in Cambridge ('Professor Housman's recent address' ('Shelley' 161) gets its full title when the piece is revised for the book – similarly, in the essay on Pope, the allusion to Lytton Strachey is unelaborated in *Scrutiny* (273) but given a reference in *Revaluation* (76n)). These examples do not only show Leavis consciously assuming intimacy with his reader; they also show him working at speed. There was no time to look up the Strachey passage, no time to write out the title of Housman's lecture. The last four chapters for *Revaluation* to appear in *Scrutiny* appeared in successive numbers.

Every number of *Scrutiny* since the appearance of 'Milton's Verse' contained substantial contributions from Leavis. The conditions of production for *Scrutiny* obliged him to adopt an urgent style as well as one that was assertively of the twentieth-century context. *Revaluation* is enriched by this carrying-over of style from the journal. Leavis's first book, *New Bearings*, lacks the characteristic tension of expression that his later book derives from the pressures of its production. It remains to be shown how fundamental to the stylistic mission of *Revaluation* that tension is.


## II


One correction that Leavis does not make confirms the importance for him of *Revaluation*'s carrying over into the book the spontaneity, contemporaneity and urgency of *Scrutiny*. The opportunity for revision which Leavis declines comes in the essay on Keats, where he is speculating on Keats's knowledge of Dante in Italian:

> And, at the moment of writing, that guess gets something very like confirmation in a letter from Professor Livingston Lowes to the *Times Literary Supplement* (11th January 1936) ... ('Keats' 398; *Revaluation* 269)

*Scrutiny* readers shared a little moment of drama with the master; readers of *Revaluation* glimpse it too, because part of what the book is about is the drama of *Scrutiny* itself.

Drama in the book derives largely from its being made up of pieces written for the journal. I have already noted how its title identifies the book as a *Scrutiny* project; its style does so too, and not merely as a response to deadlines. Leavis himself describes his style in the chapter on Pope when he says that he can 'aim at little more than to suggest coercively the reorientation from which a revaluation follows ...' ('The Poetry of Pope' 268; *Revaluation* 69). Leavis combines coercion with the indirectness manifest in that reorientation towards a revaluation throughout his book. But it is a coercion that depends on the reader's sense of being with Leavis as he composes his thoughts. Take a fairly representative sentence from the chapter on Pope:

> In the passage first quoted one is not merely solemnly impressed by the striking images; their unexpectedness and variety – the 'heterogeneous ideas' that are 'yoked together' – involve (on an adequate reading) a play of mind and a flexibility of attitude that makes such effects as that of 'dregs' [line 26 of Pope's

'Elegy to the Memory of an Unfortunate Lady'] acceptable when they come: there is an element of surprise. but not the shock that means rejection (complete or ironically qualified) of the inappropriate. (71)

The way the sentence at its conclusion dwells on the necessity of rejecting the inappropriate is coercive beyond the context of Pope's poem in its assumption of a common standard of propriety, just as the disowning of the 'merely' solemn at the beginning makes the notion of adequacy raised later demanding of a more than 'merely solemn' response. If this coerciveness is not perceived as a kind of bullying, that may be because the sentence at the same time works hard at suggesting as well as at asserting. What it suggests is the author's own difficulty in expressing what it is he wants to say; the parentheses that qualify what he is saying bring the reader close up to him in the act of refining whatever it is he knows he wants to say but finds difficult to produce. 'On an adequate reading', 'completely or ironically qualified' – these phrases suggest an author anxious to be understood, an author anxious that he may *not* be understood and an author writing as he thinks, so that qualification becomes habitual as what he wants to say is modified to what he can say. This anxious author and our closeness to him make it difficult to see coercion for what it is; it suggests, does not coerce, and what it suggests is that we can identify with this scrupulous and unegotistical writer. For it is striking that the passage is couched in terms of what 'one' may or may not feel. Despite the major assertive structure of the sentence – 'one is … their unexpectedness and variety … involve … there is', its parentheses and use of the impersonal make it feel hesitant.

This qualification by suggestion of the coercive force of his sentence is present even when Leavis is at his most bullying: here is an example from the chapter on Milton:

Here, if this were a lecture, would come illustrative reading-out – say of the famous opening to Book III. As it is, the point seems best enforcible (though it should be obvious to any one capable of being convinced at all) by turning to one of the exceptionally good passages – for every one will agree at any rate that there are places where the verse glows with an unusual life. One of these, it will again be agreed, is the Mulciber passage at the end of Book I … (44)

Coercion is evident in the use of 'it should be obvious', 'every one will agree' and 'it will again be agreed'; such expressions are designed to minimize the possibility of disagreement. Yet the author presents himself as in some sense lacking the force his coercion requires. He would really like to read aloud to the reader, but that is unfortunately not possible; his prose is a second best.

'As it is' suggests a kind of throwing up of the hands, not in despair, but at least in regret. It also suggests the writer under pressure, one who does not have time to banish thoughts of what he would like to be doing in favour of what he should be doing without fuss. Leavis's prose is full of interpolated phrases of this kind: 'as a matter of fact' and 'of course' are favourites, and they do give the effect of someone not speaking but writing to the reader in a quite intimate way.

Perhaps one more example of coercion and suggestion may be helpful before coming on to the matter of what it has to do with the whole *Scrutiny* enterprise. This comes from 'The Line of Wit':

> Jonson's effort was to feel Catullus, and the others he cultivated, as contemporary with himself; or rather, to achieve an English mode that should express a sense of contemporaneity with them. This sense itself, of course, had to be achieved by effort, and was achieved in the mode. This mode, which is sufficiently realized in a considerable body of poems, may be described as consciously urbane, mature and civilized. Whatever its relation to any Latin originals, it is indisputably *there*, an achieved actuality. It belongs, of course, to literature ... (19)

'Of course' twice makes its coercive point, and 'sufficiently' plays a part similar to that of 'adequate' in the passage on Pope. This coerciveness is associated with the downrightness of Leavis's description of Jonson's mode, and manifests itself directly again in the characteristic adverb 'indisputably'. Yet this 'indisputably' is tightly linked to a gesture – '*there*' – which in its inarticulacy evokes the disallowed reading out loud of Milton in the passage previously considered. Coercion beds down with suggestion. In what other way can an 'achieved actuality' be impressed on a reader who is unaware of, as it were asleep to, its qualities?

In some ways this is a question for all criticism. Without common standards it is not possible to do much more than coerce your reader into a sharing of views. But the problem is exacerbated if what you want to do is to persuade a reader to share a feeling with you rather than an argument, 'Jonson's effort was to feel Catullus'; our effort is to feel what Leavis is feeling. Leavis's writing teeters on inarticulacy precisely because feeling is at the heart of his concerns. That is suggested by the focus on rhythm, which is by no means exclusive to the Milton chapter, and is indeed a general concern of *Scrutiny* writers. But the sense of rhythm stands for a deeper sense of things going beyond art. For *Scrutiny*, criticism was a matter of entering into a right relationship with literature, a relationship that was supportive not, for example, of anything as simple as the lucid representation in words of thought, but of the culture as a whole. Francis Mulhern describes the aim of the journal accurately when he says that

> *Scrutiny*'s strategic objective was … to *organize* the defenders of 'culture' as an effective force. As the 'Manifesto' [in the first number] put it: 'the trouble is not that such persons form a minority, but that they are scattered and unorganized.' Its organizational model was of necessity that of an *elite*. For if the industrial order was constitutionally inimical to 'culture', it followed that none of its given classes or sub-groups could provide a vehicle for 'continuity'. The 'minority' could only function as a compact, 'rootless' oppositional group formed and maintained against the natural bias of society, bearers of 'an autonomous culture, a culture independent of any economic, technical or social system as none has been before.' (76)

*Revaluation* was a kind of recruiting document for the 'elite' of which Mulhern writes here. Literary criticism mattered 'in the degree that literature was the main surviving witness of an existential integrity that had disappeared from the social world' (Mulhern 76). The tension in Leavis's style has to do not only with the anxieties of an author meeting deadlines, but with the tension inherent in the idea of recruiting for a minority. On the one hand, the reader ought to be part of the 'elite' and 'should' be coerced to join, but, on the other, that reader could not recognize Leavis's 'autonomous culture' unless he or she were already part of that 'elite' without knowing it, in which case only suggestion would do. The style picks its way through this dilemma as elegantly as Leavis knows how, considerably aided by the urgency to produce his copy which reinforced the urgency of the message.

'Milton's Verse' was the first of the 1932 lectures to be written up because it was a mark of being in touch with the 'culture' that Milton should be recognized as out of touch with it:

> the mind that invented Milton's Grand Style had renounced the English language, and with that, inevitably, Milton being an Englishman, a great deal else. (*Revaluation* 52)

The 'great deal else' is presumably the feel for the culture which comes from an adequate understanding of Shakespeare or of Donne, whose use of English in the third Satire is described as 'the use, in the essential spirit of the language, of its characteristic resources' (55). The history of English poetry that is *Revaluation* is a history of 'the use, in the essential spirit of the language, of its characteristic resources'. Milton is the great exemplar of all those artists who, despite the possession of that 'genius' which Leavis allows the poet of *Paradise Lost* (55), failed to respond to that essential spirit.

Milton is something more than that also. As a 'Latinizer' he stands for the old-fashioned study of the classics which the new discipline of English was to replace. When Leavis describes Milton it is as though he were describing the typical public school boy of his era, brought up on a diet of Homer and Cicero to serve Empire:

> His strength is of the kind that we indicate when, distinguishing between intelligence and character, we lay the stress on the latter; it is a strength, that is, involving sad disabilities. He has 'character,' moral grandeur, moral force; but he is, for the purposes of his undertaking, disastrously single-minded and simple-minded. He reveals every where a dominating sense of righteousness and a complete incapacity to question or explore its significance and conditions. This defect of intelligence is a defect of imagination. (58)

*Revaluation* appeals to the imagination in order to empower an intelligence in touch with 'essential' Englishness. The characterization of Milton as a classically-educated but insensitive public school boy implies Leavis's attachment to the new study of English as a 'modern' replacement for the classics (see, for example, Baldick 62). If 'Milton's Verse' was the first chapter for *Revaluation* to appear in *Scrutiny*, then the second was on Pope because Pope was the antithesis of Milton, a poet in touch with the culture: 'the "correctness" of Pope's literary form derives its strength from a social code and a civilization' (76). The two chapters work towards the same end by means of this contrast. That end is the upholding of the 'new' English studies as answering England's (and, to a lesser extent, Britain's) immediate needs. Wellek's apparent failure to grasp this may derive from his indifference to that aspect of Leavis's book that is a meditation on Englishness, and which led to Leavis himself becoming an icon of such Englishness in later life.

For Leavis's enterprise in *Revaluation* should be read as an extension of the work of his patron and protector Quiller-Couch who had reformed the curriculum for the English tripos which Leavis took in order to graduate. 'Q wanted "his" tripos to school undergraduates in England, of which literature was a part. He wanted it to be a school of English in a literal sense. Whitehall could not understand the national-historical orientation of the course' (MacKillop 58). Leavis's book is the evidence that he *had* understood.

The style of *Revaluation* is coercive but tentative, urgent but merely suggestive. It spans the divide between an exclusive minority and the greater number it wishes to include if only that seemed right. It invites the reader to be alongside the author at the time of writing, it invites the reader to share with Leavis in that moment which is also a moment in the rescue of English culture; it is a style about community. Because community is a matter of feeling as much as anything, argument counts for less in this style than might be expected (which is not to say that the book is short, or weak, in argument). This emphasis on feeling and on an intimacy in feeling with the writer comes to be a hallmark of the Leavis style, but it was shaped in the rapid process of writing articles for *Scrutiny*, a process whose effects were shrewdly and intelligently preserved in the book which they made up.

## Bibliography

Baldick, Chris (1983), *The Social Mission of English Criticism 1848–1932*, Oxford: Clarendon Press.

Leavis, F.R. (1932), *New Bearings in English Poetry*, London: Chatto & Windus.

Leavis, F.R. (1933a), 'Milton's Verse', *Scrutiny* 2, 123–36.

Leavis, F.R. (1933b), 'Revaluations (II): The Poetry of Pope', *Scrutiny* 2, 268–84.

Leavis, F.R. (1934), 'Revaluations (VI): Wordsworth', *Scrutiny* 3, 234–57.

Leavis, F.R. (1935a), 'English Poetry in the Seventeenth Century', *Scrutiny* 4, 158–80.

Leavis, F.R. (1935b), 'Revaluations (VIII): Shelley', *Scrutiny* 4, 158–80.

Leavis, F.R. (1936a), 'English Poetry in the Eighteenth Century', *Scrutiny* 5, 13–31.

Leavis, F.R. (1936b), 'Revaluations (IX): Keats', *Scrutiny* 4, 376–400.

Leavis, F.R. (1936c), *Revaluation: Tradition and Development in English Poetry*, London: Chatto & Windus.

McKenzie, D.F. and M-P. Allum (1966), *F.R.Leavis: A Check-List 1924–1964*, London: Chatto & Windus.

MacKillop, Ian (1995), *F.R.Leavis: A Life in Criticism*, London: Allen Lane, Penguin.

Mulhern, Francis (1979), *The Moment of 'Scrutiny'*, London: NLB.

Wellek, Rene (1986), *A History of Modern Criticism 1750–1950*, 5 *English Criticism 1900–1950*, London: Jonathan Cape.

Chapter Thirteen

# Re-reading Elizabeth Bowen

Hermione Lee

There are many scenes of reading and re-reading in the novels and stories of Elizabeth Bowen, and the negotiation over who owns the past that goes on in so many of those scenes can be applied to the ways in which this great novelist of the twentieth century has been read and re-read. Her reputation shifts, her readings change: she refuses to be fixed or finished with.

I recently re-read Antonia Byatt's introduction to *The House in Paris*, first written in 1976 and revised in 1998 for the Vintage Paperbacks reissues of Bowen's novels. Byatt talks about an 'odd, continuous and shifting' relationship with the novel over thirty years. She describes reading *The House in Paris* in different ways at different points in her life. Reading it first as a child of about Henrietta's age, she was shocked and baffled by finding out about the connections between 'children, sex and love'. Reading it again as a teenager she was much more interested in Karen and her intense emotional drama. Later she turned against the novel as being too finished, too Jamesian. And then, re-reading it more recently, she recognized Leopold's central claim to attention, and understood that her own adult experience had led her to understand his pivotal role in the novel. (Readers of Byatt's *Babel Tower* will recognize the influence of Leopold on the child Leo.) Byatt concludes: 'My reading of it in some way reflected the process it was dealing with' (7–9).

I recognize this account of re-reading Bowen in different ways at different times, and of coming to understand that returning and remembering are at the heart of her work. My re-reading of Bowen in this essay takes two forms. The first is, briefly, an account of my own returns to her work, and the changes in her reputation in the last forty years. With this as the context of the essay, I want, secondly, to describe the kind of remembering or re-membering of the self that goes on so often in Bowen's fiction through the readings of private papers – often illicit and discomforting readings.

I started reading Bowen when I was sinking my teeth as an adolescent, around the age of thirteen or fourteen, into a number of women writers – Rosamond Lehmann, Virginia Woolf, Stevie Smith, Katherine Mansfield. From Bowen and Lehmann in particular I took a very strong sense of extremes of emotion. The first Bowen novel I read was *To the North* and the first story was 'The Demon Lover'. And my first attachment to her was through a recognition (of the sort she herself talks about in *The Last September* and elsewhere) of violent extremes, breaking bonds, crashing recklessly through what was acceptable, taking bad risks and finding danger in love. Perhaps this was a suitable reading for the 1960s; it was certainly a satisfying one for a rather over-controlled middle-class English teenager.

Around fifteen years later, I came back to her as a youngish academic in my late twenties – by which time I had been overdosing on Woolf and James and Proust – thinking I might be able to turn a private passion into a subject of critical study. Only then did I become interested in Bowen's extraordinary and complicated formal manners, and in her social sense, the whole complex of cultural and literary and historical allegiances and departure points in her work. Out of this, I wrote one of the first studies of her works, in which I was very concerned to rescue her from exactly the associations for which I first fell in love with her as a teenage reader – with feminine romanticism, personal agendas, women's weaknesses.[1]

Returning to her for a revision of my book for her centenary year, 1999, and re-reading her in the light of what's been written about her in the last two decades, is to read a whole history of feminist criticism, and of new departures in writing on Anglo-Irish politics and culture – as well as, incidentally, for me to think about my life as a writer and teacher since then. As I say in my introduction to the revised *Elizabeth Bowen*, if I were writing a book about her now I would place the emphasis differently.

> Critical writing by and about women now moves much more freely between different approaches: cultural and gender studies, autobiography, historical analysis. I am much less anxious [than I was in the 1970s] about saying 'I' when I write. And I don't any longer think it a weak position to write about the 'merely' personal in women's writing.
>
> I would be more interested now ... in reading the sense of displacement and dispossession in Bowen as expressions of personal traumas and anxieties rather than as historical commentary. I think there is more to be said about sex in Bowen – repression, danger, ambivalence. I would want to give more space to the complicated feelings about mothers – intimacy with, loss of, resistance to – in Bowen's fiction. And I would feel free to spend more time than I did, without having to make excuses for it, on her brilliant use of trivia, of domestic and social detail, on *things* in Bowen: clothes, furniture, decor, the cinema, travel, meals, drinks, shopping, suburbs. (Lee 1999a, 3–4)

Much of this work has been, or is being, done since my book first came out in 1981; Bowen is now the subject of a great variety of new readings, in critical and biographical work as well as in film, with John Banville's interesting revisionary treatment of *The Last September* in 2000.

Bowen's own obsession with returns and re-readings is summed up in her 1961 'Foreword' to *Afterthought,* a collection of pieces which go back to the 1940s. The quotation reads:

> Easy to be wise after the event. For the writer, writing is eventful; one might say it is in itself eventfulness. More than any activity, it involves thought, but the thought involved in it is by nature captive, specialized and intense. One may not exactly know what one has (finally) written till one has finished it – and then only after a term of time. Then begins a view of the whole, a more perceptive or comprehensive vision; but too late. However, fortunately for authors they are seldom prey to regret. They seldom look back, for they are usually engaged upon something else. (1962, 9)

This is a typically oblique and complicated Bowen paradox: to preface a volume of essays called *Afterthought* (consisting in part of a number of pieces which *do* look back on her own earlier work) with a statement which on the one hand says, writers don't usually know what they have done until afterwards, and, on the other hand, that they don't usually look back on what they have done anyway. There is certainly some double feeling here about re-reading and remembering. Later in this volume, in a 1959 preface to a collection of her stories, she talks about how her fond memories of some of her earliest stories 'fail under the test of austere retrospect': some of her favourites turn out to have been 'mirages in my memory' (Lee 1999b [Bowen 1959], 128). Re-reading can be dangerous, disillusioning, sometimes even impossible. And this pull between the 'austere' disillusionments of re-reading and the pull of regret or nostalgia is everywhere in her critical work, as well as in her fiction.

The 'echo-track of sensation' that you get from re-reading the books you read as a child is perilous, even though alluring (Lee 1999b [Bowen 1947], 250). It is a mistake to reopen the books of childhood, she says in 'Out of a Book': 'I neither wish nor dare to touch them' (Lee 1999b [Bowen 1946], 51). Yet, almost in the same breath, she tells us that these forgotten, unrereadable books, these childhood addictions, are really the sources of all the aesthetic choices of the adult writer: 'The aesthetic is nothing but an attempt to disguise and glorify the enforced return' (Lee 1999b [Bowen 1946], 53).

'The enforced return' is an alarming phrase, and very suggestive, even for a professed anti-Freudian like Bowen, of the return of the repressed. The dangerousness of what has been (apparently) lost, obliterated, forgotten, buried, is always felt in her transactions with the past. Nostalgia, remembering, looking on the happy autumn fields and thinking of the days that are no more, is never easy or painless. Often it is resisted or diagnosed as a sign of a whole society's weakness. After the 1939–45 war, in particular, she resists what she calls 'the cult of nostalgia' or 'the sickly dominance of nostalgia in our talk, writing, and reading', so prevalent in our age, she says, as to be almost a 'malady' (Lee 1999b [Bowen 1950], 59). Yet in the same breath she shares the dominant longing of the times for books about childhood, books about the recent past, books which animate memory or which give us what we really want which is, she says, 'not the past but the idea of the past'.

When the past 'discharges its load of feeling into the anaesthetized and bewildered present' (as she says in a preface written in 1945 for *The Demon Lover* stories) it can completely paralyse the 'I' of the present, dismember it, drastically reshape it, 'at the cost of no little pain' (Lee 1999b [Bowen 1946], 98). The image of the young woman in the story 'The Apple Tree', locked up inside the trauma of her childhood, is one of the most terrifying examples of that dangerous 'enforced return'. We can easily see that moral value is attached to figures in Bowen's stories and novels who are guardians of or seekers for the past, like Matchett in *The Death of the Heart* or Dicey in *The Little Girls*, and that those who live from one thing to the next and shed the past, like Markie in *To the North* or the Quaynes in *The Death of the Heart*, are empty and queasy and untrustworthy. But guardians of the past can be baleful, too, like Mme Fisher in *The House in Paris*. There's a strong attraction to the idea that you might want to blow the whole past up, from Lois in *The Last September* right through to Jeremy in *Eva Trout*. When the re-reading of the past takes place in the fiction it comes as something enforced, resisted, unwelcome. It dismembers a constructed personality or opens a life up to something that shakes it.

* * *

Once you start looking for bits of paper in Bowen's novels and stories you are inundated: 'We shall need the waste-paper-basket', as Roderick says to Stella after she has torn up a letter in *The Heat of the Day*. There are diaries, wills, letters, photographs, schoolbooks, shopping-lists, newspapers, books, itineraries, inscriptions, writing on tombstones, letters from the dead, letters to posterity, memorandums, telegrams and all sorts of odd pieces of paper, of which my favourite are Cousin Francis's cards of 'injunctions, admonitions, and warnings', left after his sudden death stuck in the frame of an oil-painting at the County Cork house in Mount Morris. These 'clear directions' to posterity, 'here underlined, there enringed in urgent red', which embody a character, a house and a way of life, read:

> *Clocks,* when and how to wind ... *Fire Extinguishers*, when and how to employ ... *Locks and Hinges,* my method of oiling ... *Live Mice* caught in traps, to be drowned *Not* dropped into kitchen fire ... *Tim O'Keefe, Mason,* not to work here again unless he does better than last time. *Beggars*, bona fide 6d., *Old Soldiers Is* ... *Hysteria, Puppies*, in case of ... In case of *Blocked Gutters* ... In case of *Parachutists* ... *Birds in Chimney*, in case of ... In case of *Telegrams* ... In case of *River* entering *Lower Lodge* ... In case of *My Death* ... In case of *Emergency Message from Lady C* ... (Bowen 1998, 164)

As Andrew Bennett and Nicholas Royle say in *Elizabeth Bowen and the Dissolution of the Novel* (1994), her books are continually reminding us of themselves as 'writing and textuality'. The Bowen world is full of texts to be read and re-read, and all her books are in some way, even negatively, about memory. These readings are often coloured by guilt, shame and a feeling of trouble. People illicitly read something that is not meant for them, or that has been hidden, and in doing so their lives are liable to change. Once these private papers have become theirs (and there is often a debate about ownership and possession of the past) their meanings are appropriated, their effects are profound. 'The act of reading' (the phrase is used of Jane with the found letters in *A World of Love*) brings the reader to a different possible self. But there is then a space of potential, question, limbo (wonderfully registered by the hung pause of imminence at the end of *The House in Paris* and *The Death of the Heart*) where it's not clear whether that reading or re-reading or remembering is going to make any difference. Indeed there is a great horror in the last two novels that the past will prove to have had no meaning, no reality, no existence, no effect. The coffer of childhood treasures will turn out to be empty; what we say and what we remember may have no gathering significance, but be just repetition, 'repeat-remarks', as tape-recorded in *Eva Trout*:

> 'Shall I record us?'
> 'Not on any account!'
> 'It has recorded, "Not on any account." And it now records me saying, "it has recorded, 'Not on any account'".' (Bowen 1999c, 120)

Bennett and Royle write very suggestively about how what they call 'events in reading' in Bowen raise the questions of whether the past has any reality, or ever happened. What they call the 'retrolexic' is, they observe, 'a work of re-reading or re-experiencing' which may involve 'remembering what never happened. In this way the retrolexic engages with a demand for reading back, for "rereading backwards", for a rereading which at once doubles and obliterates any first reading' (89).

The dangerousness of pieces of paper in Bowen is suggested by the number of times they get torn up: like Janet tearing up the drastic letter she and Edward have just read, written about them by the dread Theodora in *Friends and Relations* – too late, though, for it not to threaten the careful decorums they have set up as defences around them, and for the reading of the letter to make 'the house fall' (Bowen 1999a, 92). Or there is the prolonged, deliberate moment in *The Heat of the Day* when Roderick finds an old piece of paper in Rodney's dressing-gown pocket and debates with Stella whether she has the right to read it, or destroy it. 'It's not yours', she says to him. 'It isn't yours, either', he echoes. She reads it and tears it up very deliberately, but we don't know what it is, only that the debate over 'this secretively-folded grey-blue half sheet became the corpus of suspicion' (Bowen 1998, 63) and invokes all the novel's painful arguments of treachery, secrets, and trust.

Many pieces of paper don't reach their destination, or remain unread: who is the rightful owner of the past is often a very important part of the Bowen story. The message written to posterity in Clare, alias Mumbo's, Unknown Language in *The Little Girls*, and buried in the coffer in Southstone in 1914, will never receive an answer, and the language is never heard again. She wrote a letter to her father in the Unknown Language, but he is killed at Mons, and the letter, as she says years later, 'got there too late'. Bennett and Royle comment: 'Clare's letter to her father is written in the language of posterity: it is both unreadable in the present, and indeed the time of its reading is indefinitely deferred' (1994, 125). Who knows how letters – or novels – will be read by posterity? The little girls ask themselves, as they are burying the message in the Unknown Language: 'And it may all be the same, by then? They may have no language.' (Bowen 1999d, 152, 125, 117.)

Eva Trout never does receive the letter, a kind of love-letter, written to her by Hugh from Cambridge; Emmeline can't give Markie the letter she has just written him because he turns up unexpectedly. Lilia never does read the recovered, uncovered letters dangerously circulating through the house in *A World of Love*. They have a strong physical presence as textual objects:

> These letters, all in the same hand, were headed by day-names only – 'Tuesday',
> 'Saturday', and so on. They had been removed from their envelopes; nothing
> showed where they had been written or when posted. The writing-paper varied
> in kind, and, though not yet so aged as to be discoloured, was soiled at the
> edges, rubbed at the folds. The rubber band round the packet survived from the
> fall from the trunk only to snap, unresilient, at the first pull from Jane – how
> many years does it take for rubber to rot? The ink, sharp in the candlelight, had
> not faded. (Bowen 1999c, 33)

But we never read more than a phrase or two of their content. Who the letters
belong to is much more the plot of the novel than what's in them. Guy's
letters, bringing with them the burden of the past reaching into and
overwhelming the present, in a sense belong to whoever finds them. This
keeps being echoed: 'Who are the letters from?' 'Those letters are mine.'
'Who are they to?' 'Naturally, finding's keeping.' 'Private letters are private
letters' (Bowen 1999c, 41–2). 'The act of reading' makes them haunt and
belong to whoever reads them. Like a number of other readings in Bowen,
the act of reading turns the reader into a possessed person, a shadow self of
the writer. So Jane falls in love with the dead Guy who appears to be writing
'to' her; so Anna half-turns into Portia through reading her diary; so Mary
becomes Sarah by reading her story in 'The Happy Autumn Fields'. For Lilia
the letters remain unreadable: 'How could I ever bear to read them again,
even if I did ever read them before?' (Bowen 1999c, 101.) There is a terror for
her in the 'enforced return' to the world of love of the letters; but even without
reading them she cannot be free of them. The danger of dead letters is allowed
a romantic, enfranchising conclusion in *A World of Love*, but it is pure horror
in 'The Demon Lover', where, like Guy's letters from the dead, the letter
from the dead lover, with no stamp, and 'today's date', arrives promptly for
Mrs Drover at the appointed time, and makes her 'remember with such dreadful
acuteness that the twenty-five years since then dissolved like smoke' (Bowen
1999f, 665).

* * *

I want to conclude with two 'acts of reading' in Bowen that embody most
dramatically the past's sometimes unwelcome pressure on the present, and
the question of the ownership of the past. I call these scenes 'The dangerous
box' and 'The empty envelope'. Typically, they are both readings which do
and do not take place, willed, imaginary readings on a strange borderland
between memory, fantasy, obsession and desire. One is the reading of what is

called 'the dangerous box' in the story 'The Happy Autumn Fields'. Mary, in her bombed London house, enters – or re-enters – the world of the Victorian family of Sarah and Henrietta through the 'unburied' box of old letters and memoirs and photographs. This object – a bomb waiting to go off – is described by her friend Travis as 'a musty old leather box gaping open with God knows what – junk, illegible letters, diaries, yellow photographs', 'some good morbid stuff' (Bowen 1999f, 677–8). Through opening her Pandora's box of the past, Mary seems to dream her way into the lives of the two (perhaps twin) sisters and their apparently enchanted, safe, but doomed and vulnerable moment in the past. The papers seem to tell Mary who she is, or was, and suggest that the past may not have ended, but (as in *A World of Love* or *The Little Girls*) may be coexistent, on a parallel plane, with the present. But, after her first rummage, the box is taken away by Travis, who, seeing its effect on her, calls it 'the dangerous box'. All she keeps is a photograph of the two sisters, which she hides next to her body, her heart. And even after the dangerous box is taken away, Mary is able to dream her way into its contents: 'at the cost' (as it says in the preface to these stories) 'of no little pain'. She loses her sense of herself and 'becomes' Sarah ('I had a sister called Henrietta') but she also takes on the losses that Sarah has not yet experienced, which prefigure the diminution and loss that the modern, war-torn world experiences in relation to the past: 'Eugene, Henrietta were lost in time to the woman weeping there on the bed, no longer reckoning who she was' (Bowen 1999f).

The other willed 'act of reading' which forces the past into the diminished present is Leopold's reading of his mother's letter in *The House in Paris*. Except that he doesn't read his mother's letter, as it has been taken out of the envelope which he has found in the handbag of Naomi Fisher, the woman who is looking after him for the day, and whose life was destroyed ten years before by the affair between Leopold's mother and Naomi's fiancé, the affair which produced Leopold. (What Leopold does read, to devastating effect, is the letter about him from his foster-parents in Italy.) Leopold presses his forehead against 'her empty envelope', in what Bennett and Royle call a gesture 'literally enacting the figurative compress of reading' (48). It's an odd anticipation of the moment in *The Heat of the Day* when the child Anne butts her forehead against Rodney's, the child trying to get as close as it can to the adult she loves and who leaves her: 'Their brain-cases touched – contact of absolute separations she was not to forget' (Bowen 1998, 266).

Leopold tells Henrietta, who thinks he has gone mad, that he is 'Thought-reading, naturally': and in a sense he is. Out of the empty envelope he wills into being the letter he wants his mother to have written. The letter which

Leopold imagines his mother having written to Naomi Fisher is a comical nine-year-old child's invention, typically characterful, eloquent, and odd.

> 'Dear Miss Fisher,' he said. 'It is kind of you to have Leopold at your house for us to meet. I shall be coming at half-past two on Thursday, so please have lunch over and be out of the way. Leopold and I shall go out, *then* you can come back as much as you want. We shall be very busy arranging things, as I am taking Leopold home to England with me. He cannot go back to Spezia as I mean to keep him, the people there must get hold of some other child. I never did mean him to go back, but did not say so for fear they would make a fuss. So they can put that in their pipes and smoke it. When I come, I shall go straight into the room where he is, so please do not be in it. I have come to the conclusion I cannot do without Leopold, because he is the only person I want. We have a great deal to say, so – ' (Bowen 1999b, 45).

Through this invention, Leopold compels his mother to make 'an enforced return' to him. This isn't, for Leopold, about remembering, although the whole book is about the past lying on and pressurizing the present inescapably. Leopold has no memory of his mother, and very little information about her. All he learns about the past is from Mme Fisher's poisoned memory-hoard. His mother is absent, we never read her letter, as we never read the piece of paper Roderick takes out of Rodney's dressing-gown, or the letters Jane reads from Guy. Leopold, pressing his head to Karen's envelope, forces her, with his ruthless solipsism and the Napoleonic ambitiousness of his will, into his present: that is his only possible way of re-membering her. And it may be that this appropriation of what is lost, absent, past, for his own need, is what we all do with our readings of the past.

## Note

1    As part of the research for that book, John Barnard and I travelled to County Cork in 1980 to look at the ruins of Bowen's Court, the church at Farahy where Bowen and her husband are buried, the landscape of the Blackwater valley, and the nearby towns, Fermoy and Mallow, which she uses and re-uses in her fiction. We talked to Bowen's cousin, the writer Hubert Butler, in whose house, Maidenhall in County Kilkenny, we saw the family portraits from Bowen's Court, hanging in the dining room. That pilgrimage made it vividly apparent how landscape, place and houses are deeply embedded in her writing: physical, geographical returns to Ireland continue all through her work.

# Bibliography

Bennett, A. and N. Royle (1994), *Elizabeth Bowen and the Dissolution of the Novel: Still Lives*, London: Macmillan.

Bowen, E. (1999a [1931]), *Friends and Relations*, London: Constable; London: Vintage.

Bowen, E. (1999b [1935]), *The House in Paris*, London: Gollancz; London: Vintage.

Bowen, E. (1998 [1948]), *The Heat of the Day*, London: Cape; London: Vintage.

Bowen, E. (1999c [1955]), *A World of Love*, London: Cape; Londo:, Vintage.

Bowen, E. (1962), *Afterthought: Pieces about Writing*, London: Longmans.

Bowen, E. (1999d [1964]), *The Little Girls*, London: Cape; London: Vintage.

Bowen, E. (1999e [1969]), *Eva Trout*, London, Cape, London, Vintage.

Bowen, E. (1999f [1981]), *Collected Stories*, London, Cape, London, Vintage.

Byatt, A.S. (1999), 'Introduction', *The House in Paris*, London: Vintage.

Lee, H. (1999a), *Elizabeth Bowen*, London: Vintage.

Lee, H. (ed.) (1999b [1986]), *The Mulberry Tree: Writings of Elizabeth Bowen*, London: Vintage.

## Chapter Fourteen

# 'Drastic Reductions': Partial Disclosures and Displaced Authorities in Muriel Spark's *The Driver's Seat*

Alistair Stead

... and the past will never be mentioned.

Near the beginning of *The Driver's Seat* Muriel Spark signals that she is going to offer some 'drastic reductions', using the economic metaphor to introduce a decadently consumerist cosmopolitan world. The phrase refers literally to the coming sales in a dress shop and symbolically to some extreme practice of her celebrated literary economy, honed to a fine satirical edge in a virtual trilogy of taut Eurofictions in the late 1960s and early 1970s.[1] 'Drastic' is transposed into 'big' when the scene shifts to another store (95), but the affinity of 'drastic' with 'dramatic' (both from the Greek word 'to act') foregrounds both the histrionic, self-reductive protagonist and a genre-affiliation of the text. Spark's novels habitually reduce to something like novellas, and texts, which incline substantially to the dramatic principle of showing rather than telling, of dialogic exchange more than narratorial analysis, often furnish fewer interpretative clues than the full-scale novel. Here, the text refuses notoriously to examine at length the protagonist's history or motivation, and any cultural context is elliptically given. Consequently, *The Driver's Seat*, almost the shortest of her longer prose fictions, is generally considered her most enigmatic. Where the book has not been dismissed as a lightweight shocker, ingenious but morbid, it has been admired as an original variation on a postmodern metafictional game. Its title indicates the mutable identity of the person behind the wheel, chiefly that of Lise, the desperate office-worker in her mid-thirties whose break-out holiday in an initially unnamed Southern city ends, as she wishes, in her violent death at the hands of a 'sex-maniac' (153). That title-phrase, a typical poetic concentration, is also a trope for varieties of contests for power, which may be, according to the aspect of reading, displaced from man to woman, from divine to human will, from omniscient narrator to rebellious character.

At least some of the problems posed for the reader by this radical laconicism may be usefully thought of in the twinned terms of my subtitle: *partial disclosures* and *displaced authorities*. The former refers to the way in which we are normally given only part of the picture and compelled to construct the story frequently out of only meagre clues. Not only are the word and syllable 'part' reverberant throughout the text,[2] but Lise's most distinguishing physical mark during her eager suicidal quest is her 'slightly parted' lips (12), symbolizing the text's manner of disclosure: subtle, gradual, metonymic. Revelations are 'bit by bit' (156), by 'a fragment' (14, 107) or 'a small fraction' (62), which may prove 'a small item of a greater purpose' (29).

My second term acknowledges the way the author of the text contrives, as in the theatre, to take a back seat, if not to efface herself altogether. As though testing the validity of the theory about the death of the author and the birth of the reader (Barthes 148), she gives us the provocative spectacle 'of power-in-exile, the parade of discredited authorial power, which has been handed over to a criminal surrogate' (Sage 16). Significantly, the word 'author' occurs once and, as we shall see, belittlingly. Displacement subsumes, therefore, not just the strategic reticence of the author, whom Spark consciously constructs, but the temporary transfer of the author-function to some anti-authoritarian protagonist staging an act of usurpation.[3] Alternatively, power may be partly displaced from author to reader, one inspired, especially after Roland Barthes's *S/Z* (1970), actively to produce rather than passively to consume a text. Lise, in this perspective, is an ironic representation of the reader as author.

However, in the exploration of some distinctive features of the novella's intertextuality,[4] my key terms tend to converge. I shall be dwelling, then, on displaced, fragmentary apparitions of more or less literary intertexts in this text, more particularly on the contexts they may supply for reading through genre. If a text is 'a tissue of quotations drawn from innumerable centres of culture' (Barthes 146), at first glance, intertextual markers in this book are sparse, with only partial disclosure of any potentially productive allusive network. Furthermore, the authorities, potential 'master' texts, adduced in a reading attentive to the markers, may be displaced; as Julia Kristeva has argued, intertextual citation always involves some displacement or transformation in adaptation to new evaluative contexts (Morgan 260). Spark's dominant modulation is parodic, working against but within genre.

Interpretation is itself always a more or less drastic reduction of all the possible readings provoked by the blanks in the text. But my reduction is simply to pursue the intertextual traces of two kinds of writing germane to this text's potential classification, highlighting its generic shiftiness by scrutiny of the 'production' of a book. Rare intertextual citations lead readers to the Scriptures and Greek tragedy, culturally hegemonic discourses acting as assumed ethical norms, thence to narrower generic framing by the Revelation of St John the Divine (apocalypse) and Aristotle's *Poetics* (tragic theory). External evidence for Spark's familiarity with these discourses is strong, but my focus is on the comparatively cryptic internal traces.[5]

\* \* \*

Let us begin with the classical context, *preposterously*, putting things back to front in the manner in which the whole text tends to unfold, with flash-forwards from early on intimating the fact of Lise's death and something of its aftermath, and in which there are prodigal reversals of expectation, large and small, from start (her demand for a dress that stains) to finish (the murderer is the victim, the ones in the driver's seat lose control). The very end of the book solicits recognition of the trace of a classical text. An unmarked quotation of a fragment of a classic passage in Aristotle's *Poetics* is enough to refocus speculation on what we have been reading. The moment is heralded by a *locus classicus* of the uncanny in the text. On a flight from Copenhagen to Rome, Richard, a putatively reformed rapist, is panicked by his realization that Lise, his garishly-dressed and aggressive fellow-passsenger, offers an obscurely familiar threat:

> He opens his mouth, gasping and startled, staring at her as if she is someone he has known and forgotten and now sees again. (40)

The narrative ends with his recognition that she has indeed sealed his fate by compelling him to murder her, with his anticipation of capture, and with that surprising last-minute allusion to Aristotle's theory of tragedy, as we move from Richard's subjective vision into narratorial discourse:

> He sees already the gleaming buttons of the policemen's uniforms, hears the cold and the confiding, the hot and the barking voices, sees already the holsters and the epaulets and all those trappings devised to protect them from the indecent exposure of fear and pity, pity and fear. (160)

It is as if the narrator recognizes, and invites our recognition of, the kind of action that has unfolded, the genre we are in, namely a tragedy. The allusion to *catharsis* draws on only the last part of the venerable definition, beginning with 'the imitation of an action that is serious, complete, and of a certain magnitude' and ending with 'through pity and fear effecting the proper purgation of these emotions' (Butcher 23). How far is 'pity and fear' *pars pro toto*? The narrow temporal scope of the action (virtually a weekend), its concentration on few locations (briefly in Copenhagen, in transit, then mostly in Rome), its tight focus on Lise's hubristic passion, all conform to Aristotelian patterns, as does the devising of 'perpetual misunderstandings' (Barthes 148), surprising recognitions ('The one I'm looking for will recognize me', 95) and reversed situations, or *peripeteia* (the victim selects her murderer, the 'driver' loses control). The last revisionary paragraph transcends the stark account of the murder and of the murderer's attempted escape, rising to a manifestly more elaborated, lyrical prose which plays the part of tragedy's concluding 'choric song'. This culminates a pattern of prolepses and minor ascents into rhetoric, as in the Beckettian opening to chapter 6, imparting a sense of imminent catastrophe, ironic detachment and gradual increase in overt narratorial control (the narrator as literary critic, as Greek chorus).

The concluding impression is of some cathartic discharge of awesome energy, whether by character, writer, or reader, and, for all its bleak (but not absolute) refusal of empathy, the story has exhibited the terrible and pitiable in the central event. Nevertheless, the conception of catharsis as a ritual cleansing, an evacuation of polluting or waste matter (Lucas Appendix II, 276), finds its travestied incarnation in Enlightenment Leader Bill's 'cleansing diet' (48), Lise's determination to be blood-stained, and the discovery of her corpse by garbage-men (144). Moreover, Lise's repeated misidentifications of her 'type' of man and semi-farcical conversations with Mrs Fiedke, Richard's aunt, envelop her grim voluntarism in buffoonery (Bill's chat-up and macrobiotic patter, his leaking bag of rice; Mrs Fiedke's conviction that men, not content with equal rights, will 'want the upper hand', 107). The savage irony of postmodern black comedy, punctuated by carnivalesque inversions, interferes with, if not wholly displaces, the 'authorized version'. Comedy, like tragedy, may turn on climactic recognition (*anagnorisis*) after cross-purposes. A later novel quotes Socrates's urging in *The Symposium* that 'the genius of comedy was the same with that of tragedy' (Spark 1992, [5]), which accords with twentieth-century preferences for the grotesque rather than the pure genre. The allusion to the tragic is challenging, given that the barely explicable climactic act (Lise's voluntary, brutal death, after her apparently stridently resisted rape) involves figures with minimal psychology and that the text is often freakishly witty. There is no missing, however, the preponderance of terror: both Lise and the text have 'frightened' (41, 46, 83, 157).[6] Although no particular tragedy serves as a model, unaccountable Lise is kin to Euripidean homicidal 'heroines' like Electra and Medea, even echoing Lyssa (personified Madness in *Heracles*). Pity enters belatedly: ambiguously prefigured in the intermittent kindness Lise exhibits toward Mrs Fiedke (81–2); most noticeable in negation, when Lise experiences a 'pitiless frustration of her will' (42). But by the end compassion *is* released, through 'a catharsis which arises from the pain of being human' (Waugh 1995, 144).

The text arguably seeks closure in returning to the narrator the dignity of an author, an identification with an aesthetic-cum-moral tradition of magisterial force, containing pathology and collective disorder in a classical frame: the narrator's signature inheres in the *preposterous* inversion of pity and fear which precedes the restored, authoritative sequence of the quoted phrase. A mere *fait divers* – what Spark had read about in an Italian newspaper (Spark 1996a) – is thus endowed with a larger moral resonance. In a return of the repressed, the author (as critic) takes back control, for, significantly, the potentially tragic perspective derives from the commentary of a superior reader on how spectators read the genre. To representations of the reader and the implications of the chiasmus[7] shaping this portentous paraph, I must return.

* * *

Generic reassignment has, in fact, already established itself as a an aspect of characterization and the reading process. Popular literary kinds, not so culturally privileged as the tragic, are parodically destabilized, since Lise appears to reconstruct her life-narrative through deceptive and contradictory rewritings of her own script (most fantastically for Carlo, 112, 114). As a surrogate novelist she mimics the Mills & Boon holiday romance, feigning to seek erotic fulfilment abroad while planning to die. Laying a trail for the authorities to identify her posthumously, by dispensing with her passport, dressing ostentatiously, behaving eccentrically, assembling a cloud of witnesses, she inverts the conventions of detective fiction whereby the criminal strives always to cover his tracks. Confronting audiences in and outside the text with the puzzle of 'the murderee', she compels readers to co-produce her text, too. Other fleetingly invoked popular genres, like the fairy tale (40) and nursery rhyme (121),[8] declare that Lise is more of an oral performer than a literary scribe, merely marking a map with a pen and addressing packages with lipstick. Travelling through genres she is a woman travelling mythologically against the patriarchal grain: a Penelope appropriating Odysseus's mobility, wiles and yarns (Lawrence 1994, ix–x), she 'spins along in expert style' (121), a parodist weaving ' a newe webbe in their [men's] loome' (Morson 112). Is it by chance that the only remotely personal touch to the Spartan furnishing of her apartment is 'a patterned rug from Greece' (19–20)? Is she weaving herself into a classical *text*?

If the rug may function punningly as minor *mise-en-abŷme*, a more obvious metafictional sign is the inclusion in the text of a book, a rather convoluted example of the intimacy between the novella's generic indeterminacy and Lise as text-in-production. Sole representative of literate culture, this unread paperback is purchased originally for the potential match of its lurid cover to the interior decor of a fellow traveller but exploited thereafter by Lise as an advertisement for her killer (31–2). The cover, depicting brown-skinned lovers wearing nothing but garlands of sunflowers (32), parallels Lise's parodied holiday romance. With the 'author's name' unspecified (31), design triumphs over content. Like Lise, the text is all brightly-coloured surface, the inside a virtual blank. She will, however, present a spectacular 'reading' of it when she eventually locates her 'type' and bequeaths it to the hotel porter:

> You can keep his luggage. You can have the book as well; it's a whydunnit in q-sharp major and it has a message: never talk to the sort of girls that you wouldn't leave lying about in your drawing-room for the servants to pick up. (151)

This is a blurb, burlesquing in advance the eventual 'directed' re-reading of Lise's story as tragedy. Her ludicrous performance of (critical) authority mocks, too, the 'authoritative' tone of Richard, making almost his last bid to be the author of his own life (150). An arbitrary, libertine reader producing her own text, Lise ignores paratext (cover) as generic constraint and indulges subjective fantasy: at first discarding classification by the idyllic cover and resorting to crime fiction, the 'whydunnit' displacing the 'whodunnit' since murderous Lise's motivation is what is unknown. The blatantly reductive 'message' recasts Lise herself as tragic Messenger, whose utterances have to be read 'between the lines'.[9] Couched in class imagery out of an Agatha Christie book, the 'message' returns us simultaneously to 'romance' in an unmarked quotation, reworking a risibly sexist and class-biased passage from the opening address for the Prosecution in the trial of *Lady Chatterley's Lover*:

> You may think that one of the ways in which you can test it from the most liberal outlook, is to ask yourselves the question, when you have read it through, would you approve of your young sons, young daughters – because girls can read as well as boys – reading this book. *Is it a book that you would leave lying around in your house? Is it a book that you even wish your wife or your servants to read?* (Rolph 17; emphasis added)

'The sort of girls' and a type of book, left 'lying around', are elided as objects which have to be disposed of. Lise's coded instruction to Richard to purge her violently of her material self mocks what John Middleton Murry claimed to see in the Lawrence: 'a cleansing book, the bringer of a new catharsis' (Rolph 83).

\* \* \*

Although Spark is self-identified as a writer of Catholic convictions, the texts do not unequivocally solicit construal according to a Judaeo-Christian, or specifically Catholic intention. In contrast with *The Mandelbaum Gate*, for example, whose Barbara Vaughan impresses as Lise's Catholic antithesis, progressing from feeling 'a spinster of no fixed identity' (Spark 1965, 45) to a new-found integrity and compatible marriage, *The Driver's Seat* reduces action overtly motivated by faith and eschews marked scriptural quotation by authentic believers. But here, as in Kafkaesque fantasy, we may perceive 'the sacred as a determinate marked absence at the heart of the secular world' (Jameson 145). 'God' makes a single appearance – in the ramblings of pious but dotty Mrs Fiedke (106). A Jehovah's Witness, she boasts that she is a 'strict believer' (101), yet her unique name probably mangles the Latin *fide et fiducia* (by faith and confidence), for she myopically approaches Lise 'confidently', with 'trusting confidence' (76, 77), and unreliable Lise is a reduced 'Elizabeth' (Hebrew: God is sworn). Two unmarked quotations from the Gospels are also partial disclosures, both implicating 'Bill the macrobiotic'. A replacement of natural with artificial sources of light in remodelling a fragment from Matthew 5:45 ('the unjust and the just alike', 135) serves as sardonic commentary on his date with Lise at the Metropole and as resiting of human justice in a Providential frame. Heedlessly urging his creed on unreceptive Lise, Bill slightly misquotes (48) from Mark 4:9, 'He that hath ears to hear let him hear.' The allusion to the Parable of the Sower, wonderfully apposite to his farcical emissions of wild rice as if it were his seed, ironically makes the point that Christ deliberately speaks in parables which remain opaque to the uninitiated.

Parable, Spark's fictional mode (Spark 1961, 63), possesses outer and inner circles of reception, its diction being aptly equivocal: superficially secular(ized) words ('holiday', 13; 'cross', 73; 'witness', 91) become ambiguous markers of the absent sacred. The past may be overtly displaced but language is enfolded, recoverable history. Even words topically oriented to 1960s cults, like 'psychedelic' (46) and 'macrobiotic' (48), insinuate etymologically the classical freight of 'mind-revealing' and 'life-prolonging'. When Lise denies she has found her type by feeling 'a presence', another intertextual node is exposed:

> 'Not really a presence,' Lise says. 'The lack of an absence, that's what it is. I know I'll find it.' (105)

Lise appears to invert both Catholic doctrine of Christ's corporeal presence in the Eucharist and New Testament promise of Christ's second coming, or *parousia*, Greek for 'presence' or 'arrival' (Alter and Kermode 670).

The division of the novella into seven chapters, along with extensive play with sevens (pp. 77–8), recalls the seven-haunted last book of the Bible. Approaching *her* last days, Lise of 'a final and a judging mouth' (12), attempts to pass judgement on herself and, an unconscious vehicle of revelation (Scourge of God), on modern decadence. Apocalyptic hope of a renewed city (mystic marriage of Church and Christ) is ultimately frustrated in Lise's violation by her 'type'. Indeed, repetition of 'type' may alert us to apocalyptyic analogy through *typological* reading.[10] In Jericho, Barbara Vaughan jestingly types herself as 'the scarlet woman' of Revelation 17:4 (Spark 1965, 232) but eventually is associated prefiguratively with St John's New Jerusalem as bride (Revelation 21:2).[11] In Rome, antithetical Lise, teasing in dress of 'an old-fashioned' 'street-prostitute' length (30, 75), more obviously plays the 'scarlet' part: 'a temptress of the old-fashioned school' (115). Since 'apocalypse' signifies an uncovering, it is proper that Lise, associated throughout with denaturing wrapped and covered objects (Waugh 1989, 216), should figure as the fallen woman-city, flamboyantly clothed like the Whore of Babylon 'arrayed in purple and scarlet colour' (Revelation 17:4):

> It is possibly the combination of colours – the red in her coat and the purple in her dress – rather than the colours themselves which drags attention to her. (74)

Mystifying herself – using different voices and languages, wearing lurid garments, presenting contradicting personae, lying – Lise (anagrammatically, 'lies') is the type of 'MYSTERY, BABYLON THE GREAT, THE MOTHER OF HARLOTS AND ABOMINATIONS OF THE EARTH' (Revelation 17:5) and of Satan, doomed accuser, who will be 'loosed out of his prison', 'And shall go out to deceive the nations which are in the four quarters of the earth' (Revelation 20:7, 8). Lise's ostentatious command of four languages corresponds particularly to the demonic Babelic mission. Finally, Lise and

Richard's attempts 'to start a new life' (160) are sad mimicries of St John's ecstatic vision of the great renovation:

> And I saw a new heaven and earth ... And he that sat upon the throne said, Behold, I make all things new. (Revelation 21:1, 5)

Lise, the ultimate 'displaced person' (90), is mirrored in the deposed Sheikh, another displaced authority, who has lost 'his throne or whatever it is he sits on' (130). She must submit to the restored authority of an enthroned divinity (Revelation 20:11; 21:5), for apocalypses are intended to reassure mankind that in spite of catastrophes, God is in control, in the driver's seat (Nineham 339).

* * *

I return now to that suspended examination of the clinching chiasmus. Spark's texts tend to close, suddenly, with some rhetorically expansive gesture involving conspicuous sound-play. Examples of completive phrases with chiasmic patterning bracket her writing career so far, from her first short-story success, 'The Seraph and the Zambesi' (1951) – 'among the rocks that look like crocodiles and the crocodiles that look like rocks' (Spark 1985, 84) – to the late novel – 'here in the tract of no-man's land between dreams and reality, reality and dreams' (Spark 1996, 160). They tend to evoke problems of distinction between normally separated entities; looking stable in a phonologically balanced structure, they inspire doubt, however, about what can be objectively established. The cathartic chiasmus may follow suit, suggesting that the paired tragic emotions may not be distinct. But chiastic disposition of Aristotle's phrase acknowledges more forcefully *dual* (moral) authority, the narrator's and the Greek's, the Catholic's and the pagan's. Since chiasmus is as much a part of the Old Testament rhetorical repertoire as of the classics (Alter and Kermode 1987, *passim*), we may register here greater convergence of mutually reinforcing intertextual frames. Merleau-Ponty's reminder that *chiasm* is 'derived from a Greek root which means to "mark with a cross"' (Burgin 117) is pertinent, for at the mid-point of the text, under the 'central light' of her hotel room Lise will mark the murder-spot on her inset tourist map with 'a little cross' (73), as if to indicate both her self-mystification (X is the unknown) and her perverted self-sacrifice. This follows hard on Lise's sudden, unexplained resolution of some crucial indecision which, taking place at the core of the middle chapter of the book, becomes the cardinal act of a chiasmically ordered sequence: arriving and departing, unpacking and packing, unfolding and folding of clothes.

While this pattern of doubled action has informed the text as a whole, with its levelling revisiting of similar urban settings and types and its close weave of iterated words like 'stain', 'pattern' and 'away', rhetorical schematization goes beyond constructing many balanced contrasts ('neither good-looking nor bad-looking', 25–6, 29; 'I'm your type and you're my type', 53) to deploying the reversed parallelism of chiasmus (the constrictive placement of Lise in the office hierarchy, with 'five girls under her and two men. Over her are two women and five men', 12; 'My brother made it clear to them. I made it clear to my brother', 108). Furthermore, *chiasm* is the 'anatomical term for the crossing over of two physiological structures' (Burgin 117), so one further possible effect of the terminal rhetorical chiasmus is to underscore a mirroring or intertwining of parts. A striking comparison tucked into the narrative detour of the Sheikh's two-by-two procession slyly combines religious and classical discourses:

> each two moving in such unison they seem to share a single *soul* or else two well-rehearsed parts in the *chorus* of a Verdi opera. (124; emphasis added)

The uncanny conception of two parts of a single soul affords a final tragic reading for *two* personages, Lise and Richard. Richard is Lise's double: unpartnered, mentally unstable, endeavouring to change; stranger to, but mysteriously aware of, the other. The language of 'partial disclosure' is a strong clue when the hotel concierge tries to explain to Lise, who has been parading her disorientation, the phenomenon of jet lag and significantly uses the masculine pronoun for Lise's 'other part':

> Yes, you left part of yourself at home ... That other part, he is still en route to our country but he will catch up with you in a few hours' time. It's often the way with travel by air, the passenger arrives ahead of himself. (65–6)

Extension of the narrative beyond Lise's death to encompass Richard's anticipation of capture and interrogation, would suggest that the story is incomplete without this implied mutuality of madness and destruction, of a fated physical commingling that achieves cross-over identifications of victor and victim, reinforcing the point that Lise is as much social symptom and casualty as criminal or sinner.

The last word should be the ambiguous 'afterwards' – what Lise wants to circumvent (postcoital sadness, 154) and to control (the aftermath of self-destruction, 158), displacing orthodox 'after-life' (ludicrous in Mrs Fiedke's application, 101) with her perceived 'finality' of physical annihilation (159). But Lise's media-managed posthumous notoriety will be short-lived. The police's suppressed apprehension of the reality of human suffering yields to 'indecent exposure', the impercipient authority of their typewriter ticking out Richard's 'unnerving statement' (159) being displaced by the compassionate recognition of those authoritative afterwords from, ironically, a *deus ex machina*.[12]

## Notes

1    *The Public Image* (1968) and *Not to Disturb* (1971). Subsequent page references to *The Driver's Seat* are to the first edition and are included in the text of the essay. The Penguin edition (1974) designates chapters by arabic numerals and corrects 'unmustered' (111) to 'unmastered' hysteria (75). The epigraph is from 108.

2    *Part* as (sb.) portion, side, role; as (vb.) separate; then *apart, apartment, departs, departures, department, partition, particular*.

3    'How could the removal of the author function as anything other than a provisional reduction?' ... 'Direct resistance *to* the author demonstrates little so much as the resistance *of* the author' (Burke 50, 172).

4    Defined as 'the ways in which any spoken or written text, literary or non-literary, is produced and interpreted through our conscious or unconscious experience' (Verdonk and Weber 248), intertextuality here sometimes indicates source, sometimes speculative analogue.

5    See allusions to Greek literature in *Doctors of Philosophy* (1962), *Symposium* (1990), 'The Messengers' (Spark 1967, 59), her review of Eliot's *The Confidential Clerk* in 1953, and autobiographical writings (Spark 1992, 146, 204; Spark 1970, 412).

6    'I understand from people who have read it that it's frightening. I frightened myself by writing it' (Spark 1970, 413).

7    '*Chiasm* [or chiasmus]: A formal patterning of any literary or rhetorical unit that preserves symmetry while reversing the order of the terms, to produce the sequence ABBA' (Alter and Kermode, 668).

8    A variant of the chorus of a popular comic song, 'The King of the Cannibal Islands', *c.* 1830 (*The Oxford Dictionary of Nursery Rhymes*, eds Iona and Peter Opie, Oxford: Oxford University Press, 1951, 211).

9    From the poem 'The Messengers' celebrating the necessary tragic servants, 'Bringing a folded meaning home, / Between the lines, inside the letter' (Spark 1967, 59).

10   Now a flexibly applied prefigurative reading derived from traditional belief that the hidden sense of an Old Testament passage or character, 'type', is made plain only when fulfilled by a New Testament 'antitype' (Alter and Kermode 672) which would be familiar to Spark from the admired writings of Cardinal Newman. Spark also uses typology in the looser sociological sense; see 'the typology of Beryl Tims', *Loitering With Intent* (Bodley Head, 1981, 25–6).

11   Barbara hears this passage from Revelation quoted by a priest in Jerusalem, 'type and shadow' of the heavenly city (Spark 1965, 214).

12 'Ironically', since Aristotle disapproved of the device (Butcher 55).

## Bibliography

Alter, Robert and Frank Kermode (eds) (1987), *The Literary Guide to the Bible*, London: Collins.

Barthes, Roland (1977), 'The Death of the Author', in *Image-Music-Text*, trans. Stephen Heath, Glasgow: Fontana/Collins.

Burgin, Victor (1991), 'Geometry and Abjection', in John Fletcher and Andrew Benjamin (eds), *Abjection, Melancholia, and Love: The Work of Julia Kristeva*, London and New York: Routledge.

Burke, Sean (1998 [1992]), *The Death and Return of the Author: Criticism and Subjectivity in Barthes, Foucault and Derrida*, 2nd edn, Edinburgh: Edinburgh University Press.

Butcher, S.H. (1951 [1894]), *Aristotle's Theory of Poetry and Fine Art, with a Critical Text of 'The Poetics'*, 4th edn, New York: Dover Publications.

Lawrence, Karen R. (1994), *Penelope Voyages: Women and Travel in the British Literary Tradition*, Ithaca: Cornell University Press.

Lucas, D.W. (1978), 'Pity, Fear and *Katharsis*', Appendix II, in D.W. Lucas (ed.), *Aristotle: 'Poetics'*, Oxford: Clarendon Press.

Morgan, Thais (1989), 'The Space of Intertextuality', in Patrick O'Donnell and Robert Con Davis (eds), *Intertextuality and Contemporary American Fiction*, Baltimore and London: Johns Hopkins University Press.

Morson, Gary (1981), *The Boundaries of Genre: Dostoevsky's 'Diary of a Writer' and the Tradition of Literary Utopias*, Austin: University of Texas Press.

Nineham, D.E. (1975), *The Gospel of St Mark* (Pelican New Testament Commentaries), Harmondsworth: Penguin.

Page, Norman (1990), *Muriel Spark*, Basingstoke and London: Macmillan.

Rolph, C.H. (1961), *The Trial of Lady Chatterley: Regina v. Penguin Books Ltd*, Harmondsworth: Penguin.

Spark, Muriel (1965), *The Mandelbaum Gate*, Basingstoke and London: Macmillan.

Spark, Muriel (1967) *The Collected Poems 1*, London: Macmillan.

Spark, Muriel (1970a), 'Keeping it Short: Muriel Spark talks about her books to Ian Gilham', *Listener*, 24 September 1970, 411–13.

Spark, Muriel (1970b), *The Driver's Seat*, Basingstoke and London: Macmillan.

Spark, Muriel (1985), *The Stories of Muriel Spark*, London: Bodley Head.

Spark, Muriel (1992 [1990]), *Symposium*, London: Constable.

Spark, Muriel (1992), *Curriculum Vitae: Autobiography*, London: Constable.

Spark, Muriel (1996a), *Reality and Dream*, London: Constable.

Spark, Muriel (1996b), *The Elusive Spark* (*Bookmark* BBC 2, 3 March).

Verdonk, Peter and Jean-Jacques Weber (eds) (1995), *Twentieth Century Fiction: From Text to Context*, London and New York: Routledge. Waugh, Patricia (1989), *Feminine Fictions: Revisiting the Postmodern*, London and New York: Routledge.

Waugh, Patricia (1995), *The Harvests of The Sixties: English Literature and Its Background, 1960–1990*, Oxford: Oxford University Press.

## Chapter Fifteen

# 'Not Undesirable': J.M. Coetzee and the Burdens of Censorship[1]

Peter D. McDonald

In an interview given in 1990, just as South Africa was poised to enter a new phase in its history, J.M. Coetzee was asked about the treatment his work had received by the censors of the *ancien régime*. His reply was disarmingly candid: 'I regard it as a badge of honor to have had a book banned in South Africa ... This honor I have never achieved nor, to be frank, merited' (Coetzee 1992, 298). Characteristically – he has never been one for easy ways out of ethical difficulties – this put the burden of responsibility as much on himself as on the censors. And yet the five novels he published during various phases of the censorship era – *Dusklands* (1974), *In the Heart of the Country* (1977), *Waiting for the Barbarians* (1980), *Life & Times of Michael K* (1983), and *Foe* (1986) – were not exactly innocuous. So just how did they manage not to get banned? How was it that Coetzee, unlike many of his contemporaries, was deprived of that particular 'badge of honour'?

The essential details about his treatment by the censors have always been a matter of public knowledge, at least in South Africa. The fact that *In the Heart of the Country* and *Life & Times of Michael K* were embargoed – that is, withheld from distribution, read, passed, and then released by the censors – was reported in local newspapers. Conversely, in the absence of any such reports, it has always been considered likely that *Dusklands*, *Waiting for the Barbarians* and *Foe* escaped the censors altogether. New evidence from archives of the former Publications Control Board (hereafter PCB) confirms this. There are detailed files on *In the Heart of the Country* (P77/7/103) and *Michael K* (P83/10/168) but none on the other three novels. More importantly, as the archival records of the day-to-day workings of the PCB also show, there is no single, or simple, explanation for the official response to Coetzee.

The fact that *Dusklands* and *Foe* failed to reach the censors could, for instance, be attributed to the inefficiency of the system or its various functionaries (the police, especially); to the particular circumstances of their production (both were published and printed locally for the South African market); to the refusal of Ravan Press, Coetzee's politically radical South African publishers, to collude with the censors by submitting books prior to publication; to inaction on the part of local readers who could (and often did) lobby the PCB; to Coetzee's 'indirect' and 'rarefied' literary methods; or, in the case of *Foe*, to the more nuanced censorship policy of the 1980s.[2] About *Waiting for the Barbarians* we can be a little more definite, in part because of the particular way the local edition was initially produced and distributed. First published in 1980 by Secker & Warburg, Coetzee's British publishers from 1977, it appeared in South Africa in January 1981 under the Ravan imprint. (Between 1977 and 1986 Secker generally ceded Coetzee's South African hardback rights to Ravan.) Importantly, the first impression of the local edition (but not the second) was printed in Great Britain and then exported to the country. In all likelihood, then, *Waiting for the Barbarians* never came to the attention of the PCB because, unlike *In the Heart of the Country* and *Michael K*, it survived the scrutiny of the customs officers, the first agents in the chain of distribution for imported books.

This admittedly only shifts the puzzle further down the line. How did it manage to get past customs? Local newspaper reports about the fate of *Life & Times of Michael K* two years later suggest a plausible solution. The embargo procedure initiated by customs was, one report noted, a 'formality, applied to all books *about South Africa* coming into the country' (*Argus* 3, my italics). Another claimed customs officers 'automatically' sent such books to the PCB, a revelation which led one sardonic local journalist to comment: 'The day is not far off when a South African gardening book, about, say, the cultivation of proteas [the national flower], will find itself in the illustrious company of *Michael K*' (Botha 14; Grütter 20). Clearly, for the Cape Town customs officers, who no doubt routinely judged books by their covers, *Waiting for the Barbarians* was not a 'South African novel'. This was a reasonable enough assumption. Neither the book, with its simple, non-pictorial cover design, nor the non-realist narrative, which the blurb noted was set simply on 'an outpost of Empire', displayed any obvious signs of 'South Africanness'. Yet, while the blurb accurately described the novel's oblique methods, it was not itself over-subtle. It referred directly to state-sanctioned torture, and concluded with this remark about the central protagonist:

> The old Magistrate is not simply a man living through a crisis of conscience in an obscure place in remote times; his situation is that of all men living in unbearable complicity with regimes which elevate their own survival above justice and decency. (Coetzee 1981)

That the customs officers overlooked this adds further irony to the novel's opening question, asked of a state functionary: 'Is he blind?' (Coetzee 1981, 1).

Customs made no such mistakes about *In the Heart of the Country* or *Michael K*, and for obvious reasons. Despite the arrangements with Ravan, Secker initially exported its own editions of the two books to South Africa. Their covers made no particularly national statement either: while the former had the same abstract design as *Barbarians*, the latter was pictorial but non-committal (it had a sepia-toned negative portrait of a racially indeterminate man in a bowler hat). Their blurbs, however, were direct and confrontational; indeed, in the case of *In the Heart of the Country*, even provocative, given that the Immorality Act (1950) was still enforced in 1977. It began:

> Stifling in the torpor of colonial South Africa, trapped with his serfs in a web of reciprocal oppression, a lonely sheepfarmer makes a bid for private salvation in the arms of a black concubine, child-bride of his foreman. But this lurch across the colour-bar marks the end of the uneasy feudal peace.

It also downplayed the novel's metafictional preoccupations, describing it as having a 'sensational plot' about 'violence and madness' and 'bloody revenge' (Coetzee 1977, dust-jacket). The opening sentence of the blurb for *Michael K* was equally forthright:

> In a South Africa whose civil administration is collapsing under the pressure of years of civil strife, an obscure young gardener named Michael K decides to take his mother on a long march away from the guns towards a new life in the abandoned countryside.

It then went on to mention how he is 'tracked down and locked up as a collaborator with the rural guerrillas' (Coetzee 1983, dust-jacket). For all the indirections of his texts, then, these paratexts, which were either written or authorized by Coetzee, left little doubt about the oppositional stance of the two novels. For the Controller of Customs the simple mention of 'South Africa' was enough. Using powers accorded to him under Article 113 (3) of the Customs and Excise Act (1964), he applied to the Director of Publications for a decision about *In the Heart of the Country* on 11 July 1977, and about *Michael K* on 31 October 1983, a few days after it had been announced that Coetzee had won the Booker Prize for the first time.

On reaching the PCB, the books were processed according to a strict bureaucratic schedule. After a file was opened on each they were taken to one of the Director's deputies who assigned them to readers approved (and paid) by the government. (The appointment of readers, it should be noted, was the responsibility of the Minister of the Interior, not of the PCB.) This was a fairly random business. The archival records show that *In the Heart of the Country* was, rather unusually, posted to three readers: H. van der Merwe Scholtz, Professor of Afrikaans and Nederlands at the University of Cape Town; F.C. Fensham, Professor of Semitic Languages at Stellenbosch University; and Anna M. Louw, a professional Afrikaans novelist living in Cape Town. Following a more common practice, *Michael K* was sent only to one: Mrs E.H. Scholtz, a cultured, university-educated Cape Town housewife. That both novels were sent to literary specialists was predictable; that they were sent to the more open-minded among them was probably lucky. All four readers belonged to the small world of the apologist Afrikaner intelligentsia which dominated the censorship committees in the 1970s and 1980s – indeed, Mrs Scholtz was (and remains) the Professor's wife. Their establishment credentials were impeccable: they were graduates of reputable Afrikaans universities in their fifties or sixties; they were members of the N.G. Kerk, active in various mainstream Afrikaans cultural and academic organizations; and they came with the highest recommendations. Professor and Mrs Scholtz were, for instance, proposed as readers by J.T. Kruger, then Deputy Minister of the Interior.[3] Yet this did not automatically make them defenders of conservative Afrikaner opinion, at least on literary matters. Indeed, in what became a *cause celèbre* of the era – the banning in 1977 of *Magersfontein, O Magersfontein!*, an iconoclastic historical novel by the Afrikaans writer Etienne Leroux – Professor Scholtz and Anna Louw found themselves among an embattled, culturally-progressive minority. They were members of the committee – Scholtz was in fact the Chair – that originally passed the novel in January that year, a decision which was subsequently appealed by the Minister of the Interior, Connie Mulder, and then overturned by the Publications Appeal Board, the PCB's final adjudicator, then under the chairmanship of the elderly Judge J.H. Snyman. (As eight thick files of letters in the archives reveal, the Minister and the PCB were lobbied by outraged ordinary Afrikaners and N.G. Kerk groups.) When the novel was ultimately banned in November – on the grounds of 'unsavoury [*ongure*] language and descriptions in a book of acknowledged literary merit' – both Louw and Scholtz resigned as readers, though they continued to serve on the Appeal Board (PCB 77/1/97; IDP 1/5/3).

The *Magersfontein* episode suggests that Coetzee was indeed fortunate to get the readers he did – Scholtz and Louw were again overruled when they tried to unban *Lady Chatterley's Lover* in July 1977 – but it also shows that

that was not enough to save a book from banning. The readers' statutory powers were too limited. The only area in which they could exercise some provisional freedom was, of course, in the application of the law to particular books. This was their first key function. On standard report forms they were required to give a 'synopsis of the contents' of each book, to indicate with detailed page references which parts of it 'may possibly be regarded as undesirable', and finally to make and justify their recommendation. The forms listed the six subdivisions of Section 47 (2) of the Act (1974), according to which any publication could be 'deemed to be undesirable' if it

(a) was 'indecent or obscene' or was 'offensive or harmful to public morals';
(b) was 'blasphemous or … offensive to the religious convictions or feelings of any section of the inhabitants of the Republic';
(c) brought 'any section of the inhabitants of the Republic into ridicule or contempt';
(d) was 'harmful to the relations between any sections of the inhabitants of the Republic';
(e) was 'prejudicial to the safety of the State, the general welfare or the peace and good order';
(f) disclosed anything which was 'indecent or offensive or harmful' from 'any judicial proceedings'. (*Gazette*, 61–2)

These were the legal criteria with which readers had to work. In practice, they also had to consider their responsibilities as custodians of community standards. This second key aspect of their remit imposed limits on the first by obliging them to operate as (ideally self-effacing) adjudicators between the book, the law and a putative reading public. This additional measure was intended to bypass general problems of relativism in questions of value, and to allay specific concerns about subjectivism on the part of reading committees.

What this 'public' meant in legal and practical terms was, however, among the most contested issues of the late censorship era. Indeed, the changes in censorship practice, instigated by the furore over *Magersfontein* and then facilitated by the appointment, on Snyman's retirement in 1980, of the young criminal law professor, J.C.W. van Rooyen, to the Chair of the Appeal Board, centred principally on its legal definition. Under Snyman's conservative dispensation of the 1970s, the 'public' meant a hypothetical 'average reader'; while in van Rooyen's more nuanced later phase, it meant the 'likely reader' of the book under consideration.[4] These radically different definitions had far-reaching consequences at every level of the system, beginning with the meaning of the Act's various criteria. In theory, the word 'obscene' – to take just one criterion – meant, for Louw, Fensham and Professor Scholtz in 1977, 'that which would be obscene in the eyes of a supposed average South African reader'; whereas, for Mrs Scholtz in 1983, it meant 'that which would be obscene in the eyes of the likely reader of *Michael K*'. Just how these elaborate exercises in triangulation and supposition worked in practice can only be determined on a case by case basis.

The readers' first task, after attempting a brief summary of the narrative, was to identify parts of the text that might be 'undesirable', and to classify them under the Act's six criteria. This was left somewhat vague in the case of *In the Heart of the Country* because all three readers provided only a list of problematic pages without reference to the Act. A more or less clear idea of their views can, however, be inferred from some of their comments – all originally in Afrikaans – and from the novel itself. Their 'doubts', as they put it, centred on 47 (2) (a), the obscenity criterion.[5] Yet, as most of the sex in the novel occurs 'across the colour-bar', they could conceivably have been concerned about 47 (2) (d), in effect the race relations criterion, at the same time. Significantly, the only episode that seemed to all three problematic in this regard was the sexual assault in sections 206 to 211, according to the novel's own numbered sequence of textual fragments. This is where Hendrik, the black farm labourer, repeatedly rapes Magda, the white spinster-daughter and the novel's first-person narrator. Or so it seems. In a move characteristic of 1960s and 1970s literary experimentalism – John Barth's 'funhouse' of fiction is pertinent – the novel, as all three readers recognized, never discloses whether the events Magda recounts are real or only figments of her increasingly deranged imagination. Yet, if they all thought the rape 'possibly undesirable', they had very different interpretations of its overall significance in the novel. Knowingly or tellingly, Professor Scholtz, who emphasized Magda's alleged patricide, all but ignored it: 'Hendrik becomes increasingly uppish [*vrypostig*], later sleeps with her (the sexual intercourse between the two is, seen from her side, affectingly pathetic, with absolutely no fulfilment).' Fensham was more matter of fact and optimistic on this issue: 'Magda is raped [*verkrag*] by Hendrik, but she later achieves a sexual awakening with him.' And Louw, who identified strongly with Magda whom she saw as a tragic heroine of the spirit, noted:

> To avenge himself, to humiliate his former mistress as much as possible, Hendrik rapes [*verkrag*] her, makes her his kept woman. Even out of this ruin Magda tries to rescue a little of the regard she has had to forfeit for so long in her life,

as well as spiritual rewards for all three of them [herself, Hendrik, and Klein-Anna, Hendrik's young wife]. To no avail.

About all the other potentially doubtful passages there was no unanimity at all. The only other section Louw identified, no doubt also under 47 (2) (a), was no. 64 where Magda, the postmodern Electra, thinks about the odd intimacies between her father and herself made inevitable by their shared use of the farm's 'bucket-latrine'. She imagines how their excrement becomes 'looped in each other's coils, the father's red snake and the daughter's black embrace and sleep and dissolve' (Coetzee 1977, 32). This also concerned Scholtz, but not Fensham. The two men, who were either more vigilant or more conservative than Louw, were, however, in broad agreement about most of the novel's other explicit moments. They both listed Magda's thoughts about her body and her speculations about her sexual destiny (no. 87), her baffled glimpse of Hendrik's erect penis and his sexual advances on Klein-Anna (no. 144), and her less brutal but still empty sexual encounters with Hendrik after the rape (nos 217 to 222, and 228). Fensham alone found the description of the father's seduction of Klein-Anna (no. 75), as well as Hendrik's provocative striptease before Magda (no. 196), potentially problematic. And only Scholtz drew attention to Magda's anxieties about what Hendrik might tell Klein-Anna about her sexual needs (no. 167), to the detailed images of the father's putrefying corpse (nos 157 and 182), and to the black comedy of the burial scene (no. 182). The passages giving concern which were not classifiable under 47 (2) (a), or a combination of (a) and (d), were no. 248, mentioned by Scholtz, and no. 259, singled out by Fensham, both of which include comments on God's indifference to, or active part in, human suffering. Here the blasphemy criterion, 47 (2) (b), is most likely to have been the issue, but it is also worth remembering the Act's foundational principle which was to recognize the 'constant endeavour of the population of the Republic of South Africa to uphold a Christian view of life' (*Gazette*, 7).

There was, in other words, much in the novel that could be deemed 'undesirable' in terms of the law, and no doubt in the eyes of the 'average South African reader' whose putative values Scholtz, Fensham and Louw were supposed to be upholding. Yet, in their separate reports, they all designated it, according to the official litotes, 'not undesirable', and strongly recommended it be released for circulation. Their individual justifications for this ranged from the steadily predictable to the inventively idiosyncratic. All agreed, for instance, that the rape was wholly functional. As Louw characteristically put it, 'the rape scene ... becomes a baptism of fire for the soul rather than a description of sexual activity'. For her, too, the 'description of the latrine' was 'a function of Magda's painful love-hate relationship with her father'. In different ways, they also agreed that this functionality was largely a triumph of style over content. For Scholtz, who found it a 'difficult read', 'the terrible murder episode, the father's death throes, the lugubrious "burial", the sexual intercourse between white and black are so firmly interwoven, even overwoven, by the sometimes almost hermetic style, that it won't give any offence'. For Fensham, the novel's remarkable verbal texture tempered its provocative content – importantly, he detected 'traces of protest literature [*versetliteratuur*]'. It was 'so outstandingly well-written that the sexual act is never over-emphasised', he noted. In her typically florid Afrikaans prose, Louw, by contrast, felt the functionality was an effect of the narrative method:

> Owing to the striking technique employed by the writer the reader is made to see the events taking place as if through a bell-jar [*glas stolp*] so that details and incidents that might, in a different context, be questioned as being undesirable function, by means of the distancing achieved, solely as parts of the mystery of being human.

This emphasis on Magda's interiority, reinforced, Louw thought, by the title, also freed the novel from the burdens of local history in her view. Going against the provocative specificity of the blurb, she argued it was 'essentially' about what happens 'in the secret human heart – that seat of emotion and consciousness – and not only to people of a specific time and place'.

Fensham produced three further, particularly inventive, motivations for his recommendation. First, pointing to the experiments with narrative epistemology, he noted 'it is difficult to abstract the reality out of the spinster's flights of imagination'. By implication, fantasized 'sex across the colour-bar', no matter how precisely detailed, was, it seems, less offensive than the fictionalized reality. Second, appealing to the contrary ideals of realism, he observed:

> The circumstance of the spinster who is cut off from all life's comforts, who sits alone on a farm, can develop into a situation when things [*dinge*] across the colour-bar can occur. The same goes for Magda's lonely father.

(Such a pragmatic appeal to plausibility would not typically have been welcomed by Christian nationalist ideologues of the 1970s.) Finally, taking a more sociological turn, he concluded that the novel was so 'intellectually and powerfully written' that it would be 'read and enjoyed only by intellectuals'.

This was also Scholtz's final opinion: 'The story is really so densely written, sometimes apparently so over-written, so over-compromised, that it won't be accessible to just anybody.' This was arguably their most controversial motivation, given the larger debates in the air at the time. It implied that the legal fiction of the 'average reader', and all it entailed, could be discounted, on the simple grounds that no such reader would read the book, and it looked towards the 'likely reader' test of the 1980s.

Mrs Scholtz's individual report on *Life & Times of Michael K*, which she wrote in English, followed the same format. After giving a brief plot summary, she identified four 'portions that may be regarded as undesirable' this time with reference to the Act. Under Section 47 (2) (a), she created sub-heading 'language', and noted 'fuck off as used by policeman' (Coetzee 1983, 105), and 'pussy-fucking' (Coetzee 1983, 126).[6] The first of these curses is directed at Michael K, the second at the army guards at the Jakkalsdrif Relocation Camp outside Prince Albert by Oosthuizen, the local police captain, who also says 'fuck the army' (Coetzee 1983, 126). Scholtz seemed especially concerned about the fact that the police were using such language, as she overlooked the 'fuck' casually uttered by young Visagie, the army deserter, in an earlier conversation with Michael K (Coetzee 1983, 87). Also under the obscenity criterion, she drew attention to the 'mention of cunnilingus' (Coetzee 1983, 243–4). In this scene towards the end of the novel, a prostitute fellates Michael – Mrs Scholtz was endearingly confused about sexual practices – who has, by then, become an object of charity for a gang of drifting carousers. Finally, under 47 (2) (c), the ridicule or contempt criterion, she identified the description of the 'police raid' on the Relocation Camp (Coetzee 1983, 123–9). Though this is a labour camp for men, women, and children officially classified as 'vagrants', Oosthuizen ransacks it in a brutal reprisal for an attack on Prince Albert. His men and their dogs move through it 'like a swarm of locusts', creating havoc, beating and terrorizing the inmates. Yet it soon becomes clear that Oosthuizen has little evidence that they are, in fact, to blame – though he calls them 'Criminals and saboteurs and idlers!' (Coetzee 1983, 125) – and that he is driven mainly by feelings of professional *ressentiment* against the army. He sees the Free Corps guards at the camp as loafers and debauchees.

For all this, Mrs Scholtz, too, considered the novel 'not undesirable'. The 'crude words' were, in her view, 'completely functional', and the 'description of fellatio' – she got it right by the end – was 'not in the least offensive' on the same grounds. 'When Michael K submits to this act,' she commented, 'it is the ultimate stage that he has reached as an object of pity.' Yet, in 1983, her principal arguments were based, not on functionality, but on the 'likely reader' test, or, more accurately, on her assumptions about this supposed reader's attitudes to literature. Her detailed motivations are worth quoting in full:

> This brilliant novel deals with sensitive political issues in South Africa. It contains derogatory references to and comments on the attitudes of the state, also to the police and the methods they employ in the carrying out of their duties.
>
> The likely readers of this publication will be sophisticated & discriminating with an interest in literature. These readers will experience the novel as a work of art & will realise that although the tragic life of Michael K is situated in South Africa his problem today is a universal one not limited to S-Africa.

To justify this final claim, she went on to quote some of the medical officer's words about Michael: 'He is like a stone, a pebble that, having lain around quietly minding its own business since the dawn of time, is now suddenly picked up and tossed randomly from hand to hand' (Coetzee 1983, 185). Used as evidence of the novel's legitimizing universality, this unsituated quotation – she made no reference to the medical officer's questionable point of view – harmonized well with her interpretation of the whole. As her summary made clear, she saw *Michael K* as a study in 'alienation'. The novel could be 'read on many levels – as a fable, as a comment on the human condition in South Africa or as a protest novel: in the sense that it protests against the way in which people are caught up in processes beyond their control'. Michael was, in her view, a 'puppet … thrown from one situation into another'. Given this, the 'probable reader' would 'only feel compassion & sympathy' when reading the fellatio episode where Michael's status as an alienated victim of forces beyond his control is conclusively dramatized. This tendentious, universalizing reading not only reduced the force of the novel's specifically South African setting – in this Scholtz echoed Louw's reading of *In the Heart of the Country* – it also ignored Michael's own refusal to accept the identity of the victim. Having been classified and reclassified throughout the novel by all those in power with an interest in defining him – as a 'vagrant', a 'criminal', a 'guerrilla', and so on – he remarks at the end, in a discreet warning to future readers: 'I have escaped the camps; perhaps, if I lie low, I will escape the charity too' (Coetzee 1983, 249).

These individual readers' reports and recommendations represented the first stage in the PCB's decision-making process. Once they had been returned with the books, one of the deputy Directors set up an *ad hoc* committee, again from the list of government-approved censors, to make final recommendations. In the case of *In the Heart of the Country*, the committee comprised Professor

Scholtz (Chair), Fensham and Louw as well as Professor F.C. Gonin and Professor W.J. du P. Erlank – three members were required to make a quorum, but four or five were common. They met on 9 September 1977, and agreed to endorse the readers' recommendations. Gonin and Erlank simply added their signatures to Fensham's report, saying, 'Let through' and 'No ban'. On the same day Professor Scholtz submitted the following Chair's report (in Afrikaans):

> In many respects an obscure, densely textured novel that is therefore extremely difficult to penetrate. And according to three (expert) readers unusual and even outstanding; indeed, according to one of them [Louw] 'one of the few works of stature in the world of South African English letters'. Sex across the colour bar occurs, but the characters are historico-geographically so situated that it is perfectly acceptable. Above all the sexual act is never described so as to cause titillation, provocation or lustfulness. Indeed, the reader does not always know where the boundary between reality and the rich, afflicted imaginary world of the spinster-narrator is. In any case, as has already been said, a difficult, obscure, multileveled work that will be read only by intellectuals, which will not reveal all its 'levels' even to them. The committee has decided with conviction to let it through. For detailed comments see the three readers' reports.

Two days later one of the Under-Directors of Publications, S.F. du Toit, who was empowered at that stage to appeal the committee's decision, authorized the release of the novel after further study and consultation with one of his colleagues, Mrs M. van der Westhuizen. In all, then, the process took exactly two months, involved seven principal figures, and required the production of just over 2,000 words.

The final deliberations on *Life & Times of Michael K* followed the same pattern, but the process was significantly quicker. The *ad hoc* committee of four – Mrs Scholtz (Chair), Mrs A.M. Theron, Dr D. Meinert and J.H. Uys – met on 14 November 1983, and endorsed Mrs Scholtz's report. Meinert and Uys briefly acknowledged their agreement, but Mrs Theron, a sixty-five-year-old former teacher, and a long-standing member of the PCB, noted (in English):

> I fully agree with excellent report of reader. A book of such merit can carry the cunnilingus [sic] description on p. 243–244. The likely readers will only be those with a literary interest.

As Meinert also referred to its 'obvious literary merit', it seems likely that the Booker award had some effect on their decision. In her chair's report, submitted on the same day, Mrs Scholtz simply referred to her individual account and indicated that the committee's decision was unanimous. The following day du Toit, and two colleagues, Mr Etienne Malan and Dr Abraham Coetzee (then the Director), confirmed that there would be 'No Appeal' from the Directorate. In one of the more enigmatic official statements, Malan added, in Afrikaans, 'Against the army and the SAP [South African Police], but ...'. The fact that the entire process took only two weeks suggests that the PCB might have been concerned about the international embarrassment the embargo was causing, an issue raised repeatedly in the local press.

For a book to circulate in South Africa with the censors' formal approval a number of conditions had to be satisfied. To begin with it had obviously to enter the censorship bureaucracy through one of the PCB's channels of primary surveillance: the police, the publishers, the reading public, the Directorate itself or, as in Coetzee's case, customs. Once in the system it had to pass the scrutiny of the readers, the committees and the Directorate. Finally, the decision to release the book for circulation had to remain uncontested. At every point in the process the decision could be reversed and a ban imposed. With *In the Heart of the Country* and *Life & Times of Michael K*, it so happened that the initial readers were relatively open-minded and that their views prevailed.

Yet this was not simply because they alone managed to persuade the committees and the Directorate that, despite some potentially undesirable episodes, neither book would cause offence or threaten the order. Other factors beyond their control also affected the process. The first of these was Coetzee's growing reputation. This was especially true in the case of *Michael K*, when his international status was assured, but it had already been an issue with *In the Heart of the Country*. Louw ended her individual report with a reference to *Dusklands* where, she claimed, Coetzee had already shown 'evidence of his unquestionably enormous talent'. Scholtz, too, noted that the first novel had been 'highly acclaimed' (locally), adding that the second was 'serious work that will certainly get attention' (perhaps locally and internationally). Moreover, with *Michael K*, it was not only Coetzee's Booker-size reputation that mattered. The changes in censorship practice after 1980 were also a major factor. In applying the more nuanced 'likely reader' test in 1983, Mrs Scholtz was working according to the new rules, not expressing her own views. All these factors, combined with the constraints imposed by the practice of reading by triangulation and by the bureaucracy itself, significantly reduced the initial readers' power to influence an already over-determined process.

For all this, however, it would be difficult to see Louw, Fensham and the Scholtz's merely as the hired eyes of the PCB (and the apartheid state). The evidence in the archives suggests they were also individuals who brought particular interests and assumptions to their job that inevitably affected their ways of reading and hence their recommendations. The first of these was their commitment to literature *per se*, and their belief that literary merit was a trumping value. This was not the official line in 1977. As the *Magersfontein* appeal decision showed, literary merit was considered only one relevant value among others. In their recommendation on *In the Heart of the Country*, then, the readers were going against the grain in at least two ways: first, by all but ignoring the statutory claims of the 'average reader'; and second, by insisting on the novel's literary merit. As Louw commented (and Scholtz, as Chair, reiterated), it was 'one of the few works of stature in the world of South African English letters', and, as Fensham added, 'something like this cannot be considered undesirable'. True, its potential offensiveness was, in their view, mitigated by its sophisticated, indirect approach, not least because this also limited its probable readership to an intellectual minority. Moreover, it is likely that these justifications, rather than any others, finally persuaded the Directorate against an appeal. But it is clear from the Chair's report, and the individual readings, that its 'outstanding' literary qualities were paramount in their minds.

The second influential commitment, on the part of the readers as individuals, was especially manifest in Mrs Scholtz's report on *Michael K*. While she also insisted on its literary 'brilliance', her case against its undesirability ultimately rested on traditional humanist assumptions about literature's universality. Despite its 'derogatory references' to the state and the police, the novel was in her view – which was also, in effect, the committee's – 'not undesirable' because it rose above the sordid details of local politics and history, and addressed universal themes of alienation. She claimed the 'likely reader' would reach the same conclusion. This humanist doctrine was also central to Louw's individual interpretation of *In the Heart of the Country* which, in her view, spoke to the common concerns of the human heart, and not simply to South Africans. To this extent the two novels were not banned in South Africa, in part, because the initial readers interpreted them in ways that made them not 'essentially' about South Africa. So, while critics abroad were openly championing Coetzee as a leading 'South African novelist' – a label he has always had his own reasons for questioning – local censors were secretly legitimizing him for his 'universality'. In the circumstances, this may have been the more burdensome designation.

## Notes

1    I have benefited from the assistance of a number of people in the process of writing and researching this essay. I would like to give particular thanks to Marianne George for her help in tracing the primary archival documents and for obtaining the necessary permissions for me to consult and cite them; to Rene Dinkelman for checking various details and for being so generous with her extraordinary knowledge of the censorship system; to Kareni Bannister for her assistance with the translations; and to Kinch Hoekstra, David Robertson and Mick Imlah for their astute comments and advice. An abridged version of the essay first appeared in the *Times Literary Supplement* for 19 May 2000.
2    Coetzee himself suggested his 'indirect' and 'rarefied' methods were a key factor. See Coetzee 1992, 298.
3    The biographical details are all contained in the forms each was required to fill in when applying to be a reader. PCB Archive, reference IDP 1/5/3, vol. 1.
4    For a useful discussion of this see Coetzee's own essay, 'Censorship in South Africa' (1990) in Coetzee 1992, 315–32; reprinted in Coetzee 1996, 185–203.
5    My translation. This and all subsequent remarks by the censors on *In the Heart of the Country* are taken from the PCB file P77/7/103.
6    This and all subsequent remarks by the censors on *Life & Times of Michael K* are taken from the PCB file P83/10/168. Where I have indicated that the originals were in Afrikaans, the translations are mine.

## Bibliography

*Argus* (1983), staff reporter, 'No SA ban on Michael K', *Argus*, 14 November, 3.
Botha, Amanda (1983), 'Wen-roman nou onder embargo' ['Award-winning novel now under embargo'], *Die Transvaler*, 10 November, 14.
Coetzee, J.M. (1977), *In the Heart of the Country*, London: Secker & Warburg.
Coetzee, J.M. (1981), *Waiting for the Barbarians*, Johannesburg: Ravan Press.
Coetzee, J.M. (1983), *Life & Times of Michael K*, London: Secker & Warburg.
Coetzee, J.M. (1992), *Doubling the Point: Essays and Interviews*, ed. David Attwell, Cambridge, MA: Harvard University Press.
Coetzee, J.M. (1996), *Giving Offense: Essays on Censorship*, Chicago: University of Chicago Press.
*Gazette* (1974), *Government Gazette*, No. 4426, 9 October.
Grütter, Wilhelm (1983), 'Kan SA dié soort sensuur bekostig' ['Can SA afford this sort of censorship'], *Beeld*, 9 December, 20.
Publications Control Board Archive, File references P77/1/97, P77/7/103, P83/10/168, and IDP 1/5/3, vols 1–5, National Archives of South Africa, Cape Town.

# Chapter Sixteen

# Prospero in Cyberspace

Martin Butler

In the title sequence of Peter Greenaway's *Prospero's Books*, the camera tracks Prospero walking through a set described in the screenplay as 'The bath-halls', which links the bath-house where the film opens to the library where Prospero lives. The bath-halls are a deeply confusing environment, crowded, dark and labyrinthine. A seemingly infinite array of pillars, they are ordered in parallel arcades set at right-angles to the camera, and run towards a vanishing point obscured by altars and obelisks and by the nude and semi-nude beings who fill the foreground. These figures – 'curious, ambiguous creatures of the island' (Greenaway 57) – excite and challenge the spectator's interpretation. All are engaged in intense activity, and some can be identified as mythological characters or quotations from the symbolic storehouse of Western visual art. There are Neptune with his trident, Leda and her swan, Marsyas (I think) hanging by his heels,[1] Moses in the bullrushes, three Rubenesque Graces, the whore Pornocrates as imagined by Felicien Rops, a hooded man from the paintings of Rene Magritte. Others, though, are less easily distinguished, and their significance can only be guessed at in a sequence too dense and rapid to be confidently decoded. In the screenplay, Greenaway describes them as representing the vast reservoir of characters and myths that Prospero has at his command,[2] and certainly the scene takes its coherence from his presence as visitor and observer. Passing through the crowd, Prospero is alternately obscured and glimpsed, but he always occupies the same spatial relationship to the screen. His synchrony with the camera expresses his mastery over the space and links its teeming detail to his fertile imaginative power.

But as the camera moves towards the library, so it picks up a new motif that parallels his rightwards movement. Shelves appear, from which a heavy volume is taken and passed along a line of naked figures, each briefly consulting it before delivering it to the next. Eventually it comes to characters who look like New World natives as depicted by the early settler John White. As attention is drawn from Prospero to the book being literally transmitted through the foreground, so the sequence poses the question of the link between the production and consumption of the Shakespearean text to which the film alludes. Prospero seems situated as the supreme author, source of the film's images and unity, but the physically moving book intrudes a different genetic relationship, for these figures from the world of story are themselves participating in the work of readership and interpretation. And since the sequence induces a similarly intense hermeneutic activity in its viewers, as we attempt to decipher its details, so it reinforces the perception that, as originator of the narrative's meanings, Prospero may be less authoritative and self-sufficient than at first he appears to be. It both affirms and questions his status as controller of the text over which he seems the presiding author.

In many ways, *Prospero's Books* celebrates the culture of script and print. Books and codices are everywhere. Not only does the film frame Shakespeare's story with the twenty-four arcane volumes that Greenaway supposes Prospero took to the island, but books fill its *mise-en-scène*, either as texts that Prospero writes or as props for the action. Cast adrift at sea, the infant Miranda wears a hat folded from a printed leaf; during the rebellion in Milan, scholars in the library mop up blood with loose paper; Prospero remembers his wife as a beautiful corpse, her head cradled on the open pages of a great folio. No film has more eloquently evoked the materiality of writing, or depicted books as such desirable objects, heavy with physical presence and the erotic charge of inner promise. It dwells on the translucent ink into which Prospero dips his nib, and scrutinizes the pen's progress as it taps the pot then scratches audibly across the page, making us voyeurs in the secret intimacies of literary creation. As for the film's characters, their very lives are lived within the pages of books: the mythological creatures may be the products of story, but the humans are no less fixated on texts. When Miranda first meets Ferdinand, she can barely tear her eyes from her book. Prospero's wife Susannah literally is a book, for in the film's most startling image, she opens her body to reveal its inner cavities – a gesture that visually quotes the early printed anatomies in which dissected cadavers were depicted holding open their own flesh. Even Caliban, when first encountered, curls protectively around a volume. The innermost identities of these bookish beings seem constituted by the written or printed word. Greenaway himself remarked that if his earlier film, *The Cook, The Thief, His Wife and Her Lover*, was a symbolic elaboration of the motif 'You are what you eat', 'You are what you read' would be the equivalent motto for *Prospero's Books* (Rodgers 19).

The topos at work here is, manifestly, one of the foundational tropes of print culture, that, in the words of Milton's *Areopagitica*, 'Books are not absolutely dead things, but do contain a potency of life in them to be so active as that soul whose progeny they are.' This is a trope that points, unsettlingly, in two directions. It affirms that authorial identities are preserved in the personalities of books, but it also ascribes to books an uncanny liveliness, which disturbs our sense of where the dividing line falls that separates the material from the human (see Pascoe, 185–6). Susannah's eerie self-dissection, which converts her from a living person into an object to be explored, is one of the film's many moments that draw attention to this problematic boundary. Books are much the liveliest presences in the film. They move, change and react to external stimulus, and their contents are described by an unidentified voice which, being de-localized and unexplained, speaks with compelling authority. By contrast, the human characters are inert, their words and actions ventriloquized by Prospero. They are functions rather than agents in the story, fashioned by the narrative and with their choices confined to those prescribed in the volumes on which Prospero draws. Each episode is sourced to a book which acts as the metatext for that part of the action. The 'Book of Water' appears at the outset, in tandem with the storm; Prospero's memories of Susannah are prompted by the 'Alphabetical Inventory of the Dead'; the 'Book of Motion' accompanies the masque; and so on. The effect is to situate the action within a mosaic of overlapping discourses, a Foucauldian web that predetermines the characters' subjectivities and possibilities of agency. Ferdinand does not so much fall for Miranda as act out gestures selected from 'The Book of Love'; Gonzalo's vision of the island is dreamed from the political communities anthologized in the 'Book of Utopias'; Caliban's enmity to Prospero is referenced to the 'Book of the Earth'. As autonomous entities, these characters barely signify, for their actions are literally scripted in advance. It is, rather, the books that seem volatile, mobile and pregnant with possibility.

This emphasis on the autonomy of books is reinforced by the film's other bibliographical trope, its focus on Shakespeare and the sacred bardic text. Not only does it tell the story of *The Tempest*, it shows Prospero in the act of writing it, and concludes with Caliban rescuing the manuscript from the water, together with the Shakespeare First Folio – the only two volumes to remain after Prospero destroys his library. This ambivalent conclusion simultaneously undermines and retrieves the authority of books. Prospero's return to society requires him to relinquish the superhuman technologies that his library supplies: disempowerment is the price of humanity. Notwithstanding, the loss of all this power is redeemed by the survival of the Shakespearean text, for that is the book of books which, more than any other, symbolizes the continuing hegemony of print. When all other words have gone, it is implied, Shakespeare's works will preserve the cultural inheritance, for that is the text to which all other discourses are merely sub-texts, and from which, if need be, the Babel of knowledges could be replenished. Shakespeare thus acts for Greenaway as a synecdoche for a culture in which meaning is transmitted through texts, and his casting of the archetypal Shakespearean actor John Gielgud as Prospero wittily exploits the biographical fantasies that *The Tempest* has inspired. In his screenplay, Greenaway encourages a 'cross-identification between Prospero, Shakespeare and Gielgud' (Greenaway 9), and expects the spectator to read Gielgud/Prospero as a figure for Shakespeare himself:

> Prospero is seen writing *The Tempest* ... producing a longhand manuscript that – like all other Shakespearean manuscripts – has never been seen. The film's ending interferes with chronology and history and plays a game with this loss that is lamented by every Shakespearean enthusiast. (Greenaway 32)

The text that Prospero produces shadows that most desired of artefacts and cornerstone of Western culture, a manuscript from the hand of the Bard himself.

At work in this Shakespearean topos is a deep fantasy, that of returning to a state of textual purity in which texts enact their own meanings, embodying authorial intention without the need of mediation or interpretation. If texts are imperfect vessels of meaning, *Prospero's Books* plays with the possibility of recovering an Edenic textual presence in which the gap between signifier and signified has been repaired. With Prospero both writing *The Tempest* and reciting it as he transcribes, his voicing of the words calls its action into being, the play seeming to be caught at its moment of inception. Prospero has only to speak the name 'Boatswain' for the character to appear and the text to pass into performance: more than merely imitating an imaginative world, his words distil and actualize it. Andrew Murphy has observed how this device collapses Derrida's pejorative distinction between speech and writing, in which speech is privileged as immediate and present, and writing stigmatized as posterior and absent. Instead of the written text being an imperfect echo of always unrepresentable thoughts, words are, in *Prospero's Books*, 'instantaneously made text' (Murphy 17). Moreover, as Amy Lawrence notes, the casting of Gielgud reinforces the illusion of transparency, for he was an actor admired for his almost disembodied fastidiousness of speech (Lawrence, 145). Submerging his personality into the contours of the verse, Gielgud seems to speak for the language itself, dissolving the author into the subject of his discourse. As for the written text, its status is curiously ambiguous. It is not a theatrical manuscript, as the screenplay seems to predict, for it bears none of the customary signs of playhouse use. A manuscript with scarcely a blot, its clarity echoes Heminges and Condell's over-emphatic praise of the holographs and literary transcripts they used when editing the First Folio.[3] And the film further blurs the distinction between the written and printed word by avoiding any reference to the mechanics of printing, instead treating typography and autograph as essentially alike. Indeed, it is sometimes hard to determine whether the words that appear on screen have been manually or mechanically produced, and from time to time the text seems to materialize without visible aid, like automatic writing. If *Prospero's Books* affirms the power of the bardic text, it is a text that has been curiously de-coupled from the personality of its author.

* * *

Although Greenaway's film is one of the most radical Shakespeare adaptations of the 1990s, from this perspective it seems rather nostalgic. It harks back to an idea of Shakespeare as the presiding genius of Western culture, and associates him with notions of authorial power that derive from the sacredness of the written word and the ability of print technology to preserve, order and disseminate knowledge. It represents *The Tempest* as the master-text through which an astonishing array of cultural sources can be reconnected, redeeming the fragmentation of the Western tradition by seeming to touch, at one moment or another, on every area of the literary, scientific and artistic canon. At the same time, it offers the ultimate testimonial to Shakespeare's synthesizing aesthetic. Exfoliating *The Tempest* into a kaleidoscope of related images, the film literalizes the dazzling openness of the Shakespearean text, uncovering in the play a range of reference that demonstrates its receptiveness to interpretation, its ability to absorb whatever questions can be asked of it.

However, this is not to say that *Prospero's Books* underwrites the sentimental myth of Shakespeare as the great universal, the spokesman for an unproblematically unified 'humanity' floating free of history, in which all cultures find their echo and all differences are transcended. On the contrary, by underlining the perplexing hybridity of the sources on which Prospero's story draws, it emphasizes the complex cultural transactions involved in transmitting the Shakespearean text. The film's interpretative difficulty arises from its encyclopaedic overload but also from the eclecticism of its images, which resist being reduced to any simple hierarchy. It mixes Old World and New World figures, overlays history and myth, and highlights collisions between incompatible cultural systems – such as the shocking glimpse of Claribel being sexually violated at the exotic African court into which she has married. And it further estranges the Shakespearean text by showing Prospero hard at work on it, and by displaying the almost endless variety of associations that can be unpacked from it. By surrounding Prospero's writing with a great carapace of historical and mythological allusion, Greenaway makes us feel privy to the process of selection by which the author creates his story, and foregrounds the work of inclusion, exclusion and combination that its production involves. The effect of this is to interrogate the text's hegemonic authority, preventing us from taking it either as a 'natural' synthesis of its sources or as a fixed entity that reads the same way twice. Prospero's journey through the library is one path by which his sources may be traversed, but the route is manifestly his personal choice, and the alternatives are potentially limitless. As the owner of the library, he produces the privileged narrative, but one can readily see that other users – Miranda, Antonio, Caliban? – would find competing stories there. Repeatedly, superfluous details (for example, the man with a chained leopard seen briefly in the opening sequence) leave the viewer haunted with the thought that other narratives may be happening in the background to which there is no time to attend but which potentially contradict the story that Prospero tells.

Conceived in this way, the Shakespearean text looks less like a book than a network, in which meaning circulates unpredictably: the pleasure of the story lies not so much in its narrative logic as in the richness of the imagery to which its episodes can be connected. Behind this model of textuality, as Peter Donaldson has powerfully argued, one readily senses Greenaway registering the cultural impact of the late twentieth-century revolution in information technology (Donaldson 1997, 1998).[4] With its proliferating layers of 'windows', its sedimentation of imagery and text, and the amazing moving pages it invents for Prospero's books, the film imitates the conventions of electronic text production that, at the time of its release, were just beginning to impact significantly on everyday life.[5] Its astonishingly dense weave derives as much from the post-production manipulation performed on its camerawork as it does from the *mise-en-scène*. Overlaying filmed scenes with electronic enhancements provided by a wonder-working digital 'paintbox', the film identifies the computer's technical wizardry as the modern equivalent of Prospero's magic. In doing so, it situates *The Tempest* in an environment where texts circulate as virtual data rather than material objects, and where they are not so much read as used, searched non-sequentially for information-gathering purposes. In this brave new electronic world, where an infinite amount of data can be instantaneously retrieved, the function and significance of the book are radically changed, as are all the old relationships that print culture understands between power, knowledge and subjectivity. If Shakespeare's

Caliban was subjugated by his master's books, virtual technologies promise yet more awesome means of manipulation.

Greenaway's Prospero inhabits a world not so much of text as of hypertext. He seems to have immediate and enabling access to the entire contents of his library, and uses his books in a non-linear fashion, turning their pages speculatively and browsing rather than reading – as Miranda also does, when in the cornfield scene she leafs through the volume 'Endplants'. His books are, of course, not really stories but archives, banks of information and images, and are notable for their comprehensiveness and systematic arrangement. The 'Book of Colours' covers the visual spectrum from black to black; the 'Inventory of the Dead' lists every person from Adam to Prospero's wife; the 'Bestiary' describes all animals that are, have been and may be. As databases, the books can be raided for whatever purposes the user brings to them: for example, the infinitely varied political communities listed in the 'Book of Utopias' are indexed 'permitting a reader', says the anonymous voiceover, 'to sort and match his own utopian ideal' (Greenaway 24). Although there are asymmetries between the books, it is implied that they are linked by underlying concords, accessed by hidden universal codes. The 'Book of Languages' (described in the screenplay but absent from the film) is a collection of books inside books, each opening onto further layers of books nested within. Similarly, the 'Book of Universal Cosmography' arranges all known phenomena into diagrams of geometrical figures such as concentric rings, linking the solar system at one end with the body of man at the other. In its 'structured universe', says the voiceover, 'all things have their allotted place and an obligation to be fruitful' (Greenaway 24). Encountered this way, Prospero's library looks like an inexhaustible resource, which equips the mind with seemingly unbounded capacities of search and storage, and organizes infinite quantities of data into autonomous but interconnected systems. Although *The Tempest* is indeed a play about memory, it is symptomatic that the film is disproportionately concerned with the art of recollection. Nearly half the screenplay – forty-three of its ninety-one scenes – is devoted to Shakespeare's first act, and this Greenaway labels 'The Past'. The effect is to underline how much *The Tempest*'s action creates Prospero's story as a chain of links, a personal history that he makes or recovers. Greenaway's Prospero is acquiring a virtual subjectivity: his self is, essentially, his power of retrieval.

It is difficult not to feel that, in this film, Prospero's whole world has become virtual. Certainly his island is an environment where 'nature' has been completely subordinated to 'culture', where nothing exists that is not artfully created. The nearest we get to a landscape is the cornfield in which

Miranda meets Ferdinand, but this natural world is patently an artificial construct. The corn extends into the Bernini arcades beneath which Miranda and Prospero sit, blurring the boundary between inside and out, and its stalks are impossibly straight and golden: the screenplay explains it is borrowed from the paintings of Breughel and incorporates a maze pattern from Rheims cathedral. Since, like the cornfield, everything in the island is traceable to some textual or visual source, there is no detail, however small, that seems not to be 'quoted', always already digested or processed. As for the island's structure, this is even more obviously artificial, for it resembles the space of a computer game. As the screenplay explains, the island is made up of zones, adjacent to each other but sharply distinguished. There is the cornfield where Ferdinand arrives, the pit where Caliban lives, Prospero's library and bath-house, Miranda's bedroom, Ariel's pine: each is associated with one part of the action, and the home of one character who specially belongs there. Only Prospero moves easily between all zones, and the film reinforces their separations by its exaggeratedly restricted style of camerawork. Many scenes are filmed with the camera directly opposite the set, motionless, at a distance from it, and in severely symmetrical compositions enhanced by columns and arcades. This flattens the image into a two-dimensional plane, holding it with the rigidity of a cybernetic grid. The other visual signature is the long tracking shot in a parallel horizontal plane, such as we see during the titles, and later, reversed, in the bath-halls and library. This device is even more like an electronic simulation, since the camera accompanies Prospero in his horizontal movement, tracking him through the space but always positioning him on one side of the screen, as if he were the active player in a computer game. As he walks, he is accompanied by four dancers whose stilted movements, Donaldson notes (1997, 171), make them look like digital animations, and he meets figures who burst into action at his approach, as if they had no independent life outside their own zone.[6] Moreover, the island's exterior limits are puzzling: it is separate from the outside world but from the inside one cannot get out or see where those invisible boundaries lie. The island has all the ambiguous freedoms of cyberspace. A boundless yet enclosed playground, it exists simply to give pleasure to its controlling consciousness.

It is striking how isolated Greenaway's Prospero seems to be. By inventing a dead wife, the film foregrounds his lost domesticity. He is shown reaching out as if to touch Susannah's corpse, but correcting himself and drawing back: perhaps by opening her pregnant womb she implies that he was in some way responsible for her death. Prospero consoles himself with his attentions to Miranda, but she is equally remote: sleeping through all their 'dialogue' down to scene 42, she seems little more than a projection of his private anxieties and compensations. Caliban, too, is something of a missing child. In flashback we see him and Miranda as infants at Prospero's knee, but this happy family now belongs to a dead past (and the harpies' presentation of Ferdinand's corpse to Alonzo reiterates the film's preoccupation with lost children). Even when with his spirits Prospero seems aloof, absorbed in writing, communing with the off-screen spectator or gazing at the mirrors in which his visions are reflected. These mirrors define him as a split subject searching for a primal wholeness that can no longer be reconstituted: in 'Our revels now are ended', he walks away from the crowded masque into an avenue of mirrors, called by a tolling bell, until a falling curtain separates him completely, leaving him alone with the camera.[7] But if Prospero cannot relinquish this burden of self-consciousness, the knowledge of his own futility, the imagery also infantilizes him, framing the whole film as a gratification of childlike desire. In the opening sequence he is in the bath, with food to hand, telling the story like a game with the youngest of the film's four Ariels. This white-haired grandfather initiates the tale by pushing a toy ship across the water; meanwhile Ariel laughs with him and pisses at the boat, causing it to capsize. Prospero never again takes quite such naive pleasure in the plot,[8] but even its most sophisticated moments are dressed-up sensuality, particularly the masque, which Greenaway stages as an endless parade of fruits, flowers, jewels and other luxuries. These objects are ostensibly gifts offered to Ferdinand and Miranda, but they also betoken Prospero's desire to associate his power with an overwhelming, unsurpassable bounty. It is a fantasy of opulence contrived by a character whose life is, in many respects, almost entirely solipsistic.

Late twentieth-century responses to the emergent cyberculture, as Kevin Robins has argued, have been sharply polarized. If technological change always unsettles inherited notions of what it means to be human, the shift from print to electronic culture has redrawn the borderline between man and machine, and redefined the space–time frame in which the self is located by altering the individual subject's interactions with the outside world. Some (says Robins) have sought to embrace technology's promise of a new visionary reality, supposing that it will repair the mind–body divide and compensate for the disappointments of the material world. The Internet and computer game provide a space where customary limits do not apply and where new scenarios of mastery and empowerment can be created. Here the mind is free to reinvent itself 'according to the dictates of pleasure and desire', and the self returns to an 'infantile experience of power and infinite possibility' that combines 'the objectivity of the physical world with the unlimitedness and the uncensored content' of a dream. Against this are those for whom cyberculture is flawed by its narcissism, the way that it licenses the self to withdraw from the public world into a disembodied identity that has no need for external objects. In this perspective, the risk of electronic technology is its absence of 'empathy', its indifference to human relationships and its weakening of the bonds between Self and Other (Robins 85, 81; and see Kataman, Bolter and Landow).

Empathy is precisely the quality that Greenaway's Prospero lacks, and has to be educated in by the multiple Ariels. At the point where the Ariels advise Prospero to make his affections 'tender' (Shakespeare's 5.1.19), they take over the writing of his text, accompanied by cutaway images of the sufferings to which Ferdinand, Caliban and Alonzo have been brought. In response to this admonition, Prospero snaps his pen, abandons his manuscript and abjures his art, while, in a rapid montage, book after book is seen being slammed shut. After this decisive break the other characters are allowed for the first time to speak in their own voices, reinforcing the suggestion that Prospero's salvation depends on him leaving behind his fantasies of power for participation in a less self-enclosed world. Yet in comparison with what we have hitherto seen, the ensuing action seems rudimentary and impoverished. The reunion is stagey and low-key and, in the short time available to them, the subordinate characters can acquire little inner life.[9] For all that Greenaway consciously designs Prospero's outpouring of empathy to mark his release from solipsism, the film's tendency is to reaffirm how completely this human subject has become disconnected from society. It gestures towards the need for a renewed emotional mutuality but fails to invest it with much plausibility. Locked in the funhouse, Prospero seems unlikely ever to break out of his prison-house of texts.

* * *

In recent criticism, *The Tempest* has attracted predominantly dystopian readings. Critics such as Stephen Greenblatt and Stephen Orgel have turned Prospero from an enlightened patriarch into a domestic tyrant: his plots have apparently benevolent ends, but they are designed to bring all the other characters firmly under his control. Significantly, Greenaway's film echoes the current Machiavellian emphases: in no other production has Prospero's surveillance seemed so complete, or his knowledge been equated so emphatically with his power. With Prospero speaking all the lines, the life of each character is literally ventriloquized. Their seeming freedoms are manifestly determined by him, and their subversions are allowed only for the sake of their eventual containment. The library's comprehensiveness means that Prospero can never be surprised or wrong-footed: all political systems are anticipated in the 'Book of Utopias', and there are pornographies alongside 'The Book of Love'. Prospero's own perspective on his power is quite disenchanted. The flashbacks to Antonio's rebellion show his grasp of *realpolitik*, and he acts with total ruthlessness even towards Ferdinand, who is reduced to a tortured victim on the library stairs. The film takes for granted that violence is intrinsic to organized social life, and the prevalent nudity underlines the vulnerability of the human body, its susceptibility to coercion and biological flaw. Greenaway may showcase the glories of Prospero's culture, but makes it apparent that 'civilization' is only one more name for power.

Does this mean, then, that Greenaway's film endorses the despairing politics of New Historicism, that see the modern subject as radically disempowered and possessing 'subversion, no end of subversion, only not for us' (Greenblatt 65)? This is certainly how many commentators on the film have taken it. For example, Donaldson has argued that, although Prospero is separated from his books, the closing images reinstall him in a position of incontestable authority and affirm his total control over the film's world. After Prospero speaks the epilogue, his face is freeze-framed, then zoomed back towards the screen's vanishing point. This device, says Donaldson, puts him at the locus of visual origin and most dominant cinematic position: he 'seems to suffuse the space', and becomes 'the originator of the film in an enhanced, permanent way'.[10] Yet I have been trying to suggest that in many respects the film's representation of the emergent cultural technologies unsettles the totalizing models of authority with which Prospero is identified, and no more so than in this concluding image. Rather like the characters in the influential computer simulation movie *Tron* (1982), who find themselves caught in the electronic matrices of a video game, Prospero seems to have been absorbed into the machine. Dwindling into a tiny TV frame, he appears just as trapped as are the characters whose lives he writes, his frozen image uncoupled from his material reality, his status as the originator of meaning not confirmed but dissolved. Instead, the movie's future meanings will depend on the spectators whose consumption is the final term in the chain of transmission, and, since its images are so various, these meanings remain open and plural, even in repeated viewings by the same spectator. The excess of content over form, the richness of its links and pathways, and the abdication of its apparently controlling author, make *Prospero's Books* a film that is reassembled every time it is seen. Situating the viewer as the ultimate producer of its meaning, it offers its consumers pleasures of choice and mastery that, within the diegesis, seem to be exclusively Prospero's property.

In the film's penultimate sequence, Prospero casts his books into the pool, where they disintegrate with astonishing violence. Attacked by water, fire and acid, they shatter, burn and corrode, to the accompaniment of screams and explosions. It is as if, in abandoning his books, Prospero releases their energy, returning their data to pure electricity, fission without form. All that are left are the Shakespeare Folio and the manuscript of *The Tempest*, and these, when dropped in the water, are salvaged by Caliban. This concluding gesture has been taken for an allegory of the director himself, rescuing Shakespeare for a cinematic *avant-garde*, but the idea cannot be recommended, for there is little in the film to connect Caliban with Greenaway.[11] Rather, like the Third World characters who in the title sequence inherit the book, Caliban's intervention signals a transfer of power from author to readers, and that future meaning will inhere not in Shakespeare's *Tempest* but in the *Tempest* that our readings make and remake. And it encapsulates the film's ambivalence towards the cyberculture that it embraces, the possibilities of which seem at once so liberating and so unsettling. Hesitating between an all-powerful centralizing technology where everything is known, and a decentred consumerism where anything is possible, the unresolved tensions of *Prospero's Books* bespeak the opportunities and anxieties of the new electronic age.

## Notes

1   The screenplay identifies the third of these figures as a naked woman hanging head-down in a waterfall (Greenaway 58). But there is no waterfall, and it is difficult not to see Titian's 'Flaying of Marsyas' as standing at some level behind this motif.

2   The scene introduces 'the spirits and images and mythology of the island', and the gigantic *Book of Mythologies* down which we see a young child slide is 'the template for Prospero's imaginings to people the island' (Greenaway 54, 57).

3   It should be noted that although Prospero's text is written out in an autograph that looks archaic, the letter-forms are not taken from the sixteenth-century secretary hand which Shakespeare himself wrote, since they would have been undecipherable to a twentieth-century cinema audience. Instead, the calligraphy is cleaned up and rendered transparent to modern eyes. In point of fact, the one Shakespeare holograph that does survive, *Sir Thomas More*, is full of blots.

4   I am very grateful to Professor Donaldson for his help in providing me with access to 'Digital archives and sibylline fragments'.

5   The electronic connection is even more evident in Greenaway's immediately prior project, his *TV Dante*, which surrounded Dante's text with footnotes, marginalia and talking heads in small windows imitating the conventions of electronic media. See Kinder, 160–82.

6   Similar crossovers happen in 'The Book of Motion' and 'The Ninety-two Conceits of the Minotaur', which quote images from Eadweard J. Muybridge's *Animal Locomotion* (which analyses the movement of the human body as a sequenced series of still images); and in the very final moments, when the film appears to slow down to its single images.
7   There is a detailed Lacanian reading of the film by Hotchkiss, 8–25.
8   Later moments of playfulness include the 'Book of Architecture', with pages that fold out like a pop-up book, and the image of Prospero physically miming the 'sad knot' into which he imagines Ferdinand wreathing his arms.
9   The lack of consistency in this sequence is most apparent in Miranda, who, in a jarring moment, turns out to have a Scottish accent.
10  Donaldson 1997, 175; and see also Murphy 18.
11  Lanier 1996, 201–2; and see the summary statement in Lanier 1998, 52.


## Bibliography

Bolter, J.D. (1984), *Turing's Man: Western Culture in the Computer Age*, London: Duckworth.
Donaldson, P. (1998), 'Digital Archives and Sibylline Fragments: *The Tempest* and the End of Books', *Postmodern Culture* 8: 2.
Donaldson, P. (1997), 'Shakespeare in the Age of Post-mechanical Reproduction: Sexual and Electronic Magic in *Prospero's Books*', in L. Boose and R. Burt (eds), *Shakespeare, The Movie*, London: Routledge, 169–85.
Greenaway, P. (1991), *Prospero's Books: A Film of Shakespeare's 'The Tempest'*, New York: Four Walls Eight Windows.
Greenblatt, S. (1988), *Shakespearean Negotiations*, Oxford: Oxford University Press.
Hotchkiss, L.M. (1998), 'The Incorporation of Word as Image in *Prospero's Books*', *Postscript* 17:2 (winter/spring), 8–25.
Kataman, S. (2000), 'Terminal Penetration', in D. Bell and M. Kennedy (eds), *The Cybercultures Reader*, London: Routledge, 149–74.
Kinder, M. (1997), 'Screen Wars: Transmedia Appropriations from Eisenstein to *A TV Dante* and *Carmen Sandiego*', in J. Masten, P. Stallybrass and N. Vickers (eds), *Language Machines: Technologies of Literary and Cultural Production*, London: Routledge, 160–82.
Landow, G.P. (1992), *Hypertext: The Convergence of Contemporary Critical Theory and Technology*, Baltimore: Johns Hopkins University Press.
Lanier, D. (1996), 'Drowning the Book: *Prospero's Books* and the Textual Shakespeare', in J.C. Bulman (ed.), *Shakespeare, Theory and Performance*, London: Routledge, 187–209.
Lanier, D. (1998), 'Now: The Presence of History in *Looking for Richard*', *Postscript* 17:2, 39–55.
Lawrence, A. (1997), *The Films of Peter Greenaway*, Cambridge: Cambridge University Press.
Murphy, A. (2000), 'The Book on the Screen; Shakespeare Films and Textual Culture', in M.T. Burnett and R. Wray (eds), *Shakespeare, Film, Fin de Siècle*, Basingstoke: Macmillan, 10–25.
Pascoe, D. (1997), *Peter Greenaway: Museums and Moving Images*, London: Reaktion Books.
Robins, K. (2000), 'Cyberspace and the World we Live in', in D. Bell and M. Kennedy (eds), *The Cybercultures Reader*, London: Routledge, 77–95.
Rodgers, M. (1991), '*Prospero's Books* – Word and Spectacle: An Interview with Peter Greenaway', *Film Quarterly* 45, 11–19.

# Chapter Seventeen

# Texts and Worlds in Amitav Ghosh's *In An Antique Land*

Shirley Chew

Returning 'from an antique land' with a tale to tell of ruins and the futility of earthly power, Shelley's traveller concludes:

> Nothing beside remains. Round the decay
> Of that colossal wreck, boundless and bare
> The lone and level sands stretch far away.
> ('Ozymandias')

The lesson Shelley's sonnet teaches depends for its final impact on a number of familiar properties in European narratives on the Orient, such as the desolate landscape and the feelings it calls up of loss and inevitability. 'Nothing beside remains': here, not only is Ozymandias (the Greek name for Ramses II, the Great) a stereotype of the Eastern tyrant but Egypt as time–space is flattened out, emptied of its history, peoples and cultures, and laid open to the scrutiny of the visitor from the West. In this respect, Shelley's vision of the East can be said to shadow forth 'the conquering European spirit' (Said 1985, 87) that was to overtake a large part of the globe in the nineteenth century and the first half of the twentieth.

Indeed, so Edward Said contends, 1798 already stands for a significant beginning in the textual production of the modern Orient. To Shelley, Napoleon was prefigured in Ozymandias and 'merely another form of despot' (O'Neill, 2).[1] But, as well as a military venture, the French occupation of Egypt (1798–1801), given its 'monuments' such as the *Déscription de l'Égypte* and the Institut de l'Égypte, was 'the very model of a truly scientific appropriation of one culture by another apparently stronger one' (Said 1985, 42). Fragments and inscriptions of the kind alluded to in 'Ozymandias' were precisely the objects of study among the cohorts of scholars at the Institut. As *Orientalism* makes clear, whether it is Napoleon's Egyptian projection, or Britain's Indian empire, or, more recently, the United States' 'oil encounter' in the Middle

East, an interlocking relationship exists between territorial conquest and cultural usurpation.

How then can 'new objects for a new kind of knowledge' be produced in 'a setting that is deeply inscribed with the politics ... and the strategies of power' (Said 1997, 129)? In the discussion which follows of Amitav Ghosh's *In An Antique Land*, I view the work with its consciously derived title (the traveller 'in', not 'from', the land) as a studied and dexterous experiment in the textual recovery of a portion of this appropriated ground. I explore in particular the distinction the narrative makes between 'History' and 'history';[2] the self-reflexive attention it brings to the reading and transmission of texts, that is, its problematizing of its claims to knowledge of the past even while engaged in the retrieval of that past; and the play it enacts between the decentred consciousness of Ghosh and the creative instabilities of his fictional form.

The imaginary terrain of *In An Antique Land* comprises the countries which border upon the Indian Ocean, the Arabian Sea and the Persian Gulf, and which together mark the location of two main systems of commerce – the spice trade of the Middle Ages with its principal centres at Fustat-Cairo, Aden and Mangalore on the Malabar coast of India, and the modern oil industry in the decade leading up to the Iraqi invasion of Kuwait (31 July 1990) and the Gulf War (January–February 1991). Paradoxically it is Ghosh's concern with the 'barely discernible traces that ordinary people leave upon the world' (1992, 15–16), rather than 'grand designs and historical destinies', that has made possible the mapping of this geographical and temporal expanse. The minute detail, the trace, which precipitated his interest in the histories of 'ordinary people', occurs in S.D. Goitein's 1973 edition and translation of *Letters of Medieval Jewish Traders*, in a letter sent by Khalaf ibn Ishaq, a Jewish merchant in Aden, to his friend Abraham Ben Yiju, of Fustat but resident in the 1130s and 1140s in Mangalore. It consists of Khalaf's 'most plentiful greetings' which he wished to be conveyed to Ben Yiju's Indian slave.[3] A conventional courtesy offered to what must seem an unusual recipient, its curiosity was to determine the kinds of research which Ghosh set out to pursue in Egypt in 1980, and which are rewritten in *In An Antique Land* as, respectively, an account of his experiences as an ethnographer in the villages of Lataifa and Nashawy, and a historical reconstruction of a medieval world of trade and cultural exchange. Ghosh completed the field work for his doctoral thesis in social anthropology in 1981. Research on Ben Yiju and the Slave was put aside until 1988.

A key episode in *In An Antique Land* is the dismantling of the Geniza[4] of the Synagogue of Ben Ezra in Cairo in the second half of the nineteenth century, and the dispersal of its 800-year-old collection of documents. At a time when the Orient and its traditional disciplines were being re-created by the scientifically advanced techniques of Western research, this tremendous storehouse of manuscripts and, from the sixteenth century onwards, of books and other printed matter, became an object of interest to collectors and dealers in antiquities. The outcome is a tangled tale of greed, dishonesty, and complicity, involving local employees, foreign buyers, high-ranking British officials in Egypt, the religious and social elite of Cairo, and members of the Western academy. Starting off in piecemeal fashion, the removal of the material to private collections and libraries in Europe and the United States culminated in the bulk transplantation of 140,000 manuscripts and fragments that became the Taylor-Schechter Collection at the University Library at Cambridge. A phenomenon of cultural uprooting, it left behind 'no trace of [the Geniza's] riches: not a single scrap or shred of paper' relating to an important strand of Egypt's past (95). As for the documents themselves, 'having come to Fustat from the far corners of the known world, a second history of travel carried [them] even further' (95).

If a principal theme in *In An Antique Land* is that of loss, another is the intimation of presence, in this case a pre-colonial world of 'accommodation and compromise' which, for so it seems to Ghosh, survives still and is 'in some tiny measure, still retrievable' (237). On the Slave's trail once more in 1988, Ghosh found two important resources available to him. As is evident from the extraordinary number of 'Notes'[5] appended to his text, thirty-seven pages in all, he was able to rely upon a wealth of scholarly and literary material. His references range freely across the works in Persian or Arabic of twelfth-century travellers, geographers, historians, diplomats and poets, and those, in English mainly, of present-day scholars, in particular S.D. Goitein's extensive *oeuvre* on the Jewish communities of the Mediterranean and Indian Ocean trade.[6] This material apart, there are the archival documents that lie preserved at Cambridge, Oxford, Princeton and other Western universities. One of the difficulties here is the paucity of the primary evidence relating to Ben Yiju, and, of the few dozen manuscripts which exist, only some half-dozen mention the Slave. Another difficulty is the language used by Ben Yiju and his trading associates. Known today as Judaeo-Arabic, it was 'a colloquial dialect of medieval Arabic', derived from the language of the Muslim armies which conquered the Middle East and North Africa in the seventh century. Unlike other Arabic dialects, however, it was a written language, transcribed in the Hebrew alphabet. As Ghosh moved from library to library, it was this strange hybrid, the product of multiple historical and cultural crossings, which he must learn to read and decipher in the hope that some precise idea may be gained of the identity of the Slave, his background, and the nature of his relationship with Ben Yiju. The examples below, in which the two modes of research often complement each other, highlight a number of the problems Ghosh met with in his attempts to interpret this small clutch of Geniza documents.

Richard Kerridge has drawn attention to a category of nature writing in which 'the wild object' of the quest (his examples include Peter Matthiessen's snow leopard and Rick Bass's grizzly bears) provides 'a never-to-be-reached threshold which draws the traveller on' (1999, 175). The proximity of the animal which is rarely, if ever, glimpsed is registered in marks and traces, such as 'spoor, claw-marks, skulls, bedding-litter, hairs, scats (excrement)', intermediary objects that are studied by the explorer-traveller 'with an intensity displaced from the animal itself' (1999, 176–7). I see in Ghosh's tracking of Ben Yiju and the Slave, a narrative sustained upon some of the strategies Kerridge has underlined, in particular the interplay of absence and presence that is 'the characteristic paradox of quest literature'. There is, for example, the close, almost cherishing, attentiveness Ghosh brings to the materiality of the Geniza fragments; the half-ironic displays of pedantry in the weighing of evidence and the advancing of possible conclusions; and the affecting of a formal, disinterested tone. All part of the scholar-researcher's performative act, this parodic practice calls into existence 'the presence of the past' even as it calls into question any claim to knowledge of that past outside its texts, its traces (Hutcheon 1988, 125).

Consider, for instance, Ghosh's speculations upon the eighteen or more years Ben Yiju spent in India. The reason for the prolonged residence was probably raised in a letter which Madmun, the Chief Representative of merchants in Aden sent to Ben Yiju. But 'a cryptic letter' (160) and, in its existing form, a fragment ripped from the original, it yields very little in the way of hard fact. Of course, as an object from the past, it is amazingly reassuring still in its tangibility.

> This particular piece of paper is quite large, about eleven inches long and more than five inches wide, but it is still only a fragment – a scrap which Ben Yiju tore from a longer sheet so he could scribble on its back. The little that remains of the original letter is badly damaged and much of the text is difficult to decipher. Fortunately the scrap does contain the name of the letter's sender: it is just barely legible and it serves to link the fragment with this story for it proves that the writer was none other than Madmun ibn al-Hasan ibn Bundar, of Aden. (160)

And of course there are concrete explanations as to why Ben Yiju was given to recycling old letters. Paper being difficult to come by in India – 'the material most commonly used for writing at that time was the palm-leaf' (268), it had to be imported from the Middle East; and it had to be of fine quality to satisfy Ben Yiju. Obviously, not an item to be squandered. The message itself, however, is hedged about with uncertainties, not a few of these springing from the ambiguity of Madmun's words. How, for example, is 'dhimma', 'one of those Arabic terms that can spin out a giddying spiral of meanings' (161), to be translated?

> Used as it is here, the word could mean that the ruler of Aden had agreed not to prosecute Ben Yiju for a crime he had committed, or been accused. Or it could mean that he had pledged to protect him from certain people whose enmity Ben Yiju had cause to fear. By Arab tradition this was the kind of guarantee that was extended to a man who had killed someone: it was intended to protect him and his relatives from a vengeance killing so that they could raise the murdered man's blood-money. (162)

The skills of the researcher connect with those of the writer of detective fiction in this instance to create mystery and suspense. And comedy, too, as after the dark hints of unlawful deeds and retribution comes the bathos. 'For all we know', Ghosh has to admit, 'it could just as well have been a matter of unpaid taxes' (162).

At times leading to a dead end, at others, as my next example shows, the fragments of text betray a fascinating multivalency by accruing new meanings to themselves when they are made to travel across temporal, geographical and discursive boundaries. Hoping to reconstruct Ben Yiju's itinerary on the occasion the trader departed Fustat for Aden, Ghosh borrows freely from the *Travels* of an Andalusian Arab who was to pass that way some sixty years later. Very likely this is what Ben Yiju also experienced when, after moving up the Nile valley to Qus, he headed east towards the Red Sea port of Aidhab, at that time 'one of the most important halts on the route between the Indian Ocean and the Mediterranean' (176).

> Over the next seventeen days they progressed slowly through the desert, on a south-easterly tack, camping at night and travelling through the day. A well-marked trail of wells helped them on their way, and all along the route they passed caravans travelling in the opposite direction so that the barren and inhospitable wastes were 'animated and safe'. At one of the wells Ibn Jubair tried to count the caravans that passed by, but there were so many that he lost

count. Much of their cargo consisted of goods from India; the loads of pepper, in particular, were so many 'as to seem to our fancies to equal the dust in quantity'. (175)

Revisited by Ghosh in the steps of Ibn Jubair and Ben Yiju before him, the emptiness begins to fill once again with the passage and activities of innumerable travellers. Likewise the port of Aidhab, which had 'simply ceased to be' in the middle of the fifteenth century, is briefly called back to life by the words on a piece of twelfth-century paper and the voice of an old man complaining of Ben Yiju's refusal to meet a particular debt. An angry and importunate letter, first sent to Madmun at Aden, then redirected to Ben Yiju at Mangalore, and finally carried with other correspondence home to Fustat, a fragment kept today in the University library at Cambridge, it tells us something, when relocated back, of the trader's tactics. In addition it reinforces our idea of the influence Madmun exerted and the organization of the Indian Ocean trade. Finally, it hovers, like the trace of a butterfly or petal of flower that gleams from some piece of shard amid the 'few ruins' and 'great quantity of buried Chinese pottery' which is all that is left of Aidhab, to give us a fleeting sense of livelier days.

My last example concerns the deciphering of the Slave's name, and the question it provokes as to how far Ghosh's conclusions are the product of 'the scientist's devotion to austere fact' and how far of 'the artist's sense of the superior beauty that resides in what might have been' (Altick 1993, 27). Faced with these 'two opposed inclinations', Altick and Fenstermaker are convinced that 'our choice, as scholars, is clear'. But equally clear is the lesson which Ghosh's young narrator was given by his uncle in the earlier work *The Shadow Lines*, and which serves as an expression of Ghosh's aesthetic: '[Tridib] told me once that one could never know anything except through desire, real desire … that carried one beyond the limits of one's mind to other times and other places (1988, 29).

As I have noted, words, particularly names, are a constant source of interest in *In An Antique Land*, close-woven as they are of strands of cultural history. 'Masr', by which Egypt as well as Cairo is known to Egyptians, is one example. Similarly the Slave's name, were it to be ascertained, would provide an important clue to his identity. Written originally in Judaeo-Arabic as 'B-M-H' (or 'B-M-A' since 'H' in Arabic is not a consonant but an open vowel), this is rendered in Goitein's *Letters* as 'Bama', and glossed as a diminutive of Brahma.[7] We can assume that the attraction of the Slave for Ghosh is his probable racial identity. But, while he is prepared to concede that 'B-M-A', however vague, is more likely to be Indian than Arabic or Semitic in its provenance, Ghosh resists emphatically the link Goitein has set up between 'B-M-A', 'Bama' and 'Brahma'. In his own decoding of the 'mysterious acrostic', he steers the name, lightly but firmly, away from high Sanskritic culture and 'History' towards a more fertile ground, the 'vast network of foxholes where real life continues uninterrupted' (16). A sleight of hand but enough, as can be seen, to undermine any pretense on Ghosh's part to scholarly interpretation.

> After puzzling over those three characters for a long time, one last possibility suggested itself to me. In Judaeo-Arabic (as in Arabic) a doubled letter is often represented by a single character. It was possible then that the single 'M' in the name was actually doing duty for two of its kind. If that were so, it would mean that there were actually four letters in the name: 'B-M-M-A'. If I then filled in a short vowel after the first letter, the result was 'Bomma' or 'Bamma', names which I knew to be common in certain parts of India. (249)

In the excerpt above, while phrases such as 'it was possible', 'if that were so', 'it would mean' serve to lead steadily forward to the moment of breakthrough when effort is crowned with success,[8] there is, running against the movement, an unmistakable current of the mock-serious so that searching for the Slave's name is at times not unlike doing a crossword puzzle. Add to this the teasing ambiguity in the grammatical status of the last phrase, and it is debatable whether 'names which I knew to be common in certain parts of India' should be taken as strictly descriptive in function (that is, as a noun clause in apposition) or elliptically explanatory (that is, an adverbial clause of reason) and hence reflecting back upon Ghosh's tendentiousness in naming the Slave.

Like Goitein, Ghosh defers to the opinion of an expert, in his case an authority on local folklore rather than mainstream cultural history. Once it is established that 'Bomma' is a name rooted in the landscape of Tulunad (as the area around Mangalore is called), in its social history (the several matrilineal communities) and indigenous culture (the Bhuta-cult), a 'local habitation' for the Slave becomes imaginable, a figuring forth that depends as much upon the seductive provisionality of Ghosh's prose as the precision of his seeing.

A key date in *In An Antique Land*, 1498 marks the arrival of Vasco da Gama at the Malabar coast, and the subsequent erosion of the 'ancient trading culture' of the Indian Ocean by Portuguese commercial ambitions and force of arms. Among the casualties of the new aggressive power was the medieval city and port known to Bomma and Ben Yiju. Ghosh's remaking of the lost world of the Mediterranean and Indian Ocean trade conjures up a Mangalore long since vanished but which was once the hub of a global trading community as well as the crossroads of the cultural and spiritual life of the Malabar. Various ploys are used in the narrative to induct the reader into the landscape and its 'intricate network of differences'. We are shown something of the hinterland, travelling with Ghosh towards the little towns in the foothills of the Western Ghats by river-boats and palanquins, as we imagine Ben Yiju and his family would have done, and, as we would do so nowadays, along roads that run 'through vast plantations of cashew and rubber, with low-slung motels and lavish residences', until a town, like Srikandapuram, 'when it arrives', is a recreation wonderfully suspended between the two temporal moments.

Secondly, Ghosh invites us to speculate on the language, now lost, which Ben Yiju would have used in his day-to-day dealings with people so different from each other as his wife Ashu, his associates Madmun and Khalaf, and his slave Bomma. Necessarily it would have to reflect the qualities of reciprocity and compromise that typify the trading community.

> Common sense suggests that in an area as large and diverse as the Indian Ocean, business could not possibly have been conducted in Tulu, Arabic, Gujarati, nor any tongue that was native to a single group of traders; to function at all the language of everyday business would have had to be both simpler and much more widely dispersed than any ordinary language. Given what we know about the practices of Arab traders in other multilingual areas (like the Mediterranean for example) it seems likely that the problem was resolved by using a trading argot, or an elaborated pidgin language ... one that was compounded largely of Perso-Arabic and north Indian elements, and was in use amongst merchants and traders all along the coast. (281)

Finally, it is within this 'contact zone', to borrow Mary Louise Pratt's phrase (1992, 7),[9] that Ghosh locates the relationship between Bomma and Ben Yiju. The key, as might be expected, depends upon the interpretation we bring to a particular word, to 'slavery' in this case. Reconceptualized as a 'principal means of recruitment' to service (260) in numerous areas of life, such as apprenticeship to a trade or craft, probation in the civil service, training in a particular discipline of art, and personal devotion to God, 'slavery' constitutes a practical or moral or spiritual bond. Read in this light it makes understandable the trust, akin to that bestowed upon a business agent, which Ben Yiju and his friends placed upon Bomma. It makes credible that Bomma should have stayed on as a member of Ben Yiju's household when in 1152 the merchant finally returned, after brief sojourns in Aden and the Yemen, to

Fustat. The evidence for this is preserved among the Geniza documents at Dropsie College, Philadelphia, and consists of a torn fragment of paper on which is a set of accounts entered in Ben Yiju's handwriting, 'for household purchases such as loaves of bread of various kinds' (349). One of the items it lists is a sum of money owing to Bomma the Slave.

In his carefully elaborated essay on *In An Antique Land*, Javed Majeed lays stress upon 'the main opposition to emerge in the text between the "medieval" and the "modern"' (1995, 45), that is, between the affluent and cosmopolitan communities of the Indian Ocean trade and the economically and socially restrictive Egyptian villages, and between the hegemonic nation states of the present day and the rich cross-cultural societies of the Middle Ages.

Accepting the presence of these broad contrasts, I would propose that subtle lines of contact also exist between the two narratives. Aside from the prologue and epilogue, Ghosh's work is in four sections, the headings of which – 'Lataifa', 'Nashawy', 'Mangalore', 'Going Back' – highlight the contemporary story rather than detract from its significance. Furthermore the structural links between the narratives are carefully forged to underline the interconnections between the 'medieval' and the 'modern'. Take, for example, the envisioning of twelfth-century Mangalore. In terms of the formal arrangement of the book, this comes after the quarrel between Ghosh (or Amitab, as he is known among the villagers) and the truculent Imam Ibrahim, and has to be read as Ghosh's attempt at expiating what he understands to be his betrayal of the 'histories' he quested after. In their ferocious exchange, both he and the Imam have tried to outface each other with vaunting of their countries' superiority in the technology of modern warfare: 'Our guns and bombs are much better than [yours]. Ours are second only to the West's' (236); and, positioned ostensibly on opposite sides, they have been speaking the same language all the time, the language of 'History', in particular of militarism and global domination in which the Western powers traffic.

Finally what the narratives have in common are the motifs of loss and recovery. *In An Antique Land* ends with the Iraqi invasion of Kuwait; with the disappearance of Nabeel and several other young men from Lataifa and Nashawy, foreign workers no longer wanted in Iraq; and, in the villages themselves, with the 'unfinished shell' of new houses (318) standing like curious ruins, the money from Baghdad having run out and jobs being hard to come by for those who manage to make their way back to Egypt. What remains then of the world Ghosh came to know as a research student? And of his own participation in that world?

It had sometimes seemed to Ghosh in those earlier days that, between them, he and Shaikh Musa, a village elder, had created a Lataifa and Nashawy of their own out of their conversations. In his subsequent visits in 1988 and 1990, the conversations are picked up again, with Ghosh's reminiscences answering freely Shaikh Musa's reports of the changes which have taken place over the last ten years – the departures, the making good, the disillusionment, the homecomings, among a small rural population driven to make use of whatever opportunities for betterment it gets. Beating back and forward in time, the narrative crisscrosses personal recollections, gossip, the latest news, the stories of Ben Yiju and Bomma, and, transcribed from Ghosh's doctoral thesis, descriptive accounts of, say, rural markets, *mowlids*, kinship systems, myths of origin. This play of voices and stylistic registers evokes an idea of Lataifa and Nashawy as they used to be, a coherent community though touched even then by the spirit of change, and the bereft places they have become in under a decade. But, something else remains and, despite his attempts to pin them down, Ghosh knows too well that, having since the first days of his arrival shown a resistance to being studied, Lataifa and Nashawy will continue to elude definition.

One reason for this can be attributed to Ghosh's anxieties regarding his role as an ethnographer. A person from the Third World, not the West, a South Asian, not a white man, a secular Indian, his feelings of inauthenticity become underlined when Ghosh tries to author his text so that to write as an ethnographer is to find himself, consciously or otherwise, subverting the conventions and the main concerns of his narrative. Examples are: the recurrent intrusions of the personal into the descriptive fieldwork;[10] the undermining of the subject position of the researcher with the result that the observer is constantly switching places with the observed, the interrogator is dogged with questions from his audience and the gatherer of knowledge is exposed as sadly lacking in answers; and finally, the gaps of knowledge left unfilled and the concealments, the most glaring of which relate to the religious life of the villagers.

On one occasion at least, Ghosh's attempt to hold his own with the villagers ends badly. This occurs when the guests at a wedding, Muslims all, set about bombarding 'the doktór al-Hindi' with questions concerning his background. Some of these questions are worn counters by now. There is, for example, 'what do you do with your dead?' And equally predictable is the expression of shock at his response, 'They are burned.' Ghosh is by now resigned to the absence in Arabic of a word such as 'cremate', and to being restricted in his reply to 'the verb "to burn"', which was the word for what happened to firewood and straw and the eternally damned' (168). In this instance, however, his predicament is exacerbated by the impossibility of distinguishing in Arabic between 'to circumcise' and 'to purify', and he is compelled to say what amounts to 'No ... women are not "purified" in my country' (203). Whereupon the curiosity turns personal: '"And you, ya doktór?" "What about you ...?"' And, innocent in itself, the question returns Ghosh to memories of unspeakable violence, and the trauma of a homeland partitioned and lost.

A second reason for the resilience of the villages is the spirit which they embody and which makes them the heirs of the medieval societies of Ben Yiju and Bomma. Not the most 'modern' of places as far as material comforts go, they are, in Ghosh's experience, 'far gentler' and 'very much more humane' in the conduct of human relationships than the majority of the modern world. It is Nabeel, the young student, who by an act of the imagination intimates what it must mean for Ghosh to live as a stranger among strangers. And it is Khamees, the fellaheen, who in perfect good humour and reasonableness diverts Ghosh from his self-recriminations after the set-to with the Imam. And, above all, it is Shaikh Musa, that most faithful of men, who makes of Ghosh's second visit to Lataifa and Nashawy a true homecoming. In short, if it is the case, as Ghosh claims, that there is 'a world of accommodations ... still alive, and, in some tiny measure, still retrievable' (237), its accessibility to the imagination must be possible precisely because of its rootedness somewhere in the actual.

## Notes

1   'Ozymandias' was written in late 1817 and published in the *Examiner*, 11 January 1818. An earlier sonnet, 'Feelings of a Republican on the Fall of Bonaparte', makes a similar point in a direct address to Napoleon: 'thou didst prefer / A frail and bloody pomp which Time has swept / In fragments towards Oblivion' (Bloom 1966, 58).

2   'History' is here 'the construction of knowledges which all operate through forms of expropriation and incorporation of the other' (Young 1990, 3). An episode from *In An Antique Land* was published in *Subaltern Studies*, VII, 1992; Ghosh's focus upon 'history' in his work has strong affinities with the claim of the Subaltern Studies group for a historiography which is narrated not from a colonialist and elitist point of view but from that of the indigenous subaltern (Guha 1988, 35–6).

3   Besides the Slave, two other Indians are mentioned in Goitein's *Letters*: 'the nakhoda Tinbu', a Tamil shipowner, between whom and Ben Yiju 'there are bonds of inseparable friendship and brotherhood' (1973, 64); and Ashu, a slave girl whom Ben Yiju manumitted in Mangalore and who 'might have become his wife and mother of his children' (1973, 202).

4   A geniza is a special chamber where discarded writings on which the name of God was written were deposited, so that they would be preserved from accidental desecration to be

ritually disposed of later. The Geniza of the Synagogue of Ben Ezra had never been cleared out since the Synagogue was rebuilt in 1025AD.

5   Ghosh's 'Notes' make wonderful reading in themselves. Referencing and explaining the matter in hand, they also gesture towards other stories and other pathways. All in all, the items convey a vital sense of a landscape already traversed and known and mapped long before European expansion.

6   See, for example, S.D. Goitein, *A Mediterranean Society: The Jewish Communities of the Arab World as Portrayed in the Documents of the Cairo Geniza*, 6 vols (Berkeley, 1967–94).

7   Goitein's footnote reads: 'Yiju's slave and business agent, a respected member of his household. In another letter (*India Book* 57), Khalaf calls him "Brother Bama." Bama, as I learned from Professor A.L. Basham, is vernacular for Brahma' (1973, 191).

8   For comparison, see Erik Iversen's account of how, by piecing together two of the names from the inscriptions from Abu Simbel, the Egyptologist Jean Francois Champollion was able to establish beyond doubt the alphabetical nature of the hieroglyphs (1961, 142–3). Iverson appears in Ghosh's 'Notes'.

9   Pratt uses 'contact zone' to refer to 'the spatial and temporal copresence of subjects previously separated by geographic and historical disjunctures, and whose trajectories now intersect' (1992, 7).

10  The accepted practice in ethnographic writing has tended to keep distinct the formal ethnographic description and the personal narrative, the latter being regarded as a sub-genre of the former. Mary Louise Pratt's essay (1986) calls this convention into question.

## Bibliography

Altick, Richard D. and John J. Fenstermaker (1993 [1963]), *The Art of Literary Research*, 4th edn, New York: W.W. Norton.

Bloom, Harold (ed.) (1966), *The Selected Poetry and Prose of Shelley*, New York: New American Library.

Ghosh, Amitav (1988), *The Shadow Lines*, London: Bloomsbury.

Ghosh, Amitav (1992), *In An Antique Land*, London: Granta Books.

Goitein, S.D. (ed. and trans.) (1973) *Letters of Medieval Jewish Traders*, Princeton: Princeton University Press.

Guha, Ranajit, and Gayatri Chakravorty Spivak (eds) (1988), *Selected Subaltern Studies*, Oxford: Oxford University Press.

Hutcheon, Linda (1988), *A Poetics of Postmodernism: History, Theory, Fiction*, London: Routledge.

Iversen, Erik (1961), *The Myth of Egypt and its Hieroglyphs in European Tradition*, Copenhagen: Gec Gad Publishers.

Kerridge, Richard (1999), 'Ecologies of Desire: Travel Writing and Nature Writing as Travelogue', in Steve Clark (ed.), *Travel Writing & Empire: Postcolonial Theory in Transit*, London: Zed Books, 164–82.

Majeed, Javed (1995), 'Amitav Ghosh's *In An Antique Land*: The Ethnographer-Historian and the Limits of Irony', *Journal of Commonwealth Literature* 30: 2, 45–55.

O'Neill, Michael (1989), *Percy Bysshe Shelley: A Literary Life*, London: Macmillan.

Pratt, Mary Louise (1992), *Imperial Eyes: Travel Writing and Transculturation*, London: Routledge.

Said, Edward W. (1985 [1978]), *Orientalism*, London: Penguin Books.

Said, Edward W. (1997 [1985]), 'Orientalism Reconsidered', in Bart Moore-Gilbert, Gareth Stanton and Willy Maley (eds), *Postcolonial Criticism*, London: Longman.

Said, Edward W. (1994 [1993]), *Culture and Imperialism*, London: Vintage.

Young, Robert (1990), *White Mythologies: Writing History and the West*, London: Routledge.

# Chapter Eighteen

# Congratulations

Christopher Ricks

In 1973 there appeared *I.A. Richards: Essays in his honor*. One of the trustiest tributes came from William Empson, honouring his old teacher. Empson was nearing seventy, Richards was eighty, but then as Empson once remarked, one trouble with getting old is that you all become the same age.

A volume in someone's honour is a text in transmission. More, it is a congratulation. Or rather, it is congratulations, since the word belongs among *pluralia tantum*, nouns that – in some given sense – occur only in the plural. There the word is, in the company of thanks, regards, credentials, auspices, and, it must be admitted, amends.

How, though, might a contributor to such a book avoid self-congratulation? To be invited to join in honouring: this is, after all though not above all, an honour. Yeats, anxious to give credit where credit is due, namely to himself, ends his grand tour, 'The Municipal Gallery Revisited', roundly:

> You that would judge me, do not judge alone
> This book or that, come to this hallowed place
> Where my friends' portraits hang and look thereon;
> Ireland's history in their lineaments trace;
> Think where man's glory most begins and ends,
> And say my glory was I had such friends.

Is this what friends are for?

But then what is so bad about self-congratulation? Don't several self-prefixing words manage to preserve the possibility that they are not simply self-serving? True, it is a charge against Malvolio that he is 'sick of self-love', but had he been a man of good will not of ill will then his self-love might have been of a good kind. You are to love your neighbour as yourself, not not-love yourself. Milton was aware that pride can come not only before a fall but before a right rising. Self-esteem likewise. But:

> weigh with her thy self;
> Then value: Oft times nothing profits more

Then self-esteem, grounded on just and right
Well manag'd; of that skill the more thou know'st
The more she will acknowledge thee her Head,
>                                   (*Paradise Lost*, viii. 566–70)

Disapproval of the male chauvinism that frames these admonitions from Raphael to Adam ought not to move us to disown what is here of profit, just and right, well managed, and alive with skill. Not, 'Nothing profits more than self-esteem'; rather, that 'Oft times' this is so, but only provided that the self-esteem is 'grounded on just and right' – and that even this is not enough, for round the corner there is a further warning sign:

>       grounded on just and right
>   Well manag'd;

Even the old-world indistinguishability of 'then' from 'than' (a textual nicety that I retain here, as is not always called for when preserving old spelling) makes its modest contribution. The move from the consecutive 'Then' to the other 'Then' (as 'Than') is a scruple of cautioning, there at the head of successive lines:

>   Then value: Oft times nothing profits more
>   Then self-esteem, grounded on just and right

Why then should self-congratulation be intrinsically any more obnoxious than self-esteem, on occasion estimable? Because of what ought to be the unignorability of the prefix 'con-'.

For congratulation is, from the start, from its start, a 'together with another'.

**congratulate** [con- together + *gratulare* to manifest or express one's joy]
+1. *intr*. To rejoice along *with* another; to express to a person one's pleasure or gratification at his good fortune, success, or happiness.
+2 *trans*. To express sympathetic joy on the occasion of;
>       b. to celebrate *with*.
4. To address (a person) with expressions of joy or satisfaction on an occasion considered fortunate; 'to compliment upon any happy event' (Johnson); to felicitate.

When we say 'to express to a person' or 'To address (a person)', do we really have in mind that the addresser may as well be the addressee as well? Well, people do talk to themselves. But that way madness lies. Again, when the *OED* includes within the definition of 'congratulation' 'the expressing to anybody in a complimentary way gratification at his success, fortune, or happiness', does 'anybody' there really include oneself, as against 'the expressing to somebody else'? The dictionary cites Thomas Fowler in 1887: 'To the act of "rejoicing with others" there is no single term appropriated . . The outward expression of the feeling is, however, known as *congratulation*'. A good point, and one that rests on specifying 'rejoicing with others'.

Yet it might seem that '*congratulation* 3 (*Obs.*)', 'on one's own behalf", is evidence that long ago 'congratulation' had slipped free of others. Yet how could there be '*Grateful* and glad acknowledgement on one's own behalf' except by the acknowledgement of something or someone other? Self-gratitude would be a teaser.

But then self-congratulation is a teaser, a perplexity. Its con- (together with another, not just with, not just the con- of, say, 'confidence') is paradoxical at root; yet the reflexive use is ancient and should warn us against waxing politico-moralistic about a modern degeneration. So *OED* '4b. *refl.*' presents a challenge: 'To call or account oneself happy or fortunate in relation to some matter'. The citations, though, particularly the early ones, are wary. Henry More in 1664, in *A Modest Enquiry into the Mysteries of Iniquity*: 'To congratulate our selves that we are neither Turks nor Papists' (*OED*). It is not themselves whom Christians should congratulate that they are neither Turks nor Papists. 'The Pharisee stood and prayed thus with himself, God, I thank thee, that I am not as other men are, extortioners, unjust, adulterers, or even as this publican'. Or even as those Turks or Papists. But then 'not as other men are' admits the other.

For the reflexive 'congratulate' was promptly averse to what was spotted, as when it is the disgusting Gulosulus whom Johnson catches:

> as he thought no folly greater than that of losing a dinner for any other gratification, he often congratulated himself, that he had none of that disgusting excellence which impresses awe upon greatness ... (*Rambler*, no. 206, 7 March 1752)

Conversely but complementarily, when we find in Dr Burney's *Memoirs of Metastasio* in 1796 (this, too, cited in the *OED*) the words 'Congratulating myself for the good fortune which has procured me such valuable friends', it is the thanks to fortune, which is not of one's own making, that may make 'congratulating myself' something other than self-contradictory folly.

One way to get your mind round a word is to muster its opposite, or rather its opposites. One opposite of taking pleasure in people's happiness is taking pleasure in their unhappiness. English-speakers are reluctant to admit that English has any truck with such nastiness, falling back upon the undomesticated Schadenfreude (harm joy). R.C.Trench schuddered:

> What a fearful thing it is that any language should have a word expressive of the pleasure which men feel at the calamities of others, for the existence of the word bears testimony to the existence of the thing. And yet in more than one such a word is found. (*On the Study of Words* 1852 edn, vol. ii, 29)

In more than one language, but not, thank somebody, in ours. The more humane opposite of congratulation is the one that Samuel Beckett summoned:

> 'Nelly is in heat,' she said, without the least trace of affectation, in a voice both proud and sad, and paused for Murphy to congratulate or condole, according to his lights. (*Murphy* 1938, 98)

How unaffectedly 'heat' arrives in the end at 'lights'. There could be lights without heat.

Beckett's later French for this is 'ses condoléances ou de ses félicitations'. In that order, partly for rhythmical reasons. The French 'félicitations' will escape the problems that lurk within the connerie of 'congratulations'. Littré, *Dictionnaire* (1873): '*congratuler* REMARQUES On dit *féliciter* ou *complémenter*, sauf quand il y a une nuance de plaisanterie, cas où congratuler est employé; il n'est pas rare en français qu'un mot qui vieillit se dégrade et passe dans la catégorie du langage de plaisanterie'.

Beckett has an eye for our congratulating ourselves. There is a chastening instance in *Murphy* (1938, 227): 'Miss Counihan congratulated herself on having closed her eyes when she did. With closed eyes, she said to herself, one cannot go far wrong. Unless one is absolutely alone. Then it is not necessary to – er – blink at such a rate'. In *Molloy* (1955, 149): 'I went out. But as with delicate steps, almost mincing, congratulating myself as usual on the resilience of my Wilton, I followed the corridor towards my room, I was struck by a thought which made me go back to my son's room'. And in *Malone Dies* (1956, 40): 'There are rabbits that die before they are killed, from sheer fright ... And you congratulate yourself on having succeeded with the first blow, and not caused unnecessary suffering, whereas in reality you have taken all that trouble for nothing'. In all these cases, *se féliciter* strikes a different chill.

It is 'condole' that is the complementary opposite of congratulate. For its formations make clear that con- must call up others.

> **condole** To grieve *with*; to express sympathy *with* another in his affliction. (The only extant use.)

> **condolement** The expressing of sympathy with another on account of loss, bereavement, or other grief.

> **condolence** Outward expression of sympathy with the grief of others.

Self-congratulation ought to announce itself as no less contortionist than would be self-condolence. (Self-pity is something else.) The *OED* does not contain, to my eyes, any formation parallel to 'self-congratulation', self- followed by co-, con- or com- in the sense of together with another. Such self-cooperation, say, would baffle the mind. The language does not permit of self-commiseration, commiseration being the other candidate for a complementary opposite of congratulation.

> **commiserate**
> 2. To express sympathy, condole with.
> 3. intr. To sympathize or express sympathy *with*. (The only current usage.)

> **commiseration** the expression of feelings of pity or sorrow for the affliction or distress of another.

There was once a noun 'miseration', though no verb. You used to be able to dole, but not to miserate.

The awkwardness of congratulation, both the giving and the receiving of it, remains. There is the notorious difficulty of congratulating someone on having gained an honour that you yourself already enjoy; a careful letter is called for. Unease was already audible a century ago, in the slang forms.

> **congrats** colloq. abbrev. of *congratulations*, usu. as *int*.

'Int.', perhaps, but not at ease in such intimacy and, as the first three instances in the *OED* make clear, quivering with class distinctions.

**1884** Received . . congrats on Ernest's appointment to the Royal Yacht.
**1894** 'A.HOPE' *Dolly Dialogues* So you've brought it off. Hearty congrats.
**1908** *Punch* Lord and Lady Knightsbridge . . were simply *loaded* with congrats about their brilliant son's success

The same goes for the elongated braying of '**congratters** colloq. abbrev. of *congratulations*, usu. as *int.*'

**1906** R.BROOKE Congratters on Cambridge's political enlightenment.
**1914** 'I.HAY' *Lighter Side School Life* 'Congratters!' said Blake awkwardly.
**1930** D.SAYERS Tremendous congratters and all that.
**1960** O.NORTON The Brig lifted his glass. 'Congratters my dear. Good show'.

'Congratters!' said Blake awkwardly. And so say all of us.

In self-congratulation the self is split, is both itself and another (else, why con-? 'Je est un autre'), which is not at all the same as seeing yourself as others see you. Self-congratulation may enjoy a divided self. And this, not with such self-knowledge as ruefully acknowledges that one's present self falls short of one's past self. Self-congratulation would not be the right word for Jonathan Swift in age, chastened by *A Tale of a Tub*: 'Good God! What a genius I had when I wrote that book'.

But it may be too easy to smirk when the first instance of 'self-congratulation' in the *OED* turns out to be from Joseph Addison, the man who summoned to his deathbed his stepson Lord Warwick so as to vouchsafe the words 'See in what peace a Christian can die'.

The textual transmission of this famous or notorious announcement has its own cross-currents. We famously owe it to Edward Young's *Conjectures on Original Composition* (1759, 102). Addison's thoroughgoing biographer Peter Smithers distrusts those who have distrusted the scene; he is sure that 'The words uttered would be sincere', and after a tour of the evidence concludes: 'All of these considerations seem to point to the likelihood of the famous story being true and I entertain no doubt upon the point' (Smithers 1954, 448n.) C.S. Lewis grandly left judgment to the All-Judging:

> The story that he summoned Lord Warwick to his deathbed *to see how a Christian can die* is ambiguous; it can be taken either as evidence of his Christianity or as a very brimstone proof of the reverse. I give no vote: my concern is with books. ('Addison' 1945; Lewis 1969, 157)

But Lewis's concern was not perhaps with the original book, since there are differences not only of rhythm but of substance between 'to see how a Christian can die' and 'See in what peace a Christian can die'. I have some sympathy with the early editions of the *Oxford Dictionary of Quotations*, which were so good as to sink the upper-case 'Christian' to the lower-case 'christian': 'See in what peace a christian can die'. This would claim less by way of successful *Imitatio Christi*. True, Young reports of Addison that 'he softly said' the words, but Young does capitalize in the story.

Yet Addison comes better out of all this matter of self-congratulation when his use of the word ('How many self-congratulations naturally rise in the mind', *OED*; read 'arise') is accorded its full context. For his rejoicing does make explicit how much the self owes to all that is not self, and this means that self-congratulation is refreshedly alive to and with gratitude.

> A Man, who uses his best Endeavours to live according to the Dictates of Virtue and right Reason has two perpetual Sources of Chearfulness; In the Consideration of his own Nature, and of that Being on whom he has a Dependance. If he looks into himself, he cannot but rejoice in that Existence, which is so lately bestowed upon him, and which, after Millions of Ages, will be still new, and still in its beginning. How many Self-Congratulations naturally arise in the Mind, when it reflects on this its Entrance into Eternity .... (*Spectator*, no. 381, 17 May 1712)

The point is not the personal complacency, or not, of Addison but the way in which he understands his own words, his new way of putting it. He senses that con- should be heeded. In this he inaugurates some finely redeemed uses of the paradoxical compound as it comes to the nineteenth century.

Addison sought the possibility of a proper self-congratulation, something asking that others or another be acknowledged as having played their part. This is differently valuable from the more usual warning against self-congratulation *tout court*, as when Cowper moves within a dozen lines from 'self-reproaching conscience' to its opposite, 'self-congratulating pride' (*The Task*, v. 622). The redemption of self-congratulation is a greater challenge.

Jane Welsh Carlyle rose to it. She evokes 'honest self-congratulation'. The phrase comes in the very first letter in *Letters and Memorials of Jane Welsh Carlyle* (prepared for publication by Thomas Carlyle, edited by James Anthony Froude 1883). It is to her mother in Scotsbrig, from Chelsea, 1 September 1834. Carlyle comments, in his pages introducing the letter: 'From birth upwards, she had lived in opulence; and now, for my sake, had become poor – so nobly poor. Truly, her pretty little brag (in this letter) was well founded'. (How free her own prose is from condescension can be felt in the contrast with Carlyle's affectionate diminutivery.)

> Our little household has been set up again at a quite moderate expense of money and trouble; wherein I cannot help thinking, with a *chastened vanity*, that the superior shiftiness and thriftiness of the Scotch character has strikingly manifested itself ... To see how they live and waste here, it is a wonder the whole city does not 'bankrape and go out o' sicht';– flinging platefuls of what they are pleased to denonimate 'crusts' (that is what I consider the best of the bread) into the ashpits! I often say, with honest self-congratulation, 'In Scotland we have no such thing as "crusts"'. On the whole, though the English ladies seem to have their wits more at their finger-ends, and have a great advantage over me in that respect, I never cease to be glad that I was born on the other side of the Tweed, and those who are nearest and dearest to me are Scotch.

What makes an honest woman of such self-congratulation is the acknowledgment that the self is not one's singular creation: 'In Scotland we have no such thing as "crusts"'. The gladness, the rejoicing, has to be (in its way) with others, since 'I never cease to be glad that I was born on the other side of the Tweed'. Self-congratulation does not expand into the fatuous fantasy of giving birth to oneself.

The faithful text of this letter is even better, and in details germane to self-congratulation and to honesty. For J.W.C. wrote forthrightly, not 'what I consider the best of the bread', but '... consider all the best of the bread'. She did not put within quotation marks her words to herself: not

> I often say, with honest self-congratulation, 'In Scotland we have no such thing as "crusts"'

but (without those almost mincing commas, too)

> I often say with honest self congratulation in Scotland we have no such thing as *'crusts'*.

She did not put the Scottish idiom within quotation-marks or proffer one of the flavoured spellings: not 'it is a wonder the whole city does not "bankrape and go out o' sicht"', but 'it is a wonder the whole City does not bankrape and go out o sight –'. She did not have the exclamation mark, crowing, after 'ash-pits' ('into the ashpits!'). She is briskly idiomatic: not 'glad that I was born on the other side of the Tweed' but '... the other side the Tweed'. Last but not least, it is a felicity, not an indifference, that has 'nearest' rising endearingly to 'Dearest': not 'glad that ... those who are nearest and dearest to me are Scotch', but that 'those who are nearest and Dearest to me are Scotch'.

Jane Welsh Carlyle rescues self-congratulation from dishonesty, which is exactly what she does with 'shiftiness': 'the superior shiftiness and thriftiness of the Scotch chararacter', with its pawky rhyme, is a tribute to the national character that she was so lucky as to be born to: *OED* 'shifty' – 'well able to shift for oneself' – includes 1859: 'The canny, shifty, far-seeing Scot', and, again in a Scottish context, 1888, 'shifty and business-like'. In the matter of self-congratulation, and the possibility of an honest form of it, Jane Welsh Carlyle is truly shifty.

Walter Scott, too, had the imaginative skill to invoke an honest self-reflection, and once again the faithful modern text does him more justice than did the liberties taken, in his case, by Lockhart. Again the punctuation is too pointed by an editor's tinkering.

Scott to Joanna Baillie, 23 November 1810. First, as given by Lockhart:

> But planting and pruning trees I could work at from morning till night; and if ever my poetical revenues enable me to have a few acres of my own, that is one of the principal pleasures I look forward to. There is, too, a sort of self-congratulation, a little tickling self-flattery in the idea that, while you are pleasing and amusing yourself, you are seriously contributing to the future welfare of the country, and that your very acorn may send its future ribs of oak to future victories like Trafalgar. (Scott 1837, 321–2)

As given by Grierson:

> But planting and pruning trees I could work at from morning till night and if my poetical revenues enable me to have a few acres of my own that is one of the principal pleasures I look forward to. There is too a sort of self-congratulation a little tickling self-flattery in the idea that while you are pleasing and amusing yourself you are really seriously contributing to the future wellfare of the country and that your very acorn may send its ribs of oack to future victories like Trafalgar. (Scott 1932, 402–3)

It is not only the differences in wording that count: Lockhart's throb 'if ever my' as against Grierson's 'if my'; Lockhart's 'future ribs', Grierson's sufficient 'ribs'; and the comic earnestness of 'you are really seriously contributing' (Grierson; no 'really' in Lockhart). More important to 'a sort of self-congratulation' is the movement of the two sentences. Lockhart has seven commas and one semi-colon where Grierson (and, I trust, Scott) will have none. The easy running-on by Scott is incompatible with pomposity: 'There is too a sort of self-congratulation a little tickling self-flattery in the idea that...' There is a little tickling going on, nipping along, as there is the miniature roundness of 'your very acorn'. It all has its own sly saltiness. And if your trees grow, well and good, but this is not exactly your doing, that you should grow too ripely self-congratulatory.

The contrast might be with an unsuccessful attempt to protect 'self-congratulation' against self-contradiction, this to be heard in Samuel Rogers. He means only to tell us how pleased he is, but the rhythm of his blank verse issues in a complacent climax at the word:

> Am I in ITALY? Is this the Mincius?
> Are those the distant turrets of Verona?
> And shall I sup where JULIET at the masque
> Saw her beloved MONTAGUE, and now sleeps by him?
> Such questions hourly do I ask myself;
> And not a stone, in a cross-way, inscribed
> 'To Mantua' – 'To Ferrara' – but excites
> Surprise, and doubt, and self-congratulation.
>
> *(Italy)*

The doubt in question is whether Rogers could protect self-congratulation against its propensities. The poet who most deeply set himself to do so was Wordsworth.

True, he had his lapses. Nothing protects self-congratulation or its poet in his 'Lines written on a blank leaf in a copy of the author's poem "The Excursion", upon hearing of the death of the late Vicar of Kendal':

> To public notice, with reluctance strong,
> Did I deliver this unfinished Song;
> Yet for one happy issue; – and I look
> With self-congratulation on the Book
> Which pious, learned MURFITT saw and read;–
> Upon my thoughts his saintly Spirit fed;
> He conn'd the new-born Lay with grateful heart;
> Foreboding not how soon he must depart,
> Unweeting that to him the joy was given
> Which good Men take with them from Earth to Heaven.

This is itself insufficiently weeting. Murfitt's gratitude to Wordsworth is too patently a gratification, and is not held in balance with any gratitude from

Wordsworth for anything or anybody. 'Which good Men take ...': the poet pats his chest and himself on the back. But then it is characteristic of Wordsworth to mishandle opportunities that elsewhere he delicately takes in hand. 'Self-congratulation' is finely ensconced within the felicities of 'The Old Cumberland Beggar' and its humane insinuations as to all that the poor man unweetingly effects:

> The easy man
> Who sits at his own door, – and, like the pear
> That overhangs his head from the green wall,
> Feeds in the sunshine; the robust and young,
> The prosperous and unthinking, they who live
> Sheltered, and flourish in a little grove
> Of their own kindred; – all behold in him
> A silent monitor, which on their minds
> Must needs impress a transitory thought
> Of self-congratulation, to the heart
> Of each revealing his peculiar boons,
> His charters and exemptions; and, perchance,
> Though he to no one give the fortitude
> And circumspection needful to preserve
> His present blessings, and to husband up
> The respite of the season, he, at least,
> And 'tis no vulgar service, makes them felt. (116–32)

This, in its own circumspection, is itself a monitor. It makes its blessings felt. For the thought of self-congratulation is valuable in proportion as it is transitory. Those who are not beggars are blessed to move in kindness beyond their own kindred. The source of their happiness is found outside self, outside them, and this with the double impress of 'must needs'. Each such person appreciates, thanks to the figure who moves among them, his peculiar boons; the passage speaks both of boons and of blessings, aware that these asks thanks and do not emanate from the self who may enjoy for a while a principled self-congratulation.

We are invited by such lines to revise our sense of what self-congratulation must needs be. The revision of *The Prelude* did not ask of Wordsworth any second thoughts as to the central contention, the redemption of self-congratulation.

> I spare to speak, my friend, of what ensued:
> The admiration, and the love, the life
> In common things – the endless store of things

Rare, or at least so seeming, every day
Found all about me in one neighbourhood –
The self-congratulation, the complete
Composure, and the happiness entire.
     (*The Prelude*, 1805, i. 16–22)

  I spare to tell of what ensued, the life
In common things – the endless store of things,
Rare, or at least so seeming, every day
Found all about me in one neighbourhood –
The self-congratulation, and, from morn
To night, unbroken cheerfulness serene.
     (*The Prelude*, 1805, i. 108–13)

As always with Wordsworthian revision, the gains and losses would ask patience on a Wordsworthian scale. 'The admiration' of 1805 disappears, perhaps as having put 'self-congratulation' at the old risk, yet with some sense of retreating from a boldness. The delicate line-ending –

      the complete
Composure,

– with 'complete' waiting for its unhurried and untroubled, its unprecarious, completion – was at one with the deep Wordsworthian alignment of composure, including self-composure, and composition. And how deftly the 1805 lines become entire only with the conclusive word 'entire', the adjective following its noun but in no way tardy. The 1850 lines gain in some ways by not explicitly mentioning love ('that much-mentioned brilliance, love', in the words of the poet who said that 'Deprivation is for me what daffodils were for Wordsworth'). And 'serene' has its own calmative finality. As for 1850's 'cheerfulness', we may remember that this was explicitly the subject of that essay in the *Spectator* which brought forward the first, and the proper, self-congratulation: 'two perpetual sources of Chearfulness … How many Self-Congratulations naturally arise in the Mind'.

  It matters to congratulation, and to the bizarrerie that is self-congratulation, that there were once the words 'gratulation' and 'gratulate' (expressing or manifesting joy). Wordsworth, like Milton and Cowper, was enabled to be vigilant about self-congratulation by courtesy of 'gratulate', a word that all these poets rightly valued. Scott respected the word, which is one reason not only why he could be wise about self-congratulation but why Crabbe, expressing gratitude to Sir Walter (21 December 1812), hit not only the right tone but the right word, repeatedly:

> so my want of Communication with & even of Knowledge of the Men of Genius in our Days renders the opening of an Intercourse with you highly pleasant & a motive for much Self-Gratulation and I do accordingly gratulate myself and reflect on my Acquisition with the Spirit of a Man growing rich: I have a new Source of Satisfaction. (Crabbe 1985, 94)

With characteristic modesty and firmness, Christina G. Rossetti likewise knew how to minister to a proper pleasure, not in and for herself but in and for another:

> My dear Mrs Heimann,
> It would be asking too much of boys to require them to prefer study to play: so if your young friends display no worse taste than this, I think you have cause for self gratulation. (6 June 1853; Rossetti 1997, i, 67)

Cause for 'self gratulation': and how then to give effect to the cause? Fortunately we have great exemplars. There was William Empson's remonstration that had no choice but to issue in what could then be represented as self-congratulation. Accused of perpetrating a jeering joke upon his readers (*The Structure of Complex Words*), Empson rose to the occasion:

> What I feel about the book, if there is any doubt, is easily told. I think it is wonderful; I think it goes up like a great aeroplane. A certain amount of noisy taxi-ing round the field at the start may be admitted, and the landing at the end is bumpy though I think without causing damage; but the power of the thing and the view during its flight I consider magnificent. (Empson 1955–56, 447)

Empson knew that 'This is disagreeably like writing an advertisement for myself'. But the alternative would have been his colluding in the demeaning of something that both was and was not himself: this book that he believed in. Together with something other, this being the book itself.

A different challenge once confronted James Joyce. 'Is this the great James Joyce?' asked Sylvia Beach, admiring. It was a difficult question for him to answer. 'No' would have been harsh. 'Don't know', winsome. 'Not for me to say', cadging. 'Yes', self-congratulatory. 'James Joyce', he granted, extending his hand and his imagination.

# Bibliography

Carlyle, T. (1977), *The Collected Letters of Thomas and Jane Welsh Carlyle*, gen. ed. Charles Richard Saunders, co-ed. Kenneth J. Fielding, vol. vii, Durham, North Carolina: Duke University Press.

Crabbe, G. (1985), *Selected Letters and Journals of George Crabbe*, ed. Thomas C. Faulkner with Rhonda L. Blair, Oxford: Clarendon Press.

Empson, W. (1955–56), *Mandrake*, Autumn and Winter, 2:1.

Lewis, C.S. (1969), *Selected Literary Essays*, ed. Walter Hooper, Cambridge: Cambridge University Press.

Rossetti, C. (1997), *The Letters of Christina Rossetti*, ed. Antony H.Harrison, vol. i, Charlottesville and London: University Press of Virginia.

Scott, W. (1837), J.G. Lockhart, *Memoirs of the Life of Sir Walter Scott, Bart*, vol. ii, Edinburgh and London: Robert Cadell and John Murray.

Scott, W. (1932), *The Letters of Sir Walter Scott 1808–1811*, ed. H.J.C. Grierson, London: Constable.

Smithers, P. (1954), *The Life of Addison*, Oxford: Clarendon Press.

# Index